Tropics of Desire

SEXUAL CULTURES: New Directions from the Center for Lesbian and Gay Studies

General Editors: José Esteban Muñoz and Ann Pellegrini

Times Square Red, Times Square Blue
Samuel R. Delany

Private Affairs
Critical Ventures in the Culture of Social Relations
Phillip Brian Harper

In Your Face
9 Sexual Studies
Mandy Merck

Tropics of Desire
Interventions from Queer Latino America
José Quiroga

Tropics of Desire

Interventions from Queer Latino America

JOSÉ QUIROGA

NEW YORK UNIVERSITY PRESS
New York and London

NEW YORK UNIVERSITY PRESS
New York and London

Library of Congress Cataloging-in-Publication Data
Quiroga, José, 1959–
Tropics of desire : interventions from queer Latino America / José Quiroga.
p. cm.
Includes bibliographical references and index.
ISBN 0-8147-6952-7 (hc : acid-free) — ISBN 0-8147-6953-5 (pb : acid-free)
1. Gays—Latin America. 2. Gays—Latin America—Identity. 3. Homosexuality—Latin America. 4. Homosexuality and literature—Latin America. I. Title.
HQ76.3.L29 Q57 2000
306.76'6'098—dc21 00-009851

New York University Press books are printed on acid-free paper,
and their binding materials are chosen for strength and durability.

Manufactured in the United States of America

10 9 8 7 6 5 4 3 2 1

Contents

Illustrations

Acknowledgments

A book about the theater of coding sexualities should be able to provide a key for readers to decode the show. *Tropics of Desire* is the end result of so many reconstructions that I am prone to forget the doctors and nurses who provided surgery and care when it was needed the most. The scars are all mine, but all those who tended to the patient's every need deserve credit for successful and timely intervention. The patient was a patient. It is now alive and kicking, ready to put on makeup and go out into the limelight.

To Sylvia Molloy and Daniel Balderston I give the deepest bow. This work has been marked by their conversation, support, collaboration, stimulus, and faith. Each, in their own way, has given more than I can ever hope to repay.

Friends and colleagues have supported many of these essays in all their incarnations; some of them probably are not even aware of what they did, but they have taken note of what I wrote and have engaged with this work in some way or another: Carlos Alonso, Josianna Arroyo, Emilie Bergmann, María Mercedes Carrión, Jorge Cortiñas, Damián Fernández, Jean Franco, Juan Gelpí, Gwen Kirkpatrick, John Kraniauskas, Elissa Marder, Yolanda Martínez-San Miguel, Francine Masiello, Carlos Monsiváis, Frances Negrón, Rubén Ríos Avila, Enrico Mario Santi, and Doris Sommer. Students at the George Washington University, the University of California at Berkeley, Emory University, and Columbia University provided stimulus and debate that are reflected here on every page.

Eric Zinner, my editor at New York University Press, has been patient with my delays and responsive to my calls. The colleagues at the Center for Lesbian and Gay Studies in New York have provided spaces for these ideas to be played out in front of an audience, in particular Arnaldo Cruz Malave, Elena Martínez, and Oscar Montero. Ann Pellegrini and José Muñoz are the series editors for Sexual Cultures, and I thank them for sponsoring this book. José Muñoz pays me so many compliments that I think he does it only because he himself is embarrassed at all the compliments I send his way.

Peter Johnson was generous in his help with the archives at Princeton University Libraries; Ruth Oldenziel helped me navigate some rough spots and provided the forum of the Belle Van Zuylen Institute in Amsterdam, where I first presented a chapter of this work. Jorge Salessi introduced me to Carlos Jáuregui and the activists at Gays por los Derechos Civiles in Buenos Aires, who inspired me so much. Francisco Morán, Reinaldo García Ramos, and the deeply missed Roberto Valero were stellar presences in the constellations of errant cubania; Felix Jiménez taught me how to write all the sharp sentences you may find here; Perry Miranda was the makeup artist of all my bolero nights; Jorge Morell and Yolanda have shared their home and family in New Haven and San Francisco; Joseph Massad kept me grounded when I was walking on a tightrope; Rhonda Shore and Jorge Conde offered many nights of picadillo, home repair, and music. Alejandro Varderi provided love, affection, and support, and he is the best bolero singer I know; Rafael shared many of the events that found their way into this book, and I am grateful I met him under the crystal disco ball at El Faro one night. He opened the door for only the lucky accidents in my recent life.

The George Washington University Facilitating Fund provided the initial research stimulus that took me to Argentina for a project that then turned into this book. My colleagues here at George Washington have been supportive of my work, in particular Inés Azar, who has believed most when I myself have doubted. The staff at the Instructional Technology Lab tried to smooth over my relative ignorance of computer capabilities; from Rutgers, Larry La Fountain-Stokes read very quickly and provided comments that were sharp and good. The communities in Washington, D.C., where I have lived for the past nine years, have been gracious and supportive: Nancy Rivera, Lana Shekim, Lamis Jarrar, Adeeb Jarrar, José Gutiérrez, and others who provided small talk, hummus, and Cuba libres.

My family deserves more than just the simple token of gratitude that one writes at the beginning of a book. No words could describe how fortunate I am to have them with me at all times. I am the luckiest man alive for them. *Gracias.*

And at this point, before I spoil the show with tears, I would like to dedicate this book to Licia Fiol Matta, Rafael Rosario, and Robert Vázquez Pacheco. That is just strict alphabetical order, because I cannot describe in one sentence how generous they have been, how many wounds they have helped to heal, and how fortunate I am to count on their loyalty and their support.

Some of the essays here have been published in other collections, and others have been delivered as conference papers. They have all been revised. "Outing Silence as Code: Virgilio Piñera" was delivered as "The Weight of the Flesh" at a New York University conference on "Hispanisms and Homosexualities," and parts of it appeared in *Hispanisms and Homosexualities*, ed. Sylvia Molloy and Robert McKee Irwin (Duke University Press, 1998). Parts of this essay are also contained in "Fleshing Out Virgilio Piñera from the Cuban Closet," in *Entiendes? Queer Readings, Hispanic Writings*, ed. Emilie Bergmann and Paul Julian Smith (Duke University Press, 1995), 168–80.

"Revolution: *Strawberry and Chocolate*" is a revised version of a paper delivered at the Americas Society conference "Margin/Center: Emergent Discourses in Latin American and Latino Literature and Culture" and of "Homosexualities in the Tropics of Revolution," in *Sex and Sexuality in Latin America*, ed. Daniel Balderston and Donna Guy (New York University Press, 1997), 133–51.

"Tears at the Nightclub" is a much-revised version of the essay that appeared as "(Queer) Boleros of a Tropical Night," *Travesía: Journal of Latin American Cultural Studies* 3, nos. 1–2 (1994): 199–213.

"The Mask of the Letter" was delivered as a paper at the Center for Lesbian and Gay Studies in New York in October 1996, at the Modern Language

Association conference in December 1996, and in Caracas, Venezuela, at the Instituto Internacional de Literatura Iberoamericana in June 1996.

"Queer Desires in Lydia Cabrera" was originally written for the sixth Conferencia Internacional de Literatura Hispánica Femenina. I thank all those responsible for urging me to present this work in these venues.

Preface

In Drag

> Through your peripheral vision you see young men frolicking in the water, but you had your share and you pay little attention. As you relax and take in the gentle waves, a young man, that you met the night before, brings you a cold drink and lies besides you.
>
> —SEÑOR CÓRDOVA (PSEUD.), *A Man's Guide to the Caribbean*

The tourist book calls itself a guide to the Caribbean but does not confine itself solely to the islands. Roughly, it covers an arc extending from Key West in the north to the Virgin Islands in the east and Veracruz in the west. Even within these limits—which are not limits, nor borders, but rather transient spots—the guide plays off cultural similarities and difference. The islands are scattered like so many one night stands, with flower curtains, cheap reproductions of the Masters, and wicker chairs, but they are all part of the same circuit of desire. They are divided according to country into different chapters in the book. But then, after one notices the differences (islands like punctuation for the vast currents of the Caribbean sentence), some kind of sameness sets in. On the islands, you get the cities, the tourist locales with the grand hotels and high-class service, and, on the slumming end of the spectrum, the cheaper locales for the budget traveler. Chapters may or may not form imaginary communities, but nations certainly do. Here they are not the sites where diaspora plays with imperial history but simply chapters—momentary flings. The "national" has its own specific "weather," its "national holidays," its "local" cuisine. One can already hear the budget travelers' complaint: "It's all the same rice and beans." But the men are a different thing. When it comes to men, there seems to be a pecking order. It is part of an itinerary called "the tourist trail," and it goes from spot to spot and from island to island with some very well defined protocols.

In the nineteenth century the Romantics yearned for the unspoiled, or at least for the ruined traces half hidden in a jungle that always reclaimed what civilization had borrowed. With a new age of sensibility in which the unspoiled has been lost from the radar screen of time and space, the traveler demands the difference of the "local" within the onslaught of the same. Nature is a franchise with different values pegged on the dollar. This traveler is seeking not the absence of all that civilization may offer, but the space where nature and culture collude: the air conditioner and the unspoiled beach; sex on demand but also the cabana chair.

Pedro, Julio, Félix are some of the local delicacies that the guide book says can be sampled at will. They are pictured at the beginning or the end of the chapters, lounging next to a swimming pool or striking a pose on the beach as their glistening bodies are hit by the waves. They will make your stay a pleasant one. They will make sure that your drink is well served and cold to your lips, and that your vacation is not interrupted by cheap and unwelcome hustlers. At the same time, they will keep a proper distance if you so choose—to sample the local delicacies, that is.

And that is why the guide book provides two glossaries for each country it describes: one allows the tourist to sample the local dishes, and the other offers the illusion, the privilege, of engaging in conversation on sex in the local language, with the local metaphors (which generally concern food) clearly explained. This is the language of love, the language of lovemaking. But recall that even if you memorize those words, the boy's talent lies in taking you out of the glossary for one night or two, so that you may return to the glossary in order to reminisce, once the experience is over.

The blinding light of Key West is where the curtain opens, and the story ends in Veracruz. There are Spanish fortresses under blinding sun, modern amenities, and screeching parrots. "An academic discourse in Havana," as Wallace Stevens would say, with an idea of order borrowed from Key West. The curtain is only a mask: it conceals how those behind the curtain play with the ones who look.

Introduction

Interventions on Code

Decoding the Mask: Buenos Aires, 1993

At the 1993 Marcha del orgullo gay (Gay Pride March) in Buenos Aires, the organizers distributed masks to those who wanted to march without being recognized. As the Argentinean gay and lesbian organizations assembled in a central plaza, several men and women went into the crowd in the streets and tried to convince many to join—not as open and visible members of the community, but as *openly masked* members in support of that community, as part of a body count manifesting solidarity with the cause of civil rights for a disenfranchised minority.

This open masking was a brilliant tactical move, in ways that had nothing to do with the standard epistemologies of the closet. The closet was part of the equation, but it was not the *only* part of the equation. The mask spoke of broader circuits that did not necessarily end with an "outing", or an identity as conclusion. It was part of a complex dynamic of subject and identity, and the closet was one element among many. There were men and women there who lived openly with partners, but could not afford to be recognized by their employers, nephews, aunts, or uncles. There were those who held their sexuality as a kind of "open secret" in their families, who had in turn accepted their partners as such. But in these families the social fabric depended on something that would have been destroyed had the very notion of homosexuality *as identity* been put on the dinner table. To expect men and women to choose family exile as the price of homosexual identity was certainly too much to ask in such a tightly knit context of relations, and the organizers of the march knew that.

There were, of course, other reasons for those masks, especially in a country that had recently come out (pun intended) of one of the most ferocious military dictatorships in Latin America. Can anyone belabor the desire *not* to be recognized when the faces of the disappeared were still part of a nation's emotional reckoning? The mask at the lesbian and gay march was overdetermined by circumstance, social context, even culture. What was interesting to me, as one of those whose sense of privilege (as a foreigner) allowed open and "unmasked" participation, was the way taxonomies seemed to be created and recreated precisely from the space created by the mask. If the march parodically reconfigured society, the option of the mask ruptured the borders of the stage. Those masked bodies reached out to observers on the sidelines: they "homosexualized" all those who merely watched, they turned them all "queer." The act of *not* wearing the mask turned you into a homosexual, while *wearing* it absolved you of responsibility. How many of those masked participants were homosexual? How many were not? From the moment the mask was deployed, those on the sidelines became the ones whose sense of shame did not allow them to join.

The mask entailed a liberatory act in its own right. It destroyed the dialectical opposition between the visible and the invisible, between the *visibility* of homosexuals and their *invisibility* in the population at large. It turned the actors in the public drama into representations. By allowing the invisible to incarnate, as a presence, the social polity in itself construed its own public rite. It produced a zone of contact that mediated rupture; it operated from the point of view of structural play, instead of from the blinders given by systems and taxonomies.

. . .

Visibility precedes memory. That is why historians are seduced by the give and take of the visible and the invisible: they understand that for something to be memorialized, it first of all has to be *seen*. It has to be seen when it proclaims itself invisible, because that is when it most urgently demands an *other*, different vision.

Tropics of Desire examines visibilities within forms of social praxis in the Latino American context as modes of intervention that allow different publics to participate in the social sphere. The march in Buenos Aires rendered identity as one more component—and not the most important one—of a complex equation in which civil rights are seen as a need, not part of a circuit of "special" interests. The covered and uncovered marchers gave meaning to the situations studied in this book, the forms of intervention the authors studied here chose to enact, and the practice of Latino homosexuality at large. They defined the cultural phenomena as well as the context that surrounded certain authors I was interested in. They validated their sense of cultural praxis as one that always sought linkages, blurrings, and chiaroscuros for the sake of progressive action.

The interventions in this book collide with identity narratives deployed in the United States. The book also challenges the sense of unproblematized visibility created in those narratives. The space of the mask goes beyond the certainties of assumed identities; it aims, on the contrary, to blur them. At many points readers will notice that I seem to validate practices that are very different from the ones that are now prevalent in writings about homosexuality in the United States. In one chapter I read the work of the ("closeted") Mexican poet Xavier Villaurrutia as one that liberates us from the sexual conservatism put forth by certain sectors of the U.S. gay and lesbian movement. Another chapter seeks to question "outing" from within a context where state mechanisms erase individual agency; at another point still, I *seem* to demand that precursors not be classified as "gay," nor outed, since this "flattens" their work—it consigns them to the gay niche market and thus collaborates against their work's broader progressive aims.

These positions can be classified as ambivalent, tentative, or even antiprogressive. This is so, of course, depending on the way one frames the dialectics that underlie such arguments. I can only *partly* claim a sense of cultural difference to explain this social praxis. I do not wish to hide under the mantle of culture in order to ascertain difference, and I am not interested in creating a facile distinction between "white" Anglo American culture and the "mestizo" Latin American "essence" as terms whose oppositions are clear-cut. Certainly there is a cultural continuum between many Caribbean societies and those of the American South, just as there is a broad swath of territory in the southern and southwestern United States that is part of Latino America, although its political and economic structures may differ from those in the rest of the continent. I just think that homosexual praxis is *effective* in these contexts in ways in which homosexual identity is not.

Let me also clarify from the outset that were it not for those courageous women and men who marched uncovered, and who risked very real persecution and threats, there would have been no march in Buenos Aires to begin with. Without the work of activists like the deeply missed Carlos Jáuregui in Argentina (as one example among many), the civil rights demanded by the march would never have been gained. The brilliance Jáuregui brought to his work as tactician and as public figure and his refusal to be tied down to a position or a politics that was not consistent with a sense of praxis cannot be underscored enough. Activists like Jáuregui refuse to be outmaneuvered by a social imperative that insists they speak only in one register and become spokespersons for one issue to the exclusion of all the other issues of class, race, ethnicity, gender privilege, and homophobia. Jáuregui understood that at his time and place it was necessary to engage society as a whole, and that he could do that only by arguing for civil rights that *all* society wanted. In this way, Jáuregui avoided a common trap: he never forfeited his right to speak on broad social issues; he did not limit his radius of action when he proclaimed his own visibility. He refused the normative space of the balkanized social polity.

The figure with the mask is strategic in a way that Carlos Jáuregui was not. Jáuregui was the tactician; the masked figure I present as my tactic. The figure memorializes its own absence, insisting on its own presence as erasure. It responds to the demands of identity with the silence of No One. This is the praxis that I want to decode in this book.

Threading Desire

The modernists in the first half of the twentieth century excelled in the form of the manifesto. The manifesto was loosely codified—generally a statement of principles, followed by a survey of the contemporary literary and artistic scene (avant-garde movements as a rule did not believe in the separation between different artistic "genres"), and then the project for a future art that existed in the here and now, within the project that the manifesto itself displayed. Manifestos reveled in their own circularity and anticipated datedness. They did not demolish the present, but rather announced its future demolition; they created by opposition and by example, but also opened the space for other manifestos to destroy the tenets of the one that readers encountered at the moment. In short, because they were relatively open in terms of their own closures—like a letter that announces an end that can be announced only by the end of the letter as such—manifestos were textual productions of desire. They intervened in the economy of desire: the promise was more important than its fulfillment; *wanting* was more important than having; the project was more enticing than the realization of the project. To a certain extent, manifestos became repetitive because of this, even before they were consigned to the space of history or, more specifically, to the history of the avant-garde, a category that is a paradox in itself. For some literary or artistic historians, the manifesto is now pure nostalgia, evidence of a time before the desire for utopia became part of a tradition.

When I attempted to explain my use of terms such as "desire" or "intervention" in this book, I first thought of the avant-garde manifesto. Aside from the fact that manifestos are the clearest examples of literary and artistic interventions that I can think of, they allowed for definitions that did not work as definitions, but as examples. Everything becomes evidence of something else: I can point to a text and say, "That is what I mean," instead of explaining what I mean. Desire is all about intervention—about wanting to intervene—just as intervention is all about desire, about *wanting* something. The interventions that I decode in this book do not close off desire. They are not meant to end anything by means of an act of power that produces stable categories, but rather attempt to unsettle existing categories by exposing their complicities with those regulatory systems that kill desire.

Whether we like to admit it or not, queer sexualities are part of this history, a history of bodies that reclaim a sense of agency for their own desires, and a history of the desires for justice that minorities have framed as oppositional to the normative status quo. From the same-sex homophile projects of the nineteenth century to the Lesbian Avengers of the twentieth, queer sexualities are bisected by socialism, feminism, the avant-garde, and decolonization as fragments of a modernist project appearing at a particular stage of capitalism. But my framing of queer desire as part of this history is not as positive a statement as it seems at first glance. I am using the term "history" also to mean something whose very status at present is a point of contention, especially for those who would like to bracket the term in a sphere of safety. For some, the radical promise of queer sexualities is now part of a generalized stability brought about by a "history" of "identity." Because as "identities," gays and lesbians are "different," they should have a certain voice within society, they should be respected as "alternatives" and given representation within the legal, social, and economic systems that surround us.

In this scenario, identity seems to be the point of arrival after a long modernist journey—or rather, the truce declared after a battle in which the vanguard lost some of its most vocal members. Like all truces, it speaks of paperwork and negotiation, where the discrete victories are teased out of the sheer sense of exhaustion that consumes both parties—who sometimes switch sides just to see what the other side feels like. But truces are conflicted moments, and often the issues that produced the battles in the first place remain festering there, waiting for the appropriate time to come out of the closet (pun intended). The truce means that voices will be given a space, commercial venues will be established for the sake of expression. You may have access to institutions that once would not open their doors to you, and you will, moreover, insist on gaining access for the commercial and economic benefit of those same institutions that once oppressed you, for they have realized that there is much more to be gained by having you work for them, since *that* at least creates the possibility of an "alternative" market.

Tropics of Desire intervenes within the space of this contested truce. Bitterness, sarcasm, and/or even postmodern irony are the unintended effects of trying to explain the extent to which intervention and desire play off each other in these essays. But identity politics as it is understood in the United States, and then exported to other geographical and social locales, is not something that I seek to bash without understanding the very concrete gains it has produced as political practice. At the same time, it would be wrong to understand the degree of oppositional politics that I present in this book as attempting to remotivate or restart a space of utopia that has already been consigned to the "dustbin of history," to use a popular Reaganism. My understanding of social processes at this stage in time does not include rehashing the slogans that were used before: I do not want to create a literary and artistic genealogy of queer sexualities, nor do I intend to scold or exalt my precursors because they were open or not as to their gender choices. To engage in these operations at a time when the victorious project known as neoliberalism (briefly put: state devolution) in Latino America has redefined politics and turned populations into consumers merely serves to prolong a process that I disagree with and am very suspicious of.

I started this section by recalling modernist manifestos because in spite of their historical datedness, and in spite of their being texts that at this point signify nostalgia (though many of them flirted with questionable politics, like fascism), they also exist at a relative point of incompletion that beckons other interventions. In other words, the almost telegraphic efficiency of the manifesto as form—the fact that it was not a complete statement but rather a project—at least allows for the possibility of someone to say, "I can do *that*," just as Selena seemed to beckon to Chicana girls to become stars, or Ricky Martin did the same for Puerto Rican kids. There is something inherently "messy"—for lack of a better word—in these interventions that manage to join desires and acts, and that do not foreclose either one or the other with the clear distinction of theory and practice. That messy intervention where boundaries are blurred is part of the spirit of this book.

My interest is less in theorizing on the present state of gay studies than in moving about, creating a book that is a sort of traveling and movable object, one that shows and tells at the same time. I think this is the queer praxis that should animate gay and lesbian studies—the space where theory and practice meet in order to open new possibilities. I also seek to intervene within the arenas of queer U.S. sexualities by injecting Latino America as a space that blurs a political and economic border placed at what is called the Río Grande in the United States and the Río Bravo in Mexico. That the same river can be indexed with different names illustrates the overlapping structures that this book desires to engage in. Latino America as a name intends to dislocate the convenient boundaries where North and South become rigid locales—with the North always providing the theory for the South's cultural practice. In this book, North and South do not enact the space, nor the distance, between theory and praxis. To refer back to the march in Buenos Aires, if outing has been part of the cultural discourse of U.S. homosexualities, this is tempered when we look at the consequences of that discourse in other settings. The cultural practice of homosexualities in Latin America entails building bridges with other actors on the social stage, and I see this as an interesting theoretical praxis vis-à-vis the atomized and balkanized queer practice occurring in many contexts in the United States.

All politics is, or should be, queer politics, just as all forms of artistic expression should aim to queer the public sphere. Somewhere between the dilution of homosexualities and its specificities lies the future of inclusive forms of social action. I see no contradiction in appropriation as long as one factors in positionality and direction. That these interventions come *from* the space of Latino America is meant to remind readers of the qualitative difference entailed by this preposition vis-à-vis the disastrous sequence of interventions *on* Latino America produced outside its internal or external borders.

Queering the Method

Browsing at a gay and lesbian bookstore, I came across a book of photographs that allowed me to explain why Cuba carried such a specific weight in these essays, and why I was interested in documenting the change—a certain change—in the body of U.S. and Latin American culture by means of Cuba, even while insisting that this book is not specific or particular to any one nationality or cultural context. The photographic essay, titled *Somos Cubanos,* was by Benno Thoma, who lives and works in Holland. It was sold in a picture book format, while highlights from the book could also be "had" as a postcard book, with each picture a detached card, ready to be mailed. The picture that caught my attention was of two shirtless men looking at the camera from a balcony in Havana. The one on the left seems to have a more serene look; the one on the right a more "menacing" one. One of them has his arms crossed; the other has propped one leg up on the balcony and rests his hands on his ankles as if he does not know what to do with his hands, or as if to signal the fact that he is about to run. But the bodies in the picture were only part of what attracted and fascinated me; the other was that it was one of the few pictures taken outdoors, and this gives the photograph a sense of dynamism and also a sense of secret.

Benno Thoma's picture was taken from one balcony to another—not connecting balconies but perpendicular ones, and the wooden door to the men's balcony is left ajar. This seems to me emblematic of difference in terms of a cultural space that can be perceived only by means of this distance. But also the outdoor balcony allows us to feel like voyeurs who suffer a degree of vertigo. Balconies are normally spaces where the subject looks out onto a street, but here the balcony is a space where one looks out at another balcony. Thoma wants to underscore the fact that these balconies are in Havana by letting the viewer pay attention to their worn-out architectural details.

A Balcony in Havana. Credit: Benno Thomas, Somos Cubanos. © 1998 Bruno Gmünder Verlag.

Havana may not be present as a *city* in these photographs, but it is present in the peeling walls of the exterior, or in the bare interiors at other points in the sequence. This is architecture as decay, as a mask that shows the passage of time. The bodies themselves could only be placed within this architecture in order to reference the histories of revolutionary desire.

The ambivalent and even hesitant visibility of the male homosexual figure is intensely pertinent in Cuba at a transitional historical period such as this, between a socialist economy and an increasingly market-oriented one. But it is also pertinent for the local and transnational links of Latino American homosexualities. Those bodies that used to be inside the rooms that lead to those balconies were *Cuban,* while their appearance in the balcony itself allows for their new configuration as (Cuban) *gay* males. In Cuba in particular, the postrevolutionary homosexual was always outside the national body, rejected by the nationalist construct. He was the essence of discharge itself, what is not wanted, what is not accepted. In Benno Thoma's photographic essay, the Cuban homosexual rejected by the state becomes the homosexual body desired by capitalism.

In his book *Homosexual Desire* Guy Hocquenghem—following Deleuze and Guattari, and from the point of view of a liberatory politics—argues for the transnationalization of the body without organs, the body that has no limits and no boundaries.[1] The irony, of course, is that the emancipatory potential that Hocquenghem saw has appeared in the mode of capital accumulation, so that the translocalized body of the homosexual does not stand at this point so much for personal liberation as for the liberation of global capital to pursue its aims. There are specificities involved, of course, and these specificities are important for us to take into account, but overall we can say, like many of the *Village Voice* writers mentioned in Chapter 8, that "Gay is global." The national bodies are reconfigured into transnational bodies, which collaborate more effectively with capitalist ventures.

The specificities are also important to take into account. They are not merely cultural inflections, but arise from a critique that homosexuals express in their own localities. Male homosexuals, for example, reconfigure their lack of validation in their own localized sites and remotivate this into a transnational identification. After having been excluded systematically from the histories of the nation, after withstanding the continuous accusations of "foreignness" within the realm of the "not sufficiently (Argentinean, Mexican, Spanish, etc.)," gays and lesbians have turned the accusation into defiance. For the male homosexual in particular, the body becomes the signifier and signified of foreignness itself, foreignness that imitates normative masculinity to the point of parody (those bulging muscles sported by the Carlos doll studied in chapter 7), as well as in terms of a culture with its transnational dress codes and cultural figures. On the one hand, techno or techno-funk, the ABBA comeback, Madonna's career, the gym, and the Calvin Klein commercials. On the other, the mark of cultural difference that is also pan-national in the case of Latino America: the same boleros with the same retro-signification of excessive sentiment, the admiration and fandom entailed in following Ricky Martin, or the heroines of the ancien régime like La Lupe, Olga Guillot, Libertad Lamarque, or Chavela Vargas. Transpose or translate, if you will, this same strategic cultural praxis to any of the major linguistic or cultural zones in the globalized environment and you will find a similar pattern. Male homosexuals, it seems, are at the forefront of the world understood in terms of universal globalizations accented by great blocks of specificities. Those gay clubs in poor neighborhoods in Latin America, Asia, or the Middle East that suffer from constant police harassment and surveillance, may have that Friday show dedicated to the same drag queen doing the same roster of figures: for every Cuban Olga Guillot, there is the Arab Fairouz. This performance is in many instances a self-conscious and deliberate act of defiance against national exclusions. Gays and lesbians are not simply beings who engage in a series of sexual practices. They are at this point cultural constructions of capitalism and at the same time, they may represent modes of defiance that use the tools of capitalism in order to undermine its repressive paradigms.

Unpacking the Archive

In Latin America, as well as in Europe, *male* homosexuality in particular is historically bound to very concrete processes of social engineering and modernization.[2] At the end of the nineteenth century, the state defined previously untaxonomized sectors, behaviors, and practices of the population as a whole in order to regulate the "shape" of the national body. In this way, the process that Foucault noted in *The History of Sexuality* also took place in Latin American societies. If modernization entailed taxonomy, and the goal of the nation was modernity, then it follows that those practices that were "pre-modern" remnants of an atavistic past and threatened a presumably "pure" national body would be seen unfavorably. In Latin America, naming the male homosexual meant pointing at the "invert" or the passive partner, while the active partner remained "somewhat" invisible, the remnant of a nonhygienic past. In a context that repressively (and predominantly) indexed men, lesbians were consigned to an effacement that in itself belied the male-centered concerns of institutions of power.

Visible homosexuality was meant to be expelled from a national fabric that could only see itself as tenuously constructed, in view of its immense social, racial, and ethnic inequities. Power operated in this specific regard in a dual fashion: it articulated the visibility and named it as something that it believed to be *other*. The system created highly codified visibilities—once again as these related to men, although the fact that women were always already "invisible" did not mean that they were "outside" the taxonomical circuits. Lesbians were also objects of the voyeuristic and repressive actions of the state, which, in terms of its functions, was not unique to Latin America, especially insofar as its rational systems of power were derived from "universalist" models of knowledge. These models were part of broader circuits of power operating in Western societies at the end of the nineteenth century and the beginning of the twentieth, although the political contexts in which these are deployed needs to be seen more clearly.[3] The state always names collective social participation in different ways according to the politics that underlie those claims. The homosexual citizen may be marked in one state but relatively unmarked in another—and thus the very notion of an *essential* homosexual is subject to dispute. This can be seen in the questions of citizenship surrounding immigration, where legal categories may render homosexual subjects visible or invisible according to specific (ir)rationalities.[4]

Concrete situations demand their own politics of visibility, and these may undermine notions of identity as these are understood in the United States. When speaking of Latin American or Latino male homosexualities, critics and social scientists like Almaguer, Carrier, Paz, Lumsden, and Leiner argue for a universal concept of homosexualities that "translates" into specific cultural contexts.[5] For Almaguer, Latino male sexualities are part of a "Mediterranean" paradigm that marks only the passive; for Carrier, the passive-active dynamic defines both partners as homosexual (Carrier reads sexuality according to the choice of object); from a "heterosexual" perspective, Paz sees penetration as the mark that fatally defines the homosexual. Because lesbian sexuality is not touched upon by these writers, they all presume the universality of a male gender as the point of departure for an analysis of a very complex situation that, in the context of masculinist privilege in Latin America, should be seen with cautionary specificities in mind.

To argue for "Mediterranean" paradigms as modes of rendering "Latin American" sexualities is an unfortunate choice of nomenclature, one that brings to mind German travelers like the Baron Von Gloeden at the turn of the century taking pictures of Sicilian youth representing an exotic "lost time" of historico-sexual abandon. For Paz, nothing can be allowed to disrupt the paradigms under which he has rescued or "created" Mexico from within the context of masculinist crisis. Carrier, in any event, renders otherness from within the context of his own assumptions, viewed as universalist. Some sense of caution is ascertained, to a greater extent, by Roger Lancaster, Sylvia Molloy, Licia Fiol Matta, and Frances Negrón Muntaner, although in the case of Lancaster, one notices the anthropological demand that incoherent situations be defined coherently, even when they cannot be so defined, thus neutralizing some of the more disruptive codes that sexualities may use.[6] Taking at times as their point of departure notions of performativity, Molloy, Fiol Matta, and Negrón Muntaner argue for a given situationist context that in turn may more suitably explore how homosexuality deploys itself.

The deployment of homosexualities in Latino America is varied and mobile, and thus it is unfortunate that many times gay and lesbian "missionaries" draw it as a cartographical dark continent. Gay and lesbian lives take place in bars and on the streets, on the docks and at the opera, at political meetings and rallies and in private parties—strategically open or under cover of secrecy, threatened by the police and by institutions of power, or in gay bars and discos that may be threatened by those same institutions of power or may live within and even collaborate with them. These lives are also defined by issues of race, class, and access, as these are also marked by gender in a masculinist context.

In the major Latin American urban centers—Buenos Aires, México, Rio de Janeiro, and Sao Paulo—lesbian and gay rights movements have sprung up in more recent decades as a result of different factors, among them a more open public sphere after the end of the military dictatorships of the 1970s, the growing awareness of gay rights in Europe and the United States, the AIDS pandemic, and the transnational contexts of feminism that had already been in place. The same situation obtains, with differences analyzed in chapter 8 of this book, in terms of Latinos in the United States. A visitor to any of the major Latin American capitals would conclude that, even if under the law, lesbians and gays have few guarantees and fewer rights, it is possible, in some way or another, to go out to a gay bar, to "come out" in certain situations, to lead what many in the United States and Europe would consider a "gay lifestyle." This situation, of course, is tempered by geography (major capitals) and by class. Issues such as the status of "coupling" or "marriage" may or may not be culturally translated from the United States, as daily life is a series of specificities and dissimulations, of negotiated "openness" or "outing" in selective situations. Even the issue of openness should be considered within a cultural context, for "outness" itself is not a constant, universal, normative way of being.

The erotic playfulness that limns the closet is, in many cases, the result of homophobia, but statements as to the repressive nature of Latin American societies have to be qualified at times by culturally specific notions of the body and of sex. In Latino America television viewers can see a well-known astrologist adored by women—and by many men everywhere—who dresses in long robes and satin shirts and is surrounded on the set by Orientalist kitsch. Famous singers like Chabela Vargas, as Yvonne Yarbro Bejarano has recently studied, have made no secret of the fact that they are either lesbian or have had lesbian experiences.[7] No comparable figure, as far as I know, has existed in the United States unless we count Liberace's open masquerades of gender. Even within this context, the specificity of a "gay identity" has been rejected by writers and artists in Latino America, and we cannot automatically think that this rejection is due to fear or to the closet.

To insist on these differences entails always seeing Latinos as "others," and to avoid these differences generally implies falling for the universalist presumptions of U.S. identity discourse. In this sense, I would claim as my own the nuanced position on identity in *La homosexualidad en Argentina,* written in 1987 by Carlos Jáuregui. Jáuregui's book speaks of homosexuality as a political force in Argentina, while steering clear of the identity politics prevalent in the United States. For Jáuregui there is a gay historico-cultural continuum. He echoes Foucault (who mostly talked about men, as does Jáuregui, to a great extent) in asserting homosexuality as a cultural and historical construction, and he is also aware of the fact that homosexuals have been persecuted throughout history. This leads to the question of identities. Jáuregui asks, "Is there a gay identity?" and the question is posed with full awareness of its dangers:

Would it not be, in any case, dangerous if its existence were to be proven? Would we homosexuals not be falling into a trap that emphasizes our own self-esteem? Are we not playing along with a power that seeks only to straitjacket us into behaviors in order to achieve that Machiavellian "divide and conquer"?[8]

These are important words to consider when we ponder as a whole the impertinent invisibilities of Latino American gays and lesbians, including those of the marchers in Buenos Aires. Jáuregui understands that the "gay identity" can only serve as a force that isolates, and that interrupts the links between subjects within their communities. He concludes that there is no such thing as a "gay identity," but adds that if there is (or were), such a notion should be seen not as a "given" but rather as one that needs to be created and constructed, sustained by a "transformative ideology": "it is necessary that we consider, starting from that reality that is our homosexuality, what are the types of relationships that we can establish with the world, how we can go about achieving these, and what do we need to invent in order to do this."[9]

For Jáuregui, identity is always bracketed by the notion of communities and coalitions. Thus the concept of "gay identity" is here seen in relational terms. This makes sense in a book dedicated to, among others, the Mothers of the Plaza de Mayo, who also knew how to render their silent presence as one of the more effective tools of resistance against the state. For Jáuregui, as well as for all those who learned from the silent action of the Mothers, we must not essentialize identity; rather, we should privilege the network of relationships that will allow subjects to *construct* an identity. This is important when we consider that in order to claim civil rights, the Comunidad Homosexual Argentina (Argentinean Homosexual Community) also had to claim *legal* status, and in order to achieve this, it had to count on the support of transnational members of the lesbian and gay communities, as well as all members of a civil society re-created after the collapse of the military regime. When the particular situation demanded it, Argentinean lesbian and gay organizations did not hesitate to appeal to a transnational context of modernized societies, with its homosexual organizations structured around notions of identity, and they did this in order to achieve very specific goals within the emerging discourse of national civil rights. At other times (as in reference to the polemical issues of gays in the military) the transnational links were rejected.[10] Questions that are essential for many Western gay and lesbian movements may be more nuanced in terms of Latinos. Identity may be something that is used strategically in order to pursue specific social aims. As a praxis that responds to a repressively modernizing state power, these strategic forms of intervention deserve to be validated for the social gains they have produced.

Burning the Archive

Tropics of Desire addresses the ways we can puzzle out the information given by a queer performance, and how different publics decode this information. How does one read a text, or a cultural figure? How is music read from the point of view of a queer intervention? There is a queerness of methodology at the foundation of *Tropics of Desire*, as well as a queer form of organizing the book. Although at first glance the chapters move within the space of literary studies and then toward the broader arenas of cultural and political issues, this organization belies other narratives also contained in the book. The essays as a whole explore what a Latino queer presence is all about. What are we supposed to read, and how are we supposed to decode information that has been coded in order to resist the dominant structures of power? At the same time, the book poses the question of what we gain or lose by decoding that information.

Because the structures of coded and decoded information are present within the circuit of Latino American homosexualities, *Tropics of Desire* goes back to an archive in order to trace the bloodlines—the generational continuum—of the coded information. The strategic plays within the archive entail an understanding of strategic silences and an insistence on homosexuality that at the same time places itself outside the terrain of the "gay." Virgilio Piñera's novels and tales, Xavier Villaurrutia's poems, and Lydia Cabrera's anthropological texts may all seem "closeted" to a North American audience, although I think it is better to understand them as strategic texts, as queer performances that mobilize different public actors. Avoiding a confession as to identity, Piñera, Cabrera and Villaurrutia were nevertheless not lonely, marginalized figures; they were not the unhappy victims of a pre-Stonewall world. They engaged with whole networks of visible, invisible, out, closeted, semi-closeted, partly open, flaming, or circumspect lesbians and gays. They traveled and came into contact with others like them; they published in some of the more important magazines and periodicals of their time; they had as mentors and friends the most illustrious (closeted?) figures in the Hispanic world. They were government spokespersons; they engaged in, criticized, and manipulated public opinion; they inhabited a cultural space that had already been "queered" to a degree that was perhaps unthought of in the United States.

It is clear that my understanding of the strategic silences about their homosexuality entails noticing how silence is part of a political and aesthetic praxis. In ways that may be difficult for us to understand, these writers "queered" the social space where they intervened. This could take place only from within the space that is later signaled by the strategic use of the mask in the Buenos Aires gay and lesbian march, the deployment of sexuality as an image, a *play* on identity, not an identity per se. *Tropics of Desire* is less interested in the subject who proclaims his or her own sexuality than the melancholic subject who refuses the confession, the subject who chooses to mask it, while at the same time showing us the mask.

The two positions are not absolute or commensurate, and should not be simply understood as a result of open or closeted notions of identity. It is ironic, in this context, that Reinaldo Arenas could only become a renowned figure posthumously as a political dissident *outside* Cuba (more specifically, in the United States) by engaging with "queer" politics. He did this without abandoning his political fight against the Cuban government, and wishing, in fact, that gay men did not have to proclaim their own desires as an identity, since this threatened what Arenas saw as the "true nature" of homosexual desire: the pursuit of those who "were" by those who "were not." By maneuvering his status as "gay" and as political dissident, Arenas engaged the Cuban revolution within the parameters of personal liberty and collective rights that it had claimed for itself. As I mention in chapter 5, he did this in *Improper Conduct* while at the same time never once claiming allegiance to a "gay movement"—a fact that was much criticized by gay and lesbian sympathizers of the Cuban revolution at the time. These accused Arenas of manipulating public opinion against Cuba by "using" the gay angle without having ever belonged to any gay organization.

Like the marchers in Buenos Aires, many of the interviewed subjects in

Improper Conduct were masked participants, for in spite of the fact that they were in a movie that accused the Cuban government of wholesale repression against homosexuals, the interviewed subjects refused to define their own sexuality. This is one of the reasons that, as an indictment against the Cuban revolution, *Improper Conduct* was one of the most effective interventions done by a group of Cuban exiles within the context of the progressive Left, and why it took more than ten years for a coherent response to come out of Cuba in the film *Strawberry and Chocolate*, a film that is, in spite of all its progressive intentions, more conservative than *Improper Conduct*, since it insists on free expression as a question of identity (and identity as deserving of respect because it is useful in terms for culture) over and beyond an examination of the structural causes of wholesale repression. As a visible subject, the homosexual Diego in *Strawberry and Chocolate* is ineffective in a way that Arenas in *Improper Conduct* was not. Arenas related to different publics; he played with many identity categories all at once. He lashed back at the Cuban government with its own tools: if the revolution demanded the open confession of homosexuality, he refused to give it on film; if the revolution classified homosexuals as "foreign elements," as *gusanera* outside the realm of the *patria*, Arenas could be seen (and, more importantly, heard) in the film speaking perfect *French*. A more outrageous gesture in recent Cuban discourse I have yet to see.

Tracing the Network

Culture bears the mark of the social shame produced by homosexualities, and this shame places gays and lesbians always in the realm of exile. The "open secret" of same-sex attraction is imprinted in the aura of foreignness within homosexual texts, to the extent that foreignness itself seems to be the metaphor for the relationship that dares not speak its name. Oscar Wilde was the translator of French texts, Christopher Isherwood wrote coded and not so coded stories in Berlin, Federico García Lorca could allow the open expression of his homosexuality only in New York, Witold Gombrowicz embedded his homosexuality within a literary dispute taking place in Argentina, and William Burroughs, Hart Crane, and Lawrence Ferlinghetti sought refuge and release in Morocco, Cuba, or Mexico. This foreignness is but symptomatic of other forms of foreignness felt by the subject, and is in itself a coded reference to the sense of secret that can be uncovered only under the aegis of cultural exoticism as another kind of cover. One of the first novels in Latin America to treat the homosexual theme is the Chilean Augusto D'Halmar's *La pasión y muerte del cura Deusto* (1924), a story where the tragic love of a Basque priest and a young boy takes place in Sevilla. Many Latin American texts are "in on the secret," as Daniel Balderston has remarked, and partly, the history and criticism of Latino American culture have collaborated in a "conspiracy" that keeps the secret from coming out. Exotic locales may be a way of covering up sexual content, as a decoy that allows critics to notice the atmosphere of the novel and not its erotics.[11] But to notice simply the exotic locale is to betray cultural blinders that are not at all used by readers who understand the specifics of why a story may be placed in the realm of exile.

In literature the issue of homosexuality was treated by *modernismo* at the beginning of the twentieth century as something other, unnamed, occluded, and repressed—its place would be that of "crime or illness."[12] Had that cultural logic continued, as Oscar Montero argues convincingly, representations of homosexuality would have been forgotten up to the present. Literature positioned itself out of a closet after the twenties. Publishing *Contemporáneos* in Mexico after the revolution (1910–1920), Salvador Novo and Xavier Villaurrutia were openly identified as "effeminate" or "queer"—even provoking a homophobic polemic in the press as to whether Mexican literature was "virile." In the thirties and forties in Cuba, the tortured poetry of Emilio Ballagas was as close to openly expressing its homosexuality as you could get, even if Ballagas married at a later point in his life and fathered a child. Also in Cuba, during the fifties, Virgilio Piñera's homosexuality was an open secret, as was that of José Rodríguez Feo, publisher of two of the most important Cuban literary journals of this past century, *Orígenes* and *Ciclón*. These figures are studied in chapter 4 of this book. Rodríguez Feo in turn was a friend of both Piñera and Lezama Lima, whose later masterpiece, *Paradiso* (1966), contains an infamous chapter that deals explicitly, in his baroque prose, with male homosexual sex. *Contemporáneos* in Mexico and *Orígenes* in Cuba mark the active intervention of a group of (particularly) gay men who actively participated in cultural and literary polemics from the 1930s to the 1950s.

Homosexuality for these gays and lesbians was understood as a constellation—lines of flight, encounters where the code allows for its sparks to fly off in all directions. For example, Federico García Lorca was the most important poet of his time, a hit wherever and whenever he went in his tours, with his Andalusian fire and his flamboyant gypsy eyes. He was a figure whose homosexuality could be accepted and at the same time repressed, consigned to the preconscious by some epistemological feat of heroic proportions. If we want to establish an origin for the modern male homosexual ur-text in the archive, we have to go to Lorca's *Ode to Walt Whitman*, a text that damns and celebrates the homosexual, written at a period when Lorca was struggling with the question of homosexuality, an issue that, according to biographers, came into its own only with the poet's three-month stay in Havana in 1930.[13]

The first printing and only complete publication of the *Ode* in Lorca's lifetime consisted of fifty copies released on August 5, 1933, by a Mexican private press called Alcancía. The poem became the anthem for an ennobled and discreet coterie, the dramatic manifesto of an elite with "strong social sympathies toward homosexuals."[14] The sense of privacy invested in the edition allowed the particular contradictory voices later heard in the poem to be understood exactly as contradictory, and not as the "troubled, tangled or ranting voice that has been heard by later readers beyond the circle."[15] One should note from the outset the remotivation of the aesthetic avant-garde that this gesture entailed. It is as if this publication resignified the idea of a vanguard group but in this case masking the said/unsaid struggles around homosexuality at the political center of the aesthetics.

Federico García Lorca in Madrid's Residencia de Estudiantes, 1924. © VEGAP, Fundación Federico García Lorca.

The controlled publication and reception of Lorca's *Ode*, its anguished voice, and its sense of personal malaise are echoed by other long poems written by male gay writers in the Latin American tradition. I am here thinking of Villaurrutia's haunting "Nocturno de los ángeles," collected in the second edition of *Nostalgia de la muerte*; Virgilio Piñera's *La isla en peso*; Emilio Ballagas's "Nocturno y elegía," and others. All of these poets in some way or another wrote in a voice related to Lorca's, even in terms of their implicit or explicit postulation of a selected coterie of readers who would understand the language of *implications*, just as Oscar Wilde's readers were meant to understand the particular language of flowers.[16] What is important here is the constitution of the selected coterie itself, the community of readers, its sense of diasporic self-identification. Lorca met the Mexican poet Salvador Novo in Argentina in 1933, and the account of that meeting, presented in Novo's *Continente vacío,* is a full-fledged exercise in the limits of careful—but also flaming—outing. In Novo's account, published in a newspaper at the time (not as part of a memoir, or as a letter), Lorca appears first of all in bed, dressed in white and black striped pajamas, with a coterie that includes a very quiet and serious young male secretary, attending to his every need as if he were a movie star diva. It is clear from Novo's *public* account that he and Lorca *read* each other as only two flaming queens can, and it is also clear that at least some readers were meant to understand the secret language of this mutual tease. Meeting later on in one of the restaurants that overlooks the Río de la Plata, Novo thinks back on Lorca's *Ode,* and this publication is outed for the public record:

Federico and I, alone, like two friends who have not seen each other in many years, like two persons who are going to compare their biographies, prepared at different extremes of the earth to enjoy each other. At what moment did we start using the familiar "tu"? I had his Ode to Walt Whitman *fresh in my memory, virile, courageous, precious, that Federico had not seen but had just been printed in a limited edition by the boys from Alcancía. But we did not talk about literature. All of our Spain flowed from his lips in that conversation with no witnesses, avid to approach our Mexico, which he saw in the small Indian that he discovered in my eyes.*[17]

This erotic encounter between Spain and Mexico is astounding for all the raging cattiness and the ruffled feathers that can be decoded on the very surface of the writing. It may be superfluous to stress that their sense of identification is not predicated on literary aesthetics, but on what is named as an allusive camaraderie where serious literature becomes also the item placed in the gossip column. Novo is like Miss Mexico and Lorca Miss Spain (Novo later reproduces Lorca's speech by tranzcribing Lorca'z Andaluzian Zpanish as I have just done now), and they share a *quiet moment* with no witnesses

(Novo underscores this). This encounter, then, is predicated on the common bond of a screaming anthem of faggotry (Lorca's *Ode*) that Novo *just so happens* to describe with the terms "virile" and "courageous." These terms seem pertinent as self-descriptive if we consider the readers that the "muchachos" of Alcancía had in mind—readers who would fawn over the silhouette of the two naked boys that appeared on the cover. The question of the homosexual voice here is not necessarily a question of the closet. The public that knows and can read the code will know exactly what to read, while the writers go on with their social affairs.

The line of flight that starts with Lorca and Novo can be followed a bit further, and it leads to many authors and cultural figures studied in this book. When Lorca went to Havana in 1930 he met with Lydia Cabrera, a young, wealthy Cuban socialite who had met him in Spain in 1926 at the house of José María Chacón y Calvo. Cabrera had visited Spain and Paris in 1925, and had returned to Cuba briefly before returning to Paris in 1927. Aside from a couple of trips back to Cuba, she lived in Europe until 1938, when, as she says, she discovered the world of Afro-Cuban culture. This turned her into the foremost authority on the subject and the writer of the *Contes nègres de Cuba* (1936)—first published in French and then in Spanish (1940)—and of *El monte* (1954), perhaps the best book on Afro-Cuban religion to date. What is important in this context is that Cabrera met the Venezuelan writer Teresa de la Parra on the latter's stop in Cuba in 1924 at a particularly difficult juncture in Parra's life. Parra, in fact, was on her way back to Venezuela from Paris and was in mourning for Emilia Barrios, who was her Parisian companion and, as Sylvia Molloy states, "possibly the greatest influence in her life."[18] The epistolary exchange that ensued between Cabrera and Parra, as Sylvia Molloy recalls, reflects "the difficulty of stating a sexual identity and, more generally, of expressing gender unease" and allows the reader to notice "the way that desire sees itself, the detours to which it resorts in order to name itself, the simulation it must engage in in order to 'pass,' the codes it uses in order to be recognized even as it masks itself, and even the repression it exerts against itself as it internalizes conventional prejudice."[19] Culture was a way of talking and not talking, it was the code and it was also the mask. The frank and "not unsympathetic" renderings of lesbianism in a book by Collette disturbed Cabrera and Parra, but what is important is that the book was there as a mode of filtering, a way of engaging in a conversation that could not be had by any other means.[20]

Cabrera knew and shared a cultural space with two Cuban gay men who, after 1944, started working on one of the century's most important Latin American literary and cultural journals, *Orígenes*, which was directed by José Lezama Lima with the funds provided by José Rodríguez Feo's considerable fortune. *Orígenes* was an example of intellectual consistency in a country in which all attempts at institutional order seemed doomed to fail—graft, corruption, and sheer venality dominated public life. Because the political and social life of the country seemed to be condemned to a change with no change, *Orígenes* presented the unruffled surface of a timeless present. The roster of artists, writers, and essayists who were published in the journal yields a list of the most impressive names of the moment. Rodríguez Feo's sojourns outside Cuba enlisted for the journal, among others, Vicente Aleixandre, Luis Cernuda, Aimé Césaire, Gabriela Mistral, Octavio Paz, W. H. Auden, T. S. Eliot, Witold Gombrowicz, Saint-John Perse, Wallace Stevens, and William Carlos Williams. It is clear that Rodríguez Feo saw his own role in *Orígenes* as much more than that of a simple financial sponsor.

Given the centralized space that *Orígenes* had in Cuban culture, it is surprising that the issue of the homosexuality of many of its members (including, but not solely, Rodríguez Feo and Lezama Lima) did not assume the center of debate as it had in the case of the Mexican journal *Contemporáneos*.[21] Undoubtedly, this was due to the very different contexts in which the journals subsisted: *Contemporáneos* belonged to a time of debate within Mexican revolutionary cultural politics, whereas *Orígenes* was in many ways the product of the general indifference to issues of culture in prerevolutionary Cuba. A revolutionary society is one that demands visibility: Mexican traditions and culture were examined in postrevolutionary society in a way that was not found in the Cuban context before 1959. Cubans lived in a relatively unexamined cultural space until the revolution inaugurated a new debate on Cuban culture.

As I explain in the first chapter, it was through and by means of culture-as-work that writers coded their information. The American poet Hart Crane's belabored and cultured poetry at some level entailed the "sweating out" of poetry as a mechanism of production; Rodríguez Feo is very clear on the fact that his travels throughout the United States needed the economic excuse of the magazine and the personal excuse of education (he studied for a time at Middlebury College) in order to compensate for the "sensual" periods themselves. Within a culture that at the same time values and dislikes poets and writers, and that totally rejects homosexual ones who in turn feel isolated because of issues of class, culture becomes a kind of lingua franca, to the extent that everything is expressed through and by means of it. The spectacle of *Orígenes* precisely depended on the coded silence within this elliptical circuit of affections, as if *Orígenes* were not only a metaphor but rather a kind of pre-text. "I know," Lezama says to José Rodríguez Feo, "that you haven't done anything, and you let yourself be drawn into insensate and sensuous periods."[22] "You haven't done anything," says Lezama, and by this we are meant to understand the code: "you've only been having sex." José Rodríguez Feo will explain: "After six days in Firenze, I am bathing on this delicious beach, contemplating those Italian beauties who come out of the sea like that Tadzio in *Death in Venice*."[23] If culture was understood as the way of remotivating unproductive sex, it may be that we can, to a large extent, read *Orígenes*, for Rodríguez Feo, as a way of pursuing sex by other means. In this way, we could say that the exquisite elegance of *Orígenes*, after all, could only be born out of the gutter.

Tour Guide

Tropics of Desire studies cultural relations, but it tries not to forget the gutter that in some measure sustained Rodríguez Feo's enterprise. The latter chapters of the book concern the representation of homosexuality in a recent Cuban film, the codes that allow us to read questions of sexuality in Latino music, the representation of Latinos within the broad culture of U.S. male homosexuality, and the actions of queer Latinos in U.S. and Latino American politics. I did not intend to divide the book in such a clear-cut fashion, and this is not a book that profits from a reading that distinguishes literature from other questions of cultural studies. Like other books and cultural practices examined within it, *Tropics of Desire* engages in a queer methodology and works in a queer fashion.

From the outset, identity, desire, and revolution allow me to explore the dialectics of visibilities, geography, and politics. These three axes may never be seen in isolation from each other if the book's broader theoretical implications are to be understood. The "tropics" of the title refer to a space centered in Cuba and Mexico but that is in no way limited to these countries. It speaks to the imaginary constructions that allow many citizens of the United States to unanimize the world south of the border. "Tropics" has to be seen, then, as a tongue-in-cheek, ironic response to the mode in which the geographical variety of Latin America is perceived in the United States as a unanimized land of "heat," as the *gumbo* of sensuality that meshes in some way with a world in which repression renders subjects as children, rather than discerning subjects of national polities of erratic legalities. Because any book on sexuality is always a book about desire, it is important to at least take note of a desire that defines Latin Americans for Western consumption, even if in the mode of irony.

The book is more flexible in terms of its organization than what it seems to be at first. Literature and art here form a constellation of signs, a kind of ideogrammatic archipelago completed by the one who gazes. Instead of argumentation, I have opted for recurrence; instead of pursuing one historical line, I have chosen to explore and contest at times the notion of filial continuity. In the first four chapters of the book—on correspondence, Xavier Villaurrutia, Lydia Cabrera, and Virgilio Piñera—I have grounded these authors' ways of coding themselves as a mode of praxis. In the latter part of the book, I have examined the different publics mobilized by the praxis of homosexual interventions.

The latter chapters of the book prolong the play with the audience that I see used by many of the writers in the first part of the book. The gay audience for the boleros, the gay consumers of Billy and Carlos dolls, the varied population that grooved to Ricky Martin are all related to the cultural interventions that I saw in Villaurrutia, Cabrera, and Piñera. What readers will find in all the essays is a mode of praxis that interpellates difference and community. The different publics recognize each other as part of a community bounded by affect. *Tropics of Desire* wants to be within that border, where the nightclub yields the usual roster of stars that invite you to go past the ballroom to the dressing rooms, where nostalgia breeds affect with a self-conscious, melancholic gaze.

1 The Mask of the Letter

Envelope

When Elizabeth Bishop arrived in Brazil in 1951 and met Lota Macedo de Soares, she took a bite of a cashew nut and got sick. By the time she recovered, she was in a relationship with Lota Macedo that kept her in Brazil for the next fifteen years, in a home in the mountains above Petropolis in Samambaia. Bishop was protected from neighbors by miles of land, as she confessed in a letter. "[T]he scenery is unbelievably impractical . . . it is a sort of dream-combination of plant & animal life. I really can't believe it at all. Not only are there highly impractical mountains all around with clouds floating in and out of one's bedroom, but waterfalls, orchids, all the Key West flowers I know & Northern apples and pears as well."[1] While Bishop's life was consumed in this dream, the Brazilian "friend" and "companion" was ordering teams of workers to carry out the process of building a house.

Elizabeth Bishop writes in a haze, while Lota, who was described by Robert Giroux as having "intelligent eyes and mannish looks," fights with the workers. Elizabeth referred to these workers in her letters: "he and Lota have screamed their heads off at each other—worse scenes than usual, because carried on in the shop with twenty men hammering iron and working buzz saws and blast furnaces, etc., all around us" (241). The house was, as Robert Giroux calls it in his introduction to Bishop's selected letters, an "architectural marvel" when completed: a prize-winning "split-level, horizontal building, with ramps, sliding glass walls, and what was to be an aluminum roof" (xv) with rooms for the maid and separate houses for the cook and the gardener. On a space separated from the house and above a boulder, a running stream was transformed into a swimming pool. There Bishop had her own studio, with a wall that prevented her from being distracted by the spectacular view of the mountains. From the studio she sent "imaginary letters" and real letters while the weather changed in the course of a day: "[y]ou put on all your clothes to start with, peel off all morning, start putting on again about three, and go to bed with a hot water bottle and socks about nine, absolutely frozen" (239). The peeling off, or the adding on, was accomplished always within the context of "lofty vagueness" that Bishop liked so much in Brazil, where "a few clouds spill over the tops of the mountains exactly like waterfalls in slow motion" (243).

The isolation, the sheer exoticism (for Bishop) of the space, and the protection from the prying eyes of neighbors allowed the poet to compare herself indirectly to those clouds that came into the bedroom only to disappear. She writes surrounded by clouds that dissolve on the page on which she is writing, "where a cloud is coming in my bedroom window right this minute" (237) and where she confesses, "The intimacy with clouds may not be too good. . . . but I like it so much I don't want to move" (237). Because this intimacy with clouds takes place in that modernist dream palace, no reader should gloss over the perfect metaphor that this entails. Two women, one of them dreaming, while the other oversees the construction of a house where nature and culture coalesce in the form of a running stream turned into a swimming pool. Nature is transformed into a habitable place by elegant tampering that sometimes wants to pass as natural itself. If nature is the essence, it is always there as a construction, as a stream that calls for transformation into a swimming pool.

Bishop and Macedo de Soares are subjects who remain in a space where confession and self-disclosure are seen as tautological. There is no radical narrative in this tale, no progressive story where the closet is abandoned for realization and then self-affirmation. Nature is not going to be radically altered by these subjects, but its meaning is going to be teased out as something that is always constructed. The "coming out" (if there is one) needs the realm of perfect construction, the modernist dream palace, where the subject plays hide-and-seek with clouds, writing those real and imaginary letters where the fact of being lesbian, of having a lesbian relationship, is not even brought onto the page. It is like those clouds of which Bishop speaks, the ones important for their disappearance.

Bishop's way of not talking about sexuality in her letters is part of what Octavio Paz has termed Bishop's "enormous power of reticence" (vii) in her poetry. But the more one reads these letters the more one wonders whether reticence is truly the issue here. Bishop's letters may be important not for their reserve, but rather for the other realm of the mundane that they do not express. Who was in bed? What was love like? (I am not speaking of the banal aspects of lovemaking.) It may be that Bishop's reticence precluded these confessions, but one should also try to find other reasons that account for it.

It is important to look beyond reticence and explore the situation of the letter itself embodying the silent drama of what is and is not said, the illusion of a private space. But if this space is not private, where do we look in order to find Bishop's self-understanding as a lesbian? The spaces outside the letter and the "work" may be a better guide for this than paper itself: the architectural marvel of the house, the natural habitat that it tried to blend in and with, the reality of two women who needed that land as a buffer zone from prying neighbors, and Bishop as the only subject who has correspondents to write to—for she is the traveler, the exotic flower in the midst of that tropical landscape—inhabiting a space surrounded by clouds, where clouds in some way speak of what cannot be spoken about.

This image must be insisted on for the sake of its own aura, because the absence in the letters may only be the illusory mark of those clouds, the traces of another language that does not *need* to appear on paper. The edition of Bishop's letters that I quote from carries its own disclaimer: "selected." What has the editor excised? Or is the letter itself the mask of that absence? In these letters, homosexuality is the figure in the carpet—what is not said but is also not hidden. The mark of that absence is also the mask of the letter. Whatever it is that it covers, it also reveals.[2]

Stamp

> When we were over, I wanted my letters back. My copyright she said but her property. She had said the same about my body. . . . I took them into the garden and burned them one by one and I thought how easy it is to destroy the past and how difficult to forget it.
>
> —JEANETTE WINTERSON, *Written on the Body*

Letters are meant to be burned, destroyed, or lost. The epistolary is the most contradictory genre: it says that one owns more completely if one destroys, that one talks about things by not talking about them, and that desire is all about seeing oneself as one writes to an other. Whoever wants to explore private space will be disappointed in letters, for there is no solitude in their pages, and privacy is not a claim one can make; what we find is anxiety over what Winterson calls property and copyright. A letter is always someone else's possession. The narrative of correspondence is not really about receiving letters and writing letters, but rather about losing them, about silencing, about what happens when they fall into the wrong hands.

Letter writing brings out gay and lesbian anxieties of possession. The fiction of letters manifests illusions of ownership and possession, traits and signatures that one *acquires* in order to have, and that one *has* to acquire in order to deploy. We may think that letters talk about private life, but what they actually talk about is a code in which privacy is nothing but spectacle, secrets are told when there are no secrets to tell. What is not in the letter carries the weight of its absence, renders the letters even more present to themselves because of what is excluded. From one gay man or lesbian to another the page is no shelter but a mask for distance—the distance between writing, expression, and an ownership sacrificed in order to establish a particular kind of property. Letters call for the kaleidoscopic eyes of the voyeur, but also for the enamored gaze of the believer.

If we want to have an idea of how homosexuality was or was not expressed in the 1930s, 1940s, or 1950s, we have to dissect the space of correspondence. The more one reads, the more one understands that identity in some way or another was masked, or foiled, precisely by what initiated those letters—the sheer fact of absence. The questions one has as a reader (Did they talk about *it*? Did they go out to bars? Did they go cruising, and where? Did they have sex with each other?) all seem like impertinences to which letters only respond with silence. One could say that for the letter writers, then, identity was not an issue, or that identity and sexuality were not linked in the same way as they are for us. One way of reading this silence would be to appeal to culture, to say that sexuality was not important in the cultural context in which these writers moved. But then again, that seems like a poor answer—for how unimportant can sexuality be, when the roster of names that I will bring into this scenario reveals a kind of gay cultural network?

Elizabeth Bishop, José Rodríguez Feo, Lydia Cabrera, Hart Crane, and others lived with a remarkable degree of openness about their gender preference. These were not men and women whose sexuality is a point of contention or a secret. Their letters show an amazing range of style. Some, like Hart Crane's, speak in one code to the family and in another to friends like Waldo Frank. Others, like Xavier Villaurrutia's, replicate the poetic persona of their work: nostalgia is the theme of Villaurrutia's poetry and also of his letters. The Cuban writer Virgilio Piñera engages in funny gossip and bantering that can also be seen in his tales, while the editor José Rodríguez Feo goes on a name-dropping rampage to Lezama, that monster of culture himself, who spends quiet days in his house in Havana's Trocadero Street. It is clear that these letters in published form have been heavily censored, but even without censorship I would be surprised if more comprehensive editions revealed that editorial prudishness has excised all comments on sex, and that the writers are forthcoming about their sexual acts, as opposed to their steamy "blue periods." First, for these border crossers, privacy is a foreclosed option when it comes to writing, for there is no private space the minute one puts pen to paper. Second, writing is all about forgetting, and one cannot forget what one does not write about. This is what the absence of homosexuality in their letters shows: that the writers are not allowed the privilege of forgetting.

As a confessional object, the letter is meant to bring out anxieties of possession.[3] Oscar Wilde will endlessly fault Bosie for the careless treatment given to his letters, which end up being a matter of public record, as he states in *De Profundis*—another letter that was also not for him (Wilde) to possess. Unlike fiction, correspondence is enmeshed within a history of privacy, and as such it is part and parcel of a history of suspicion. Imprisoned for his crime, Wilde revisits the scene of the crime in the letter. Wilde could write *De Profundis* only because there was already a legal system bent on destroying him, and also because homosexuality was an item—indeed, *the* item—on the agenda.

In order to understand the language of letters we must understand three orders of communication, and these are not to be equated so simply with literary "genres." One order is the language of the "work of art," another is the language of memoirs—where the subject becomes the object of his or her own gaze—and the third is the language of correspondence. These three "languages" function and circulate within their own economies, never totally different from each other, but at the same time keeping their own borders under surveillance, since the three are predicated and centered on the fact of something that could and could not be said. The question here is not to see poems or novels as some other, more fully developed kind of "text" whose kernel is the letter. What the Mexican poet Xavier Villaurrutia writes in a letter is not simply a more developed version of what he says in a poem; rather, the letter and the poem are two situations that stand at a particular relationship of desire to each other. These are, of course, not only relations of desire but also relations of production, sites of textual pleasure. Letters are spaces of alibis where desire is both subject and object, where whatever "exceeds" the text is not figured, but rather represented.

The "work of art" does not mimic the letter, and the letter itself is not the prelude to the work of art. What is interesting here is the network, the economy that they all deploy.[4] It is a network that bleeds from one letter to the other; it allows fragmentary selves to have a point of contact. Letters are all about a circuit and not about a point of stasis. When Xavier Villaurrutia writes in a letter to his fellow poet Salvador Novo what he will then seek to express in one of the poems collected in *Nostalgia for Death*, the relations of production between one text and the other allow for a common language. Here Xavier Villaurrutia describes Los Angeles to Salvador Novo:

There is no beauty in Los Angeles except in the irresistible night. The nightclubs are beautiful and I rest in them, drinking beer before embarking on a new ascension to the heaven of my room, on the ninth floor. When you think that that ascent will be the last one of the night, a temptation, a new opportunity. I do not know what color dreams are in Los Angeles, I only know that these are blue.[5]

The letter is a form of code: Villaurrutia "rests" in nightclubs; he goes up and down the elevator. This is the same theme fully deployed in his *Nostalgia for Death*, with its constant mention of heaven on earth, angels, ascents and descents. If one wants to know what kind of weekend Villaurrutia may have had, one has to engage in the circuit, leave the correspondence altogether and look into Salvador Novo's memoirs.[6] There, Novo raves about a man called Agustín Fink. Novo explains that Ignacio Moctezuma, whom he describes as a "congressman," "lived in the Hotel Iturbide and had as a lover a young athlete of German descent, Agustín Fink, whose mammoth cock only Nacho Moctezuma himself could boast of being able to accommodate." The excerpt of the memoir concludes, of course with Novo olympically accommodating Agustín Fink, and thus beating Moctezuma at his own game.[7]

Agustín Fink was also Villaurrutia's friend and guide in Los Angeles. But Villaurrutia's reserve about these events (he does not rave about Fink as a sexual object in the published correspondence) I suspect has nothing to do with the reserve of homosexuality, or with reticence as such, as in the case of Elizabeth Bishop, but with the different forms of representation given in the letter, the memoir, and the poem. It is not an issue of the "closet" but of a subject position, a certain decorum in writing about oneself to another. It is not a failure to "come out" but a mode of representation. The secret is plain for all to see. After all, it is to Agustín Fink (Novo's olympic conquest) that Villaurrutia dedicates one of the best poems in *Nostalgia for Death*: "Nocturno de los ángeles," a poem that is perhaps more open than most about a homosexuality that it registers as an open pickup scene between angels who desire the very real bodies they encounter on the street:

> *They call themselves Dick or John, Marvin or Louis.*
> *Only by their beauty are they distinguishable from men.*
> *They walk, they pause, they move on.*
> *They exchange glances, they dare to smile.*
> *They form unpredictable couples.*[8]

If poetry plays hide-and-seek with representing or figuring homosexuality, one would expect the space of correspondence to open up the closet, to explain that which could not be said in public. But writing a letter is different from writing a memoir. One has to factor in the scaffolding that correspondence builds for itself, which is as important as the material object of the letter. In this narrative the state that demands the stamp, the paper that does not quite hold the confession, and then the empty time that it takes to send, receive, and then answer a letter—all of these are perhaps more important than the fact of what is said. This scaffold is part of the circuit of self-representation. It is not that the narrative of letters is found elsewhere, but that the space that surrounds writing is part of the narrative.

The state always demarcates the borders of correspondence. Between the letter writer and the addressee, there is always the state in the form of the postal system—the state that spies and reads, the voyeuristic state seduced by the possibilities of intimacy. A letter is an object that flies, that is handled, a visible thing. Correspondence establishes a circuit: networks, figures, decentralized movements, rhizomes, codes—and then codes that point to themselves as codes. All of these account for correspondence as a "liminal" mode of textuality. It is the place where an individual becomes a subject, and a subject becomes an "author."

Correspondence here is an emblem for homosexuality, or at least it illuminates the way we should explore homosexualities—by noticing the kinds of detours it makes, by reading a network spread out in space but localized in time. Correspondence, like homosexuality, beckons a play with liminal or marginal status, a play where readers rescue pleasure given in the form of absence.

Postmark

> I made no attempt to conceal my inclinations, but Xavier [Villaurrutia] seemed not to have discovered his, or, at least, he was not eager to acknowledge them. His surrender or self-definition finally occurred in the letters we exchanged during the last trip my mother and I undertook to Torreón. . . . His letters were exquisitely wrought and I will never forgive myself for having lost them.
>
> —SALVADOR NOVO, "Memoir"

The hypermodern house that Lota Macedo de Soares built for Elizabeth Bishop can be imagined as joined by beams that are somehow invisible to themselves and to each other, with rooms that have only tenuous hallways, always on the verge of virtual collapse. Clouds go in and out. They come from nowhere and go nowhere in turn. The house was a way of acting out, of building up what could not be said. It is a canvas, or a piece of paper, but it also expresses a desire that could not be signified on paper.

The silence, the circumlocution one finds in private correspondence written by these lesbians and gay men was not due to any sense of cultural or social repression in the way North Americans or Europeans may understand the term. Homosexual literary history in Latin America may be said to start with the nineteenth-century fin de siècle *modernismo*, a literary movement that was exquisite in terms of the Orientalist fantasies it pursued, as well as political in an anti-imperialist vein. As I mentioned in the introduction, the alienated poet and the artistic dissident were both part of the *modernista* cast of rare beings (*raros*), and we can find there homosexuality as a theme as well as a voice.[9] This literary history reminds us that even before the most important nuclei of openly gay and lesbian writers in Latin America came onto the scene during the thirties, there was already a language of homosexuality—and by language here I mean much more than simply a code: it was a library as well as a semiotics, a roster of themes and a manner of public behavior. Recall that Oscar Wilde's language in England—its petty codes, its knickknacks, its innuendos—could be understood by all those involved, to such an extent that the attorney general exclaimed to the jury, "In such a case you do not expect mathematical proof, or proof at all approaching mathematical proof. You expect such proof as reasonable men ought to act on."[10] The same, I believe, is true for Latin Americans. It may be that we have no access to the diacritical marks of the code. But there was no doubt as to the fact that the code was there.

Reading the heavily edited correspondence between José Rodríguez Feo and José Lezama Lima, one sees clearly that male homosexuality figures in some way or another in all its pages without ever being mentioned explicitly. Rodríguez Feo travels through North America and Europe meeting fabulous people whose work he will translate and/or publish in *Orígenes*. He tells Lezama of his encounters with an impressive intellectual elite. He meets T. S. Eliot and Wallace Stevens, he dines with Stephen Spender, he's hot on the trail of Luis Cernuda, he comments on André Gide, he receives a letter from Wilcock, the Argentinean writer, that he must give to Jean Genet. The names allow readers to see the cabal of the gay glitterati, but Rodríguez Feo at no point talks about their homosexuality. We only get names, dinner engagements, and afternoon teas, and this prompts Lezama, that nontraveler par excellence, hungry for any kind of gossip, to tell his friend, "I suppose your senses are all peacocked, let's say as if pomaded, with the give and take of all those signatures. What does a man dressed up as a signature look like? Many of those respectable figures that you mention, I thought they would never have gone to the same street corner I had chosen."[11] Lezama's words are exquisite in terms of their coded levity. Lezama and Rodríguez Feo are aware of a transnational configuration of writers whose identity is bisected by the claims of poetry and also by those of male homosexuality. Lezama wants more information, and faults Rodríguez Feo for treating them as mere scribbles on a surface. He shows that he understands their identity (here his coded words are important: "I thought they would never have gone to the same street corner I had chosen") but also works in a counterintuitive fashion to deflate their very sense of identity: they are signatures, "men dressed up as signatures."

Culture is decoy, it is the central element in the exhibitionist camouflage that letters deploy. As the Cuban writer Severo Sarduy pointed out in one of his more important works, *La simulación*, camouflage is all about exhibition. In order to pass, you must *show*.[12] Sarduy developed a poetics of camouflage linked to transvestism, and then to homosexuality, via French structuralist theory. This mode of camouflage illuminates the space of correspondence: openness in the act, and a certain reserve in the letter. The letter becomes the mode of camouflage as well as the exhibit of the mode. The letter camouflages something not quite localized—the point is not to name it as "homosexuality" and thus give it a concrete referent, but rather to understand its own circuitousness as pleasure. The homosexual letter is the most controlled of objects. Lezama says to Rodríguez Feo, "We are going through some Egyptian days, what is dead becomes embalmed, and the relatives continue taking food and perfumes in order to lead a petrified existence."[13] The spectacle of Egypt in Havana has no referent, no purpose other than to exhibit something that is also camouflaged.

The letter engages the closet only insofar as it names homosexuality as a presence-absence, as an ambivalent mode of presence linked to the obvious and deliberate border crossings taking place beyond the page.[14] All locales become foreign, and cities are described for the sake of those who are not there, in a language adjusted and administered for that *other* to understand. It is not that writers are in two places at the same time; rather, they inhabit *one* place in a double gaze. They see themselves looking, and they look with the eyes of the other who will receive that letter in the future tense. Hart Crane tells Waldo Frank of examining the Aztec strata that are a living presence in Mexico. He then goes to Cuba to pursue sex, to drink, and also to imagine himself as the Adamic poet who will "fertilize" American writing. This theater is contingent on the fact that it will be recounted to Waldo Frank in letters. Elizabeth Bishop is keenly aware of the sites her own subject inhabits, and her posing of desire for the other to whom she writes entails a notion of herself as living in the clouds. Xavier Villaurrutia anticipates nostalgia, and at every point in which he speaks of Los Angeles it is with the double gaze of one who remembers, before the fact, what he will then forget. For Rodríguez Feo, the trappings of culture overwhelm impressions of things that will never be seen simply as events, but rather as echoes of cultural forms.

As subjects, the letter writers all want to live in a state of oblivion, but homosexuality does not allow them the privilege of forgetting. It is hard to tell what one must read in Xavier Villaurrutia's letters to Salvador Novo from New Haven and Los Angeles, except for the banal details of going to the Schubert Theater to watch a play or chaste reminiscences about a drinking party full of Yale boys. Villaurrutia describes Los Angeles in a kind of trance: "If the city is ugly during the day, it is marvelous at night. Not even in New York do desire and its satisfaction flow like they do here. Friday and Saturday I spent almost without sleeping."[15] What the writer describes is of course not the event, for the letter is not meant to describe the event. What it describes is the memory of the event as it is being forgotten, rewritten, already processed in the mind of the melancholic poet. In Villaurrutia's letters, we don't get events, but rather moods, periods. This constant mentioning of a time without time is not only the sign of habit, but the mark of something, some event that these letters need to gloss.

The gloss comes as a result of what the word "homosexual" meant in the currency of the moment, the way it was stamped within the social circuit: a meaning that could be camouflaged in essays, poems, and newspaper articles, but that had to be faced up to the moment one put pen to paper in order to write to that other homosexual friend. These were legacies of both shame and uniqueness, and markers of class and privilege were used to cover up desires that needed to remain within the bounds of discretion. Rodríguez Feo and Xavier Villaurrutia, Lydia Cabrera and Teresa de la Parra could always enact their dreams of otherness in different settings where culture also intervened. But they could enact themselves as *others* only in the space of the letter. In a letter to Salvador Novo, Xavier Villaurrutia describes his own nostalgia for Mexico by talking about D. H. Lawrence's sense of homesickness, understanding it as a kind of "disease" that nurtures itself in the place in which one is and from the site that one abandons. The man who travels, Villaurrutia says, feels this disease, but it takes the sojourn outside Mexico for him to understand something about rejecting and assimilating some vague "habits" (*costumbres*) that are irrationally rejected: "I am not sure that I won't miss, tomorrow, in Mexico, what in the beginning I rejected here with all of the nostalgic irrational force that I felt for my habits over there."[16] One could decode these comments and insist that Villaurrutia is talking about homosexuality. But the pleasure of the code would be lost in such an unveiling. It is, and it is not—what is important here is the broad camouflage that threatens the very meaning of issues that are not bordered in any way.

In her letters from Caracas to Gonzalo Zaldumbide, Parra complains of the inevitable boredom of social engagements ("in Caracas I am not attracted even by the desire to please, and compliments mortally bore me"),[17] but it is in Paris, as she confesses in a letter to Lydia Cabrera, that Parra can allow herself to walk through spaces that reconfigure the city as an empty and protective space: "I have also felt the charm of Paris in the summer along the quays, but I was very sad and very alone, and I thought of my death and I wanted it, as I remembered the generations that had walked and suffered from disenchantment as I have suffered on these same streets, along the same Seine."[18] The Romantic description of Paris is part of a haze—a haze created by the subject, one who fashions her own representation as well—enveloped by anonymity as its desirous otherness. To be anonymous is to have a certain kind of privilege, particularly for the public personae that all these correspondents were. Villaurrutia can escape from the fractious political atmosphere that surrounds him in Mexico; Parra, already a well-known figure in Caracas, enjoys her sense of self-absence in Paris; Rodríguez Feo pursues literati without the social constraints and responsibilities imposed on a member of his class in Cuba.

This doubleness of space also pertains to the sense of *imaginary* constructed within the discourse. José Lezama Lima visualizes José Rodríguez Feo's displacements around the United States and Canada. It is a vision of movement and arrested movement: "I always see you reach the border and then retreat. You advance your restless and minute troops up to the doors of Quebec, Terranova, Bunker Hill, or New York and then, advised by your restless laziness or because of grave destiny, you desist and then look for another center of geographical explorations."[19] The word "restless" (*inquieto*) is used twice in this sentence. The traveler, as Lezama articulated it clearly in the same coded language they always used, lives continuously on the borderline.[20] The border is clearly sexual, erotic, even erotomaniacal, and its very "vagueness" (as in Villaurrutia's *vague* habits) endows it with erotic tension. This erotic tension is there in Rodríguez Feo's very coded retellings of the worldly ambiance of male literati who he meets and who invite him to summer houses in a gilded world of moonlit cruises on yachts.

The class background is related to the literary (if not financial) capital that these writers possessed in their countries of origin, for none were necessarily marginal figures within their own contexts. Some, like Novo, occupy positions of relative and always contested cultural or institutional power. They figure with a certain degree of prominence in the canon of Latin American culture, read and taught by generations of readers and academics as pertaining to the culture at large—not simply or solely to a "gay" or "homosexual" continuum, but inscribed within the very canon that they helped to shape. Perhaps the silence of homosexuality is the price they had to pay to belong, at least marginally, to this canon. But issues of sexuality are never meant to obscure other very real issues that occupy the work these writers produced. Parra is the author of veiled and not so veiled autobiographies, and Lydia Cabrera became a premier anthropologist after Parra's death; Rodríguez Feo was a publisher and translator, while Lezama wrote some of the more culturally dense poetry in the twentieth-century Latin American tradition. Novo's poetry is metaphysical and Villaurrutia's is tormented. They did not necessarily speak of "local" concerns, but rather articulated their subjectivity in such a way that many (particularly Novo and Villaurrutia) were attacked and vilified at times for their "cosmopolitanism," their lack of "national roots" within the nationalist context of Latin America in the thirties and forties.

In spite of these common forms of coding homosexuality, homosexual bonding does not allow us to read a common aesthetic in their works. This was not a community created out of artistic identification at all. Even, at times, calling it a community is doubtful. As one cross-cultural example, Crane, perhaps the most Frenchified poet in the United States at the time, lived in Mexico and fell in love with its native traditions and popular art. But he also condemned his homosexual brethren (without mentioning their sexuality) in terms that are uncannily similar to those used in the most homophobic of attacks:

What makes me rather indifferent to all of them is the fact that not one of them is really interested one iota in expressing anything indigenous; rather they are busy aping (as though it could be done in Spanish!) Paul Valéry, Eliot,—or more intensely, the Parnassians of 35 years ago. And they are all "bored"—or at least pleased to point the reference. . . . In contrast to their general directions and preoccupations, however, I still (to date, at any rate) harbor the illusion that there is a soil, a mythology, a people and a spirit here that are capable of unique and magnificent utterance.[21]

Crane always had Melville and Whitman as precursors whose homosexuality was the negative or obverse side of a moving image; Villaurrutia and Novo had models of "otherness" who were not Mexican: Cocteau, Gide, Wilde. José Rodríguez Feo was the fervent admirer not of William Carlos Williams or Frank O'Hara, but of Wallace Stevens. In a curious and perhaps ultimately sharp assessment, the Mexican poets could only see Whitman as a "poet for Boy Scouts."[22] No amount of solidarity in terms of closeted or uncloseted homosexuality would have given Crane a sense of common bond with writers who situated themselves precisely as "marginal" to the nativist traditions that so interested him.

One can create a common aesthetic space with all these queers only at the risk of falsifying the tradition, creating a homosexual continuum where there is, and isn't, one. What they all have in common, nevertheless, is their slow movement and deployment—away from a notion of homosexuality as practice to a vision of the homosexual as a subject. It is important to keep in mind Federico de Onís's account of the meeting between Hart Crane and Federico García Lorca at a party in Brooklyn. De Onís thought it would be interesting to have these two writers meet—the foremost poet in the Spanish language and the most interesting American poet of the moment. So he takes Lorca to a party in Brooklyn and introduces him to Crane. A while later, the most circumspect de Onís decides to retire from the occasion, no doubt because of the obvious homosexual tenor of the scene. But before leaving, de Onís could not help but remark on the fact that Crane and Lorca took no obvious interest in each other; rather, each commanded the attention of his own circle of sailors at opposite ends of the room.

Return to Sender

> P.S. If you receive the other letter, tear it up. If not, posterity may think that I repeated myself in my correspondence.
>
> —JOSÉ LEZAMA LIMA to José Rodríguez Feo

Some letters should never arrive, and some should never be written. There is no such thing as an innocent piece of writing, for what you write may come back to haunt you with the uncommon furies mobilized by the one who receives your confession. The letter, that most intimate of forms, is also the most public.

Betrayal assumes many forms, and there are many things that one can do, prove, or avoid with a letter. Betrayal deserves to be included in this history, and I want to conclude this space with my own act of revenge against one of these letter writers. This revenge brings us back to the circuit that colored the state of homosexualities at the time these letters were written, a time when fear of the law and fear of scandal conspired against any sense of solidarity among gay men. In the anecdote that I will retell, José Rodríguez Feo comes off as a petty, narcissistic human being, ready to be utilized by systems of power that would in other contexts seek to destroy him. But we should not judge him with a false sense of superiority for the position he took in the following homosexual scandal.

The year is 1947, and José Rodríguez Feo is at Middlebury College in Vermont, studying the Spanish Golden Age and medieval poetry. Rodríguez Feo has been on one of his whirlwind tours of the United States, allowing himself to succumb—as Lezama remarked—to periods of sensuality with a book in his hand, but then coming back to Middlebury to seek refuge with proper academics whose names all students of Spanish literature would surely recognize. It just so happens, as we can tell from the letter, that a Cuban art critic is visiting Middlebury and is slated to give a lecture. His name is José Gómez Sicre. But Rodríguez Feo, who has met Auden and Stephen Spender, talks about Gide, and will meet Jean Genet in the near future, decides to join a boycott of the critic's conference: "What's funny is that Mañach and Baralt and the Mrs. boycotted him. I didn't go either. Obviously everybody around here found out what kind of a guy he is and the story of his famous seduction was spread all around fostered by the gossipy tongue of Mrs. [Jorge] Mañach. Even Don Pedro Salinas heard the story."[23] At this point Rodríguez Feo, in his edition of his letters to José Lezama Lima (it is important here to name him as editor), adds a footnote to the text that reads as follows: "José Gómez Sicre . . . art critic, was forced to abandon the country

[Cuba] because he was accused of being a pederast" (crítico de arte, se vio obligado a abandonar el país al ser acusado de pederastia).[24]

It is clear that Rodríguez Feo recognized himself as a guilty party, one of those who would also be subjects of scandal under the law. It is because of that recognition (to purge himself of that recognition?) that he recounts the episode to Lezama—as if to say "this is us" in a coded language Lezama surely understands. And in this case, of course, the allegiance—the identification—produces a negative turn, a desire to flee, to distance oneself from any connection to this subject, who could always be *me* under different circumstances (one thinks of all those Cuban homosexuals who were later betrayed by those other homosexuals in power in Cuba after the revolution of 1959).

I would consign this episode, told in catty language to José Lezama Lima, to the realm that Manuel Puig would have called "eternal damnation." It is one thing—Rodríguez Feo seems to say—to read Oscar Wilde and meet Jean Genet, but quite another to press disgrace in the flesh, especially when that disgrace hits close to home. And it is certainly one thing not to talk to the homosexual (pederasta) in Cuba and quite another to boycott his conference at Middlebury. Actually, chances are that the pederast would have been entertained in Cuba, but not invited to dinner in polite company in Vermont.

I tried for a time to find out who this man was, this exiled and legally condemned homosexual, this José Gómez Sicre, and then finally came up with a trace that I followed as far as I could. He was the chief of the Visual Arts Section of the Pan American Union in Washington, D.C., and in the late 1950s he embarked on a project that sought to present a guide to public art collections in both the United States and Latin America. I have been able to consult only the first volume of this series. Volume 1 of the *Guide to the Public Art Collections in Latin America* (Guía de las colecciones públicas de arte en America Latina) deals with the Gulf of Mexico and the Caribbean. It is structured almost as a tourist manual—a traveler goes down the Panamerican Highway from Mexico south to Colombia and Venezuela, and then does a triple hop around the Greater Antilles. The whole book could only have been born out of a fancy for othering, for viewing Latin America from the vantage point of a certain foreignness that is glossed in no uncertain terms by the panache of culture.

Gómez Sicre introduces a museum, examines its overall structure, comments on the suitability of the space for the purposes at hand, and then names the most important works in the collection—like one of those audiotape museum guides that can be rented at the entrance to exhibits. I could comment on the hidden codes in the pictures and objects chosen for reproduction (a marked preference for the phallo-totemic, let us say) and the judgments Gómez Sicre makes—coded comments, perhaps, gossip on the artistic demimonde. But the image that sticks in my mind is that of the forced wanderer originating out of the footnote Rodríguez Feo added to his published correspondence. Gómez Sicre's *Guide* is the circumspect work of an exile, perhaps one of the coded keys to the archipelago of homosexuality. It is a bridge (Crane's *Bridge,* perhaps) that spans the community of the silenced—museum directors, or high art connoisseurs, men and women who tenuously hold on to the refuge of art as a way of talking about things that could not really be put into writing. All this, of course, articulated in code by one of the exiled members of the tribe, who felt the full force of the law.

It befits an essay about letters, their coded silences and reticence, their movement in time and space, to conclude by rescuing a man who had the letter attached to him by means of a note attached to another letter, and who was forced to move because of the stamp that was placed on him by the law. The record of the case may lie in some legal archive in Havana, where surely the record of this give and take, this plea, this option to move away rather than spend the time in Cuba in ignominy and scandal could be plotted out and revisited.

The realm of the law places its own border on the space where survival collides with solidarity. The postscript reveals the sadness that could never quite appear in the letter except as the analysis promised by the illusions of graphology. But one thing we do know is that these letter writers, in their most private moments, were never allowed to forget about what they anxiously felt that they did not own, but others did. And that is why, for all the talk about their being our precursors (which they are), it is important to notice why they could never bring themselves to rave about their one-night stands, and put the stamp on the letter for the postman to deliver.

2 Nostalgia for Sex

Xavier Villaurrutia

Past Is Prologue

Subjects always construct narratives out of the collisions between events and discourses. This is clear from Xavier Villaurrutia's, *Nostalgia de la muerte* (1946) (published in English as *Nostalgia for Death*), one of the first collections of poetry in which a Latin American male voice speaks of its own homosexuality. Villaurrutia's book is an event in Latin American literature. As such, it also shows how the subject (Villaurrutia himself or the poetic voice) traces events into a discursive flow, for others to then read and mold into their own temporalities. The historical markers are all in place within Villaurrutia's circuit, creating their own sense of discourse: Villaurrutia belonged to the Mexican group of poets and writers who published the magazine *Contemporáneos* (1928–31) and who were attacked and vilified as effeminate. They were not marginal figures, but held government posts; they were homophobically accepted and censored. As discourse, Villaurrutia's poetry is an act of courage and also a game of dissimulation: a cipher that he purposely left undone, for other voices to mimic in their own versions of drag.

All of Villaurrutia's contradictions need to be noted at the outset, for this is a poetry that plays with contradiction and paradox. That Villaurrutia held a government job even as he openly negotiated his homosexuality may have been unthinkable in the climate of the McCarthyist United States, where the witch hunt for communists and other "deviants" entailed a wholesale purging of government spheres of power (in spite of the success enjoyed by the likes of J. Edgar Hoover and Roy Cohn). In the case of Villaurrutia, we should note, he was not necessarily a powerful figure but one who benefitted from certain privileges, while at the same time—and this has to be underscored—he was also constantly harassed by power. In Mexico in the 1930s, poets like Villaurrutia and others, who may have been simply guilty by association, were subject to ferocious attacks that sought to expel the poets from their bureaucratic positions. They were called "counterrevolutionaries" and "hermaphrodites"; the attacks against them utilized a combination of Freudian psychology, revolutionary morality, and Catholic dogma.[1] By no means, however, is Villaurrutia a "forgotten" poet who we can now reclaim. On the contrary, he and his *contemporáneos* belong to the pantheon of great Mexican writing. Although their position within the canon has been in dispute at various points in history, the generation that followed his (Octavio Paz's generation) did much to settle the *Contemporáneos* role and importance to Mexican letters.

There are two reasons I think it is important to explore Villaurrutia's work at this point: first, the way he negotiated his sexuality allows me to map out one distinctive praxis of Latin American male homosexual desire; second, the way in which his figure intervenes in the United States at present allows me to explore what is at stake in reading his work as "gay." I am less interested in the debates around the word—whether we should use "gay" or "homosexual"—than in what that gesture implies in terms of identity, sensibility, and ideology. Other essays in this book, especially those on Lydia Cabrera and Virgilio Piñera, speak about the consequences of treating precursors as precursors—not allowing them to appear as lifeless subjects with no contradictions, but understanding the contradictory way they negotiated their own sexuality within society. In all these essays I am less interested in the evidence of homosexuality, and more puzzled by how it relates to their work, as a fragment of what may or may not form a complete figure. These writers are precursors, but that does not mean they are to be seen as children to our more "open" modes of understanding sexuality. I want to tease out what it is Villaurrutia says that may be so disturbing for us at present.

It is uncanny that a book with "nostalgia" in its title could be seen as a "precursor book," one that anticipates the voice of contemporary gay lyric. But one of the interesting elements in *Nostalgia for Death* is that it does not speak to "our" own sense of identity. Indeed, it is hard to look at Villaurrutia from the point of view of a future (gay identity) that he may or may not have conceived with anticipation and/or horror. I would say that even in *looking* at him as a precursor we run the risk of participating in the homophobic system that *Nostalgia for Death* sought to evaporate or dissolve. Villaurrutia was not interested in claiming for himself a more marginal role in society. On the contrary, he aimed to be heard by different audiences, some of which could decode his language along the lines of homosexual expression. He was not talking solely to this literate group, but to others who were in turn his precursors but also his contemporaries. Villaurrutia interpellates all these social actors by means of a system created within his work, a disturbing system that limns metaphysics and trash, the gutter and High Art.

It may be better, in fact, to allow Villaurrutia to look at *us* as gay men and lesbians, to turn the spectacle on ourselves and explore the way Villaurrutia deconstructs that first-person plural that "we" have carefully built over the past thirty years. In deference to the very metaphysics entailed in a title such as *Nostalgia for Death,* I will move from the present to the past, without the anxiety for creating the continuous narrative flow that Villaurrutia constructed as his form of revelation, and as his mask.

Nostalgia Translated

The most recent edition in English of Villaurrutia's *Nostalgia for Death,* superbly translated by Eliot Weinberger, also includes an essay by Octavio Paz, translated with the allusive title "Hieroglyphs of Desire."[2] Paz recounts not only part of Villaurrutia's life in the context of his (Paz's) own, but also engages in what is at this point a quasi-canonical reading of *Nostalgia for Death*. He sees the book in the context of Mexican, European, baroque, and modernist poetry. This is interesting to contrast with the reasons for this new translation found on the back cover, where American readers are expected to read Villaurrutia according to parameters given by gay identity in the time of AIDS. The blurb on the back of the book reads as follows:

Xavier Villaurrutia was one of the very few Latin American writers in the first half of this century who was openly homosexual, an important Mexican poet who wrote, essentially, one book. . . . Villaurrutia is a major poet of desire whose beloved is the death we live each day. His poems define life between the nocturnal and the diurnal and have taken on added poignancy as uncanny prophecies of individual lives in the age of the AIDS epidemic.

Closeted or uncloseted selves, desire, and death appear at the outset as categories that frame this book and this writer. In the introduction, Eliot Weinberger places us in the "present of translation," where two simultaneous wars are also taking place: the spectacle of Desert Storm and the "internal" war against "federally financed pornography." As Weinberger notes, all recipients of moneys from the National Endowment for the Arts in the 1990s were forced to sign a pledge that they would not "promote, disseminate or produce obscene or indecent materials"; indecency was defined as "including but not limited to depictions of sadomasochism, homoeroticism, the exploitation of children, or individuals engaged in sex acts."[3] These acts of censorship, as is known, were a result of the notorious 1989 outcry over Robert Mapplethorpe's photographs scheduled for an exhibit at the Corcoran Gallery in Washington, D.C., and the scandals over public moneys used to finance the artistic expression of principally—but not only—lesbians and gay men, but also all work deemed "pornographic." Weinberger as translator decries the ludicrousness of the "indecency" proposition, and states that:

beyond all the letters and petitions, all of us in a Helms America—regardless of our tastes and practices in private life, and regardless of what we normally write—had a duty to produce more such "pornography," to expose the absurdity with further concrete examples, and—with a little nostalgia for the days of the avant-garde—to work in such a way that no one would give us money for it."[4]

In a brilliant tactical move, Weinberger points out that faced with the repression of desire, we have a duty to produce more desire.

In this context it is wise to recall that the translator, as well as the historian, has a definite mission: to clarify the past as well as the present, and allow both to communicate with each other. It is fitting that Villaurrutia appears in this way within regimes that survey pleasure, desire, and sexuality. Yet if we read further into these statements, this appearance, however welcome it may be (and it is), brings out another kind of closet, where Weinberger's notion of eros collides with the issues of censorship caused by Mapplethorpe, among others: "it seemed to me evident," Weinberger states, "that the universality of any erotic art is based on the irrelevancy of its object of affection."[5]

For readers well versed with Villaurrutia's context, Weinberger's statement is and is not surprising. As I mentioned at the beginning, Villaurrutia himself was a government employee, and was threatened at various times because his and others' objects of affection were not irrelevant. In *Los Contemporáneos ayer*, Guillermo Sheridan documents the relentless attacks against Villaurrutia and his fellow poets and writers by those who thought the poets were taking Mexican literature on an erroneous, decadent, and effeminate course.[6] In 1932, for example, obscenity charges were processed against Jorge Cuesta's magazine *Examen*; as a result of these, Villaurrutia and others had to resign from their government posts.[7] It is only in this context that we can say that the object of affection is irrelevant. But it is irrelevant *even* in a system that normatizes desires along gender lines. This is not simply a moot point, and I am agreeing with Weinberger, but also claiming that the system is more perverse than he makes it out to be, and that Villaurrutia is a much more sophisticated poet. Villaurrutia, I am sure, claimed the universality of erotic affection regardless of the object. But the point is precisely that Villaurrutia manages to claim this irrelevance while all around him the circuits of power are telling him that it is not.

Villaurrutia could respond to censorship only by holding the higher ground in the networks of desire. As a way of countering public opinion, Villaurrutia could say that he spoke from a *different* point of view, and that this point of view showed the pettiness and provincialism of his heterosexual persecutors.[8] As a position of strength, of superiority, the idea that the object of affection was irrelevant was, in retrospect, the only one that Villaurrutia could take—and even this position was problematic from the point of view of those who accused the government of fostering indecency in its ranks. In other words, Villaurrutia could only stake out a *defensive* position, one that could give him some degree of parity in a heterosexist system, while at the same time allowing him to claim his own sense of exceptionality.

That Villaurrutia's poetry *does* seem to speak about the irrelevance of the objects of affection is not without irony—starting with the very "death" that appears in the book's title. In Spanish, with its distinction between masculine and feminine genders, this "universality of desire" for the Other that Weinberger talks about—a Death that is always feminine—produces a curious set of effects. This is evident in the seventh *décima* of Villaurrutia's "Death in Décimas," which I will quote in Spanish so that readers may notice the mark of gender:

¡Hasta en la ausencia estás viva!
Porque te encuentro en el hueco
de una forma y en el eco
de una nota fugitiva;
porque en mi propia saliva
fundes tu sabor sombrío,
y a cambio de lo que es mío
me dejas sólo el temor

de hallar hasta en el sabor
la presencia del vacío.[9]

Taken strictly *out* of context and in Spanish, this may be read as a love poem to an elusive woman. *Within* the book as a whole, it is a *décima* addressed to an unnamed "Death"—unnamed because there is no specific mention of it in the poem itself. From a male homosexual point of view, it could also serve to erase the elusive "other" male as the object of affection. It may or may not be, and the indeterminacy is part of the game. What is clear is the fact that context erases and at the same time inscribes the object of affection, and this object becomes "irrelevant" only if one keeps its relevance and irrelevance in constant check.

If the above statement seems tortuous, confusing, and unclear, this is because Villaurrutia is that kind of poet—he places us within the space of two mirrors, and we are constantly being asked to justify our choices and decisions. My position is that, in a curiously tortuous way, what is important in Villaurrutia is precisely how the love object *is* gendered, and not the other way around. Looked at in a different way, if gender were not important, would death still be the object?

That these issues come to the fore precisely in the dense and conflictive context that Weinberger talks about makes them much more pressing: the Helms initiative, the foreign and domestic scenarios of "war" (including, as Susan Sontag recalled, the insidious metaphor of war dominating our struggles to contain a disease), and at the center, bearing witness to lives ravaged by war and illness, a Mexican poet who speaks of homosexuality and Death—not Death himself, as Weinberger noted, but rather Death "herself." Furthermore, he speaks not of "individual lives in an epidemic" but of echoes, bodies that are surfaces, ungraspabilities, pasts and futures, memories, desires. Whether metaphysics is Villaurrutia's closet can be explored only if we return to Octavio Paz's essay "Hieroglyphs of Desire," the other gaze that the translated book offers as construction. Paz is here our mediator between Villaurrutia and the translator, in a way not unlike the mediation that Death (the feminine *muerte*) produces in terms of the male object of desire.

Mortals and Angels

From the outset, it is clear that Paz identifies with Villaurrutia, that this is one of the poets he chooses as his immediate precursor. Villaurrutia and his fellow *Contemporáneos* allowed Paz to fashion a language of desire in his early poetry, and it is interesting to recall how these poets met.

Paz is not yet twenty when he visits the Ministry of Public Education's Editorial Department in 1931. There, he sees Villaurrutia and Efrén Hernández in a waiting room outside the poet Salvador Novo's office. The whole scene, as described by Paz, must have produced a kind of homosexual panic that the young poet (as ephebe) controls, and that he does not at all register in his essay—except in the context of situating the reader within a spectacle that recalls a classier "cage aux folles." Describing Novo, Paz says that he "reigned over his two friends and subordinates with an indefinable mixture of courtesy and insolence."[10] At the same time, and again in reference to Novo, Paz says that "[w]e were stunned by his ties, his irreverent opinions, his beige shoes that were rounded at the top, his slicked-back hair, his plucked eyebrows, his Anglicisms. His mission was to astonish or to irritate, and he succeeded." It is clear that Novo astonished or irritated Paz, though we are never sure at this stage which of the two options to choose. Faced with such a character, Paz prefers to focus on Villaurrutia, the more muted presence of the two. Villaurrutia's reserve, and not Novo's flamboyance, Paz attributes to a Mexican sense of *decorum* that in this context becomes a performance of homosexuality as a form of self-control. I will quote both of the descriptions Paz gives of Villaurrutia:

He spoke unhurriedly. At times this quality became a defect: you could see him listening to himself. From the beginning I was surprised by his beautiful voice, grave and flowing like a dark river. His manners were sober and exact. There were two constant notes, one a spur, the other a brake: courtesy, and an irony that was sometimes cruel. Years later I discovered that his good manners concealed an irritable temperament. Though he was not what is called a natural person, it seemed to me that, unlike Novo and Hernández, he was not playing at being his persona. Or rather, he, too, like anyone who is out of the ordinary, was a persona, but his features coincided with his mask.[11]

While [Salvador] Novo was rather ostentatious about his sexual inclinations, Xavier was protective of his private life. He wasn't in hiding and was capable of confronting public condemnation. He was as discreet in real life as in literature; his love of form was reflected as much in his way of dressing as in his hendecasyllables. For him, excessive brilliance was the mortal sin.[12]

The more obvious distinctions between Novo's flamboyance and Villaurrutia's reserve do not quite mask the fact that Paz can see the performance of homosexuality only as a kind of hollow performance, not as a mode of intervention within a very homophobic context. Although he admires the very ethical and brave position that Villaurrutia and Novo took in relation to others' condemnation of their homosexuality, he nevertheless faults Villaurrutia, in particular, for his timidity when it comes right down to the defiant subject position of homosexuality; he also criticizes the two poets for collaborating with institutions of governmental power:

The homosexuality of certain of the Contemporáneos *(Novo, Pellicer, Villaurrutia) is no secret. They were honest with themselves about it, and confronted intolerance with integrity and humor. Nonetheless, the moral independence and intellectual coherence of a Gide or the rebellion of a Luis Cernuda cannot be found in their work.*[13]

For Paz, in other words, Villaurrutia, Novo, and the other members of that group were not sexual or gay outlaws, in John Rechy's and Leo Bersani's use of the term.[14] They may have pursued the same kind of anonymous sex that Rechy talked about, though perhaps he did not know about it, since they did not use it as a moral stance having a direct bearing on their work.[15] For Paz, homosexuality ends up being an empty show of defiance with no moral center. The reasons for this are clear for Paz: the absence of a moral stance originates from a Mexican sense of "decorum," reserve, which in the case of Villaurrutia allowed him to possess a very special kind of privacy based on self-observation.[16] But at no point is Paz able to understand that what he seeks is a rhetoric of homosexuality—a rhetoric that would have been hollow in this context—while Villaurrutia and Novo decided to *embody* that rhetoric with actions that spoke louder than words.

That they embodied this poetics is in turn ironic, considering the fact that Villaurrutia offered his public a disembodied poetics—one that accounts for the sense of "paralysis" explored, for example, in "The Paradox of Fear":

Or the fear of becoming one's self
so clearly, so profoundly,
that neither years nor consumption nor leprosy,
nothing and no one
can distract us for a moment
from the total attention to ourselves
that makes us feel our growing, irreversible paralysis.[17]

Villaurrutia aims for a particular effect, a self that can see itself only as an other—an ungraspable other, at that. Self-consciousness is a source of pleasure and pain, and the "paradox of fear" in his poem consumes subjectivity, but also allows it to come into being. In other words, the pain of loss and the paralysis of fear both create and fashion, destroy and immobilize the subject.

Moreover, the rhetorical game here is a shield meant to guard against the other's "othering" gazes, since Villaurrutia already sees his other as his self. The poem is part of a revelatory mechanism that also functions as a kind of armor: the *otherness* of the *self* will be the only source of protection, the only praxis available in a homophobic context.

This may be seen very literally as a way of closeting one's own homosexual desires, but I would rather see it as a way of escaping from the system of representation that may seek to turn Villaurrutia into a moral example. Neither the translator nor the essayist follows Villaurrutia on this crucial point: Paz turns him into an essential Mexican; Weinberger into a pan-national homosexual voice. To make such double examples out of ambivalence is baffling, to say the least. Villaurrutia, for his part, resists all those identifications that do not originate from the "paradox of fear."

This refusal to "represent" anything other than a doubled self is an important aspect in Villaurrutia's poetry. His notion of desire implies that moments of recognition are also moments of creative blindness. Unlike contemporary poets who have written about AIDS, Villaurrutia is not so interested in *how* to look at things, but rather in showing how *seeing* is a way of *not-looking*. "Nocturno de la estatua" relays a chamber of echoes where dreams are rendered in the timeless and nominal infinitive. This is the fourth poem of the collection, and it is one of the clearest indications of Villaurrutia's poetics of subject-objects—in this case, it concerns a statue (like Death, this is rendered as feminine in Spanish). The use of the infinitive allows a curiously impersonal reading—no subject seems to inhabit the sign. The landscape that Villaurrutia talks about is as elementary as one of the abstract embodiments that we can see in a Giorgio de Chirico painting: night, the street, a stairway, and then an ungraspable statue. The situation portrayed, with all its sense of delicate grandeur, actually speaks of a kind of soft-core SM. Once again, I will quote the original in Spanish in order to underscore the mark of gender:

Hallar en el espejo la estatua asesinada,
sacarla de la sangre de su sombra,
vestirla en un cerrar de ojos,
acariciarlá como a una hermana imprevista
y jugar con las fichas de sus dedos
y contar a su oreja cien veces cien cien veces
hasta oírla decir: "estoy muerta de sueño."[18]

The erotic ambiance of this poem glides over stuff that Weinberger himself understands would make Jesse Helms cringe, with its necrophiliac associations (the assassinated statue), incest ("caress it like a sister") or the more muted but still compulsively repetitive counting of "a hundred times a hundred hundred times" to the verge of exhaustion. The poem surely withstands a Foucauldian reading, where both participants become disembodied entities that act out their roles and not necessarily their individualities.[19] Except, of course—and it is quite a big "exception"—Villaurrutia proceeds from the subject in the infinitive to the echo of the statue, which the subject then finds in a wall. This is a wall that turns into a mirror from where the statue is rescued and consumed—not in death, but in sleep. The object acquires its sense of individuality in the mode of surrender, but this surrender sends us back to the first line: the statue is asleep just as the embodied voice at the beginning talks of the nominal act of "sleeping." The phrase used by the statue at the end is really a commonsensical turn of phrase: "estoy muerta de sueño" is as clichéd as "estoy muerto de frío," which Villaurrutia uses at another point in the book. These ready-made phrases send us back to the very surface of language, as if language also were the statue that Villaurrutia himself were manipulating, cajoling—literally penetrating—in order to discover its surface, its skin, and not its internal essence.

Villaurrutia's poetry turns us into elusive and illusory figures. As readers, we are also the ones who torture the statue only to find its surface, the ones who revive the statue like Lazarus in order to find that the statue itself is dying of sleep. As he implies in his "Nocturno de los ángeles," we are angels, beings of desire, of desires even unknown to ourselves. It is difficult to speak of an identity in this context—or even of an identity created in the context of a plague—for the self understands itself as a statue that is tortured until sleep allows it to produce a ready-made phrase that comes from some other voice in some other place. Claiming identity entails risk and loss in the economies of the text. But no matter how we approach Villaurrutia, we always end up turning situations inside out or upside down, and returning to the question that originated the search in the first place. To put it in a more gay male–specific context, for Villaurrutia we are all bottoms and tops, and versatility is the name of the game. As human beings we can only dream about angels, as long as we know that angels do not dream of other angels, but of mortals.

Tops and Bottoms

That Villaurrutia seems to desire a kind of "versatile" universe allows us to begin exploring the difficulties (but also the possibilities) inherent in turning this book into a site of resistance, or even of testimony. While resistance implies stopping, arresting, extirpating, pushing away, Villaurrutia predicates his book on an idea of flows, movement, an inherent absence that appears and disappears. Villaurrutia's resistance engages in a politics where flows *themselves* are the mode of resisting systems of exclusion. These flows are the flows of a desire that does not stop, but rather circulates and recirculates itself. These flows validate ungraspability as the only way to make sense of a situation.

Much of *Nostalgia for Death* concerns things that flow uninterruptedly to each other, and *on* to each other. Signifiers move on to other signifiers, starting from the first line of the first poem, titled simply "Nocturno," which opens the collection with the grandeur and totality given in its first Spanish word:

> *Todo lo que la noche*
> *dibuja con su mano*
> *de sombra:*
> *el placer que revela*
> *el vicio que desnuda.*[20]

To inaugurate a book of poems with an "everything" (*todo*) is already to speak of something that is unbounded. The first stanza leads to the second, and then to the third, and so on—they all begin with that "everything," and they are all structured in the same way. Readers understand that "todo" accounts for a circuit of desire, as if the eye were following the course of water cascading on different plateaus, or the undulating movements of a stripteaser who delivers exactly what (s?)he knows (s?)he should, so we can watch again and again. Repetition reveals and undresses the fetishes of all and none: lips, sweat, wounds, saliva, hands are all followed by a single luminous spotlight until the final reveille:

> *¡Todo!*
> *circula en cada rama*
> *del árbol de mis venas,*
> *acaricia mis muslos,*
> *inunda mis oídos,*
> *vive en mis ojos muertos,*
> *muere en mis labios duros.*[21]

Verbs and objects define the subject, even if the subject is the very poem itself—a singer (a chanteuse) who appears in a smoky bar to confuse memory and desire. Here Villaurrutia offers the erotics of a memory as pure representation of itself. "Everything" is the poem without a person, without that center that memory can use to grasp itself, to project itself onto an object. The poem aims to give a predicate for a subject that cannot be named, for it can be named only as an echo, not an event, a discourse, not a point of contact.

The letters of desire compose and recompose themselves. They flow into each other. Every poem in *Nostalgia for Death* seems like every other poem—even their titles are repeated like so many variations on a similar theme. The poems are mirrors that reflect each other with the same circuit of desire that opens "everything" to a nothing that previously justified it. It is not only that the poems blend with each other; they *bleed* onto each other just as a wound bleeds onto a piece of paper.

Unlike gay poetry collections that deal with AIDS, there is no narrative in *Nostalgia for Death*; its poems do not progress from health to sickness, from heaven to hell. They offer no site of redemption, or even a place that, in James Miller's terms, would be named an "anastatic moment," or "the illuminative climax of the personal or public struggles of the bereaved to make sense of death."[22] Miller defines "anastatic moments" as moments of awakening, of reckoning—they "deliver us from evil through a sudden imaginative breakthrough into the blessed state (however it is defined or experienced), which in turn opens new critical perspectives on the here and now."[23] If these moments occur at all in Villaurrutia's book, they are meant to show the impossibility of the disembodied subject achieving a level of positive understanding. If there is any idea of a "positive breakthrough," it happens in Villaurrutia's book by means of a negative turn. Failure constitutes the moment of truth, and only failed realizations carry the positive marks of illumination. Thcsc, however, are repeated to such an extent that there is no one moment that stands out on its own. Like the poems themselves, each moment of failure is just like the other.

Nostalgia for Death speaks for a state whose temporality is always suspect. It can only be a text of illness-as-such: a metaphysical and metaphorical illness, as opposed to a "disease." The suspicious nature of temporality—what Villaurrutia names as a state of paralysis—is also present in Villaurrutia's notion of desire, conceived and constructed as a decentered experience. Villaurrutia would have agreed with Guy Hocquenghem that "[d]esire emerges in a multiple form, whose components are only divisible a posteriori, according to how we manipulate it."[24] This is the ruling signifier in Villaurrutia's project, and this desire is at many points in the book validated as "essential," as an act that defines the subject and the book itself. Desire scatters itself while it produces an inherently decentered economy. This desire is contingent on the experience of "scattering," and is expressed in a homosexual pickup scene. "L.A. Nocturne: The Angels" (Nocturno de los ángeles) begins precisely with this sense of flow, where everything loses its sense of clarity:

You might say the streets flow sweetly through the night.
The lights are dim so the secret will be kept,
the secret known by the men who come and go,
for they're all in on the secret
and why break it up in a thousand pieces

when it's so sweet to hold it close,
and share it only with the one chosen person.[25]

No external light allows for the secret itself to be unveiled. It is held *within* the subject although it is possessed by *all* subjects. As Hocquenghem says in relation to the homosexual pickup scene, "instead of translating this scattering of love-energy as the inability to find a centre, we could see it as a system in action, the system in which polyvocal desire is plugged in on a non-exclusive basis."[26] The sense of continuous flow here is based on unanimity and repetition, stopping for a moment on the fact of selection.[27] For Villaurrutia, choice is inherently bound to a situation that repeats itself. The chosen person is chosen but for a moment, as part of a system of "unpredictable couples" (*imprevistas parejas*).[28] Villaurrutia would say, as Hocquenghem does, that in "homosexual love . . . everything is possible at any moment: organs look for each other and plug in, unaware of the law of exclusive disjunction."[29] In Villaurrutia's poem these beings of the night are not hustlers, but angels. Their encounters, as Hocquenghem remarks about the homosexual pickup scene, "do not take place in the seclusion of a domestic setting but outside, in the open air, in forests and on beaches" because these settings correspond "to the mode of existence of desire itself."[30] Villaurrutia's argument in "The Paradox of Fear" that men have experienced death in life—a moment when the perception of death is exact and definitive—comes out in "L.A. Nocturne" as the moment of sexual coupling.

Guilt in this context is not contingent on the sexual act in itself, which is seen in these poems in an erotico-religious context of acceptance, if not permissiveness. The subject looks at these figures as part of a movable dance in which he himself participates as a nonjudgmental voyeur who examines his own reactions. But Villaurrutia's emblem for desire is not Narcissus, but rather the Gemini twins, as he says in this same poem:

If, at a given moment, everyone would say with one word what he is thinking,
the six letters of DESIRE would form an enormous, luminous scar,

a constellation more ancient, more dazzling than any other.
And that constellation would be like a burning sex in the deep body of night,
like the Gemini, for the first time in their lives,
looking at each other in the eyes and embracing forever.[31]

These lines have been read by many commentators as one of the central statements in *Nostalgia for Death,* since they join many of the book's different lines. But few critics have remarked on the general sense of flow in terms of the metaphorical displacement to which desire is being submitted here. The passage itself moves from the scar to a constellation to sex, in order to then coalesce in the image of the Gemini twins. In Villaurrutia's move from scar to body, he oscillates between abstraction and materiality. The combination of materiality and abstraction, accompanied by the refusal to choose between them, allows Villaurrutia to engage a poetics that is as negative and positive, as morally indifferent as the plague itself. This is, I think, the terrible lesson that Villaurrutia may offer us in the time of AIDS. It should to be explored in more detail.

Impersonality

In *Allegories of Reading,* Paul de Man deconstructed the complicitous relationship that Rilke (or rather, his own self-figuration) has with his readers.[32] By deploying a series of oppositional categories in Rilke's poetry, de Man arrives at an almost heretical reading, one that notices the *impersonality* that surrounds this most "personal" of poets. Rilke is shown not as the poet of personification, but as one who considers objects "containers of a subjectivity which is not that of the self" since those objects are "standing in the service of the language that has produced them."[33] Statements can exist in and for themselves in Rilke, and this seems to be the point from which language—and not the subject—speaks.

To claim that this most personal of poets was truly a poet of absence amounts to an act of deconstructive heresy—it certainly accounted for the resistance that deconstruction has encountered in the U.S. "cultural wars." But de Man shows that Rilke constantly oscillates between what de Man calls a "rhetoric of figuration" and a "rhetoric of signification" in which language, emptied of referential constraints, summons an emptied subject precisely at the point at which it "abdicates any claim to truth." Hence, the structure is apprehended precisely at the point at which it unfolds negative experiences of loss. These allow for the deployment of the figure of chiasmus, which de Man validates as "the result of a void." For de Man, chiasmus is the figure by means of which the never-ending reversibility of all is "figured" in terms of "impersonal over-things." It reveals positive assertions coming out of negative experiences: falls that turn into ascents or, in de Man's words, "rising and falling motions into one single trope." It is a mode of totalizing reflection that manages to take into account both sides of the mirror, reverse negativity into a promise, and remain thus in a third plane—within and without the figural structure itself.

Chiasmus is also the rhetorical figure that Villaurrutia prefers. From the initial epigraph that he selects for his work, Michael Drayton's "Burned in a sea of ice, and drowned amidst a fire," *Nostalgia for Death* introduces us into a world where it seems that both terms of a dialectics—any dialectics—need to be seen at once, apprehended at one moment of their kinetic movement. Thus, nostalgia visualizes itself as a present only by remitting to a past as well as to a future—to a death that has always already occurred, and that will nevertheless recur within the structural unfolding of language as well as of life. The poems themselves seem to relish this kind of baroque conceit. In "Nostalgia de la nieve" Villaurrutia first exclaims, "¡Cae la noche sobre la nieve!" (Night falls on the snow!) in order to rework the line in the third stanza as "¡Cae la nieve sobre la noche!" (Snow falls on the night!). It seems to make no difference, in a world that is apprehended from two sides of the mirror at the same time, who's on top or who's on bottom.

These oppositions are maddening in Villaurrutia's work. We get the sense that two categories are apprehended by the poet, but also by a language conceived as a subject with its own sense of impersonality. Hence the word-plays, which are such an integral part of this book—games that allow language to have a sense of identity to itself. With these, Villaurrutia wants to create the illusion that by opening and closing the written and oral possibilities in language at the same time, language *itself* opens *itself* up to reveal its own sense of construction. This construction is in part a projection of Villaurrutia's own mirrored body into language, since it has to take into account, and never lose sight of, the disembodied subject that once produced it. Language—validated as the subject's anchor—is seen as a body that constitutes itself by projecting its future as something that will also reconstruct a past, as in Lacan's formulation of the mirror stage. For Lacan, since the subjective constitution of the self is both a moment of projection and retroaction, the infant assumes the upright position in the mirror and finds there the future stage of a reconstruction that comes from the outside. This is the moment of the constitution of the self, and nothing precedes it except the future construction of a body "in bits and pieces"—that flung-out body that appears in many of Villaurrutia's poems.[34] For Villaurrutia, the subject can only conceive of itself while at the same time conceiving of *itself* as a body in bits and pieces. Lacan's formulation is in itself chiasmic, as other readers have noticed—and it is also a figure, in de Man's terms. For Villaurrutia, language seems to be what it can only later become, and can only *become* this totality by constituting itself as a body that is broken in bits and pieces.

What I am arguing here is that for Villaurrutia the process of identity formation takes place separately at the level of the subject as well as at the level of language—that the subject sees itself in the mirror while language also sees *itself* in its own mirror. In other words, the chain of desire flows from the subject to language and at the same time *within* the subject and *within* language. Villaurrutia wants us to understand this kinetically. This process leads to a mutual sense of surrender, for there are no certainties in these dynamics, only reflections of self and other.

In Villaurrutia's world, events are only seen from the point of view of nostalgia, and nostalgia articulates the way the subject sees itself. This means that events already take place from within the framework of a discourse that has no point of origin. What motivates the discourse? Who controls the strings of desire? Villaurrutia does not seem to place this agency in the subject, but aims for an impersonality that will in turn motivate the discourse. The doubled subject does not look to the other in order to confirm the self, for the other already frames the self. Both are searching for a desire that will allow a moment of transcendence. When this transcendence does not take place, language becomes the only event out of which discourse originates.

Villaurrutia does not aim for a personified language; he seems to want a language *beyond* the idea of person—neither male nor female but an abstract yet embodied principle. Even if it is possible to see in Villaurrutia's semantic twists and turns a kind of avoidance, the avoidance *is* the poetics itself. If Villaurrutia desires to escape—to another realm, or to another voice, to a future-past-perfect that is also an infinitive—at no point is this escape motivated by a desire to flee from the world. Rather, it arises from the very versatility of all. Nothing coalesces, identity twists and turns and changes. Fragments are understood as fragments, and they understand their fragmented selves as what provides them with their identity.

Scattering

In retrospect—and the phrase is already charged in terms of *Nostalgia for Death*—the context in which Villaurrutia lived is much different from that of the post-Stonewall generation evoked in Weinberger's commentary. Villaurrutia, I think, would dismantle the oppositions that the gay male community has framed in order to make sense of our present situation in the age of AIDS. These positions are twofold, and they argue each other and *with* each other, not as part of a dialectics ruled by a certain amount of versatility. One position holds that any attempt at regulating sex heightens a disciplinary function present in the very discourses that name homosexuality in a straight society. The other holds that, given the realities of AIDS and the immense toll it has taken on the community, the connections between sex and identity should be dislodged in favor of new identifications that allow homosexuals to be assimilated into the "majority." The first position is voiced by Michael Warner (*The Trouble with Normal*) and also by Allan Bérubé, Douglas Crimp, Kendall Thomas, Walt Odets, and José Esteban Muñoz—these latter appearing in the collection *Policing Public Sex*.[35] The other group insists that gays must adopt the values of the "community at large," understood and privileged as monogamy, marriage, and full rights under the law. This position is the one staked out by essayists like Bruce Bawer (*A Place at the Table*), Gabriel Rotello (*Sexual Ecology*), and Andrew Sullivan (*Virtually Normal*).[36] For these latter men (let us underscore how gendered this whole debate is), identity should be remotivated from what some consider is an undue emphasis on liberation via sex; for others, homosexual identity has always already the potential to be a disruptive inscription within the social regulations of desire.

That these debates are part of a regulatory mechanism is clear. The point here is to show them as systems in motion, systems that mobilize each other. Echoing Villaurrutia's implicit refusal to engage in sequential discourse, I want to stress the artificiality of the very idea of narrative and of historical development inherent in all these versions of gay and lesbian discourse. It is a narrative that flows out of the specific constructs out of which these identities are formed.

The self-identification of gay males was not a component of Villaurrutia's world in the way it is in ours. As George Chauncey has explained in reference to U.S. society before World War II, only men who self-consciously assumed the pose and role of effeminate men were labeled "homosexual" in the public mind. The object of affection was generally not presumed to be "gay" or "queer" in any sense of the word, but rather "trade."[37] To have sex meant to have it with partners who were not "fairies" like themselves. Sex happened with an "other" who was not the same, but who was also the same—in other ways. This is not necessarily an argument for the immutability of male sexual roles—in the contexts of top and bottom—but rather for the versatility of objects of affection. From the point of view of the identity-based discourses that spread after the war, and particularly after Stonewall, this vision of homosexuality makes some gay men uncomfortable. Gabriel

Rotello, in *Sexual Ecology,* says that "Many gay men today cringe at the thought that this was a major component of the sexuality of our precursors. It seems so debasing, emotionally empty, self-loathing."[38] This hygienic stance is far from Villaurrutia's position, but the very hygiene of the statement masks its own (Rotello's) sex panic as a positive statement on identity, where "pride" (a word that carries different connotations in Spanish) entails a kind of transparency built on repressing sexual urges.

It may seem tortuous to defend Villaurrutia's metaphysical and chiasmic hieroglyphs as more "positive" than Gabriel Rotello's epistemological certainties, the former's chiaroscuros as more fulfilling than the blinding medicalized light that Rotello turns on homosexuality, and Villaurrutia's moral acceptance of death-in-life as infinitely more liberating than Rotello's "life-affirming" riposte to gay males. From the point of view of desire (if desire can be said to have a point of view), Villaurrutia is more nuanced and complex, certainly less condemnatory.

The chiasmus may now be examined on its own: how can I claim that a discourse that is more "vague," less identity-specific, is more sexually liberating than the one that dares to say the word "gay" out loud? To put it in a contemporary, North American language: how can I say that a "closeted" discourse offers more of a sense of liberation than a discourse that is out of the closet? What we are limning here has to do with an issue of translation—not in the sense of the minute, exact job that Weinberger has done, but in the sense of the cultural translation of homosexuality from one code to another, not simply in terms of space and culture (Mexico-U.S.) but also in a temporal or historical (1940/1990) sense. There *is* something vaguely prophetic and also liberating in Villaurrutia's presence and absence, in his desire to see and not to see, in the interplay between desire and nostalgia in his book. To "prophesy" is to see with different eyes—with the inner eye, if you will. Villaurrutia's other mode of seeing is in this sense another vision. It is a vision that is not without its paradoxes in terms of AIDS, since much of AIDS poetry is based on a different kind of "seeing," a "facing up to the fact," a notion of death as something that has what beings do not possess in Villaurrutia—corporeality, flesh, decay, temporality. The liberatory and prophetic stance arises from the fact that in Villaurrutia's work death is not an event but always a discourse. It happened before and it will happen after.

Death is like sex in this way: it takes place everywhere, in parks, in hotel rooms, on the streets where men cruise. Orgasm is death and life, a means to an end, and an end in itself. If we are to think of *Nostalgia for Death* as a book that is "prophetic" in the age of AIDS, we must think *like* Villaurrutia—from a position of ambivalence, or better still, from the cool performance of passionate dispassion. This is what Villaurrutia presents as the key to a liberatory stance. Contrary to much of AIDS writing, Villaurrutia writes poetry from the point of view of absence. This absence is what turns *Nostalgia for Death* into a book about sex, about the absence of the person and the presence of bodies, about the questioning of identity and the affirmation of flesh. Its sense of uniqueness is not necessarily predicated on individuality, but rather on a lack of personhood. This "hollow" subjectivity is actually a progressive stance in this context—certainly more progressive than a discourse that claims subjectivity in order to condemn its choices and its modes of sexual affirmation.[39] It is sometimes more progressive to blur the contours of an identity than to constantly affirm it as a ready-made construction. Gabriel Rotello, for example, makes a distinction between gay desire and the gay community, only to conclude that there is something out of control and ultimately wrong with gay *desire* itself. The community as identity category needs to be upheld, while it must also curb the desire for multiple sex partners.

This is not, of course, the message that is prevalent in Villaurrutia's work, where "scattering" is manifested as a key component of desire in a way that monogamy and marriage are not. In his pre-Stonewall, pre-AIDS universe, Villaurrutia, I think, would be more comfortable with a sex-positive context, where sexual liberation and the freedom to do whatever with one's own body were paramount as identificatory responses to the normatizing heterosexism of the population at large.

In one of the poems included in *Nostalgia for Death* Villaurrutia voices his own sense of identity as a disembodied voice that falls within the space of two mirrors. The poem is—significantly, for Villaurrutia and for us—titled "Nocturno en que nada se oye," translated by Eliot Weinberger as "Nocturne: Nothing Is Heard." Villaurrutia is here playing with the fact that "nothing is heard" but also "nothingness" is heard. Silence and "nothing" (*nada*) are two of the structural metaphors that he uses, as if anticipating that his reading of Silence = Death, the defining logo in the fight against AIDS, would not have been an innocent one. After all, Villaurrutia sees death as the structural precondition for identity and life. He would probably, (and with a very culturally based sense of ironic morbidity) have taken issue with the refusal, the isolation, of death as something that one has to fight against, to dislodge and oppose.

The fact that for Villaurrutia death is the subject of nostalgia, and silence is both the precondition and the aim of discourse argues for the cultural specificity of AIDS discourse. In his nocturne, Villaurrutia talks about a game of mirrors that play with each other, while voice itself falls within the space between them. In Villaurrutia's quasi-Heideggerian formulation of identity, the idea of falling is related to the very constitution of the subject, and the fall itself allows for the playful progression of a voice. I am quoting the Spanish here so readers may notice the coupling game by means of which words join and separate on the page:

> *Y en el juego angustioso de un espejo frente a otro*
> *cae mi voz*
> *y mi voz que madura*
> *y mi voz quemadura*
> *y mi bosque madura*
> *y mi voz quema dura.*[40]

This play on words allows us to see and hear the discourse of a voice as it ripens and burns with a particular harshness, a discourse in which the voice at the same time turns into a forest (*bosque*), while it is also a verb (*quema*) and a noun, burnt skin (*quemadura*). If the mirrors in the first line quoted above are playing with each other, soon enough, voice itself plays with the mirrors, allowing us to see visually a play on words that cannot be heard, since all the phrases in Spanish sound alike.[41] In this poem, sound joins what vision keeps separate, and two different versions of the poem are obtained according to whether one *hears* or *reads* it.

It is clear that for Villaurrutia identity is predicated on what is a game and not a choice, a game that does not privilege voice over vision but constructs that identity according to a sense of difference and sameness. The poem is a different event according to the mode in which it is performed. This should not be seen solely as a choice, but rather as a choice predicated on vision's ability to distinguish over and beyond the fallacies of voice—in other words, on the differential equations among voice and vision. Villaurrutia allows us access to a world where difference is perceived in nonexclusive terms. Identity recalls itself and subjects itself to dissolution within the two mirrors that it rewrites and that it brings—and seduces—into play. Anguish is opposed to the triumphalist narrative of besieged identities and the normatizing responses that these seem to command. But it is an anguish aware of its own sense of play between sleep and death as entities that have nothing to say to each other.

Villaurrutia forces an important question on us about what is gained and what is lost if we dissolve the constitution of the gay male subject as a fixed subject and a fixed identity. In this universe, there may be nothing to identity except for a sex that always happens before or after, that is always seen from the point of view of nostalgia. To conclude this after reading Villaurrutia, after allowing him to read *us* in the present day and context, is to understand the extent to which his legacy may poison the certainties that we believe in. The discourse of sleep and the event of death, like the discourse of AIDS and the event of Stonewall, in Villaurrutia's world, are entities that communicate nothing to each other. The poet reserves for himself the right to show their lack of connection while attempting to mediate between them. This mediation, in turn, constitutes the subject as always already a subject about to dissolve, not as a wall that keeps an identity within its own neurotic confines.

I realize the contradictory position at play here: rescuing Villaurrutia as a homosexual in order to let him recall, for us, the difficulty of homosexuality; allowing Villaurrutia to dissolve the subject for the sake of its future constitution, its eternal return. At other points in this book, precursors will hold forth legacies that do not allow us to ascertain the comfort of our own self-constituted visions. Villaurrutia does not offer the comforting voice of health in the midst of illness, but the poisoned ink that writes its own name only in order to erase it. In the next chapter, Lydia Cabrera's plays with absence and desire allowed her to write a book that is seen as necessary insofar as it is always written by an other. Desire comes with its own mode of authorship. The praxis by means of which identity is constantly masked, erased, or put in brackets creates a flexible body that still produces erotic tension and discomfort as we engage ourselves in the task of reading these texts.

3 Queer Desires in Lydia Cabrera

Queer Objects

Lydia Cabrera's *El monte* (1954) is one of the queerest books ever written by a Cuban author. The full range of its queerness can never be exhaustively decoded. The book itself as an object, and the authorial figure of Cabrera limn religion, Cuban politics, anthropology, lesbian sexuality, and exile. *El monte* not only allows us access to the secrets of Afro-Cuban religion, but also plays off its secrecy in a circuit of meaning where gender needs to be examined in a productive relationship to race. My intention is to mobilize theses issues, explore how they shed light on each other. I will allow Cabrera's method to guide these encounters, and reject divisions between categories of race and gender, as well as divisions between theory and practice. *El monte*'s sense of praxis illuminates secrets that at the same time will never be fully uncovered. Cabrera's mode of intervention, which I specifically name *lesbian* later on in the text, mobilizes circuits of meaning, creating communities and relations.

The cover for the 1975 edition of *El monte* is spare, almost blank. There are no drawings, no "exotic" pictures, no appeals for the reader to enter into an alien yet familiar world. Words themselves give the book more of an uncanny strangeness than the "recalled distance" provoked by a visual representation of the exotic as category. *El monte*'s subtitle is written in Yoruba. The cover reads, "El monte / Igbo. Finda / Ewe Orisha. Vititi Nfinda" and then, added in parentheses, "Notes on the religions, magic, superstitions, and folklore of the creole blacks and the people of Cuba" (Notas sobre las religiones, la magia, las supersticiones y el folklore de los negros criollos y del pueblo de Cuba). Let me underscore the impact of these words: the title *El monte* is printed in green ink on the white page, and it is followed by lines that have been deliberately left in their original language. Readers who turn to the copyright page will notice that there is no original publication date listed, only the fact that it is a fourth edition, from 1975. This seems to be a reprint of an older text, not a new edition, and there is no new prologue, no biographical information on the author, no account of the object's circumstances. At the same time, there is no attempt to pass off the book as an original edition.

Lydia Cabrera's *El monte*. Ediciones Universal, Miami, 1975.

With Lydia Cabrera nothing is hidden, but then again nothing is explained. The countless interviews the author gave throughout her life, produce many retellings of the same story. In the end, there is a strange silence—a silence echoed by the reticence of this book. It is a self-proclaimed copy that is nevertheless not a copy at all, but rather the emblem of a performance: a book that acts out its own enigma by playing off mystery and visibility. Instead of writing a new prologue, Lydia Cabrera wanted readers to face up to silence. *That* is the nature of her language, and it is also part of the language of the book itself.

El monte is a book about religion, but it is also a religious manual. It not only gives an account of a series of practices, but also puts those practices into action in carefully edited glossaries that accompany the text and guide practitioners to specific points in the book. *El monte* is, moreover, a book about religious belief and ritual in Cuba, while the religion itself (Afro-Cuban) is part of a diasporic culture. And *El monte* is a book about exile reprinted at the site—Miami—where a new Cuban diaspora had been forming since 1959.

How does the fact of exile affect a religion that is, in Cabrera's own words, based so much on land, on a particular place—on *el monte* (the mountain), on Cuba—and on a particular cultural context? How does religious practice change when one loses easy access to plants and to open spaces (*monte*) that contain the remedies for disaster and illness? The white page of the book's cover glosses the answer to this question. Its lack of illustrative material furnishes its own language. Even if the material elements that the religion needs in order to be practiced are harder to find, the need for the knowledge is never in dispute.[1]

All religious books are ultimately books about exile. They bear the trace of stories that need to be retold, practices that need to be reaffirmed and/or codified, knowledge that it is imperative to keep alive. But because *El monte* is a book about Afro-Cuban religion published in Miami, what readers face in confronting this book is a double exile—assumed not in the form of a lament, but rather as a praxis.

Santería, which is the religion to which Cabrera dedicated a major part of her life's work, has had different contextual meanings in Cuba at different times, but in the 1950s it was not the sort of culture that could be reported with a sense of distance in the evening news, as was the case with Santería during the recent visit of the Catholic pope to Cuba.[2] At the time of Cabrera's writing and throughout the course of her life, santería was something that was inexplicably *there,* though not to the extent that it was at all times openly indexed. In fact, at many points in Cuban history, santería has been a clandestine form of religious practice, a corpus of beliefs, rites, norms, actions that was everywhere and nowhere at the same time. These religious practices have always existed in visible forms as a mode of Catholicism, dating back to the slave trade during Spanish colonial times in Cuba. But they have also been prohibited and persecuted. At various times in the Cuban Republic, santería was associated with the worst forms of criminality.

Because of the semiclandestine nature of its beliefs, Afro-Cuban religion was all about syncretism and substitution. The signifier relates in a particular way to the signified (San Lazaro may be the openly visible image of the African deity Babalu Aye). The image may be the same, but the form of interpellation is different. The secrets Cabrera pursued were all about relations between signifiers and signified, relationships that were to a certain extent codified, even if the practices associated with this system were not, fully. Although santería was associated principally with Afro-Cubans, it is also clear, as Cabrera recalls, that the practices and the culture itself had more or less permeated many strata of Cuban society. Santería is an intersectional practice, a critical hermeneutics involving different components that coexist in a simultaneous manner.[3] Cabrera was invested in studying a system of beliefs that was secret, to a certain extent underground, and to a major extent "incoherent" to certain segments of the population. To her credit, as we shall see, she did not seek coherence but rather tried to explore the relative intelligibility of the system on its own terms.

Returning to the 1974 edition once again, one could claim that the internal histories of the Cuban revolution do not really have any bearing on a book that is published in Miami, but I want to argue forcefully that this is not the case. The underground knowledge that the book talks about affects the very concrete and material aspects of its publication—not only in Miami, but also in Cuba. It should be noted, as a point of reference, that the early seventies was one of the most politically sensitive periods of the revolution, named by some of its victims *el quinquenio gris,* a time when religion was banished from most sectors of Cuban life. During the first years of the revolution in Cuba, Catholic priests were expelled from the island or jailed, and their schools closed. Pentecostals, Baptists, and Afro-Cuban *babalawos* (perhaps we could call these santeria's "priests," allowing for mistranslation) were also victims of government persecution. Major *babalawos* in the early 1960s went into exile. Those in Cuba had to practice their religion, once again, as in the past—by hiding and subterfuge.

With such vital links broken, and with Cuba having experienced the collapse of the ten-million-ton harvest in the early seventies, *El monte* in 1975 seeks to openly intervene in a double setting. The book provided a link with origins (Cuba) for those who had left, and who were at a loss as to the names of plants and lacked knowledge of the old rituals. But it was also an act of political defiance directed at the geographical Cuban space itself. For those who remained in Cuba the reprint of *El monte* was a clandestine border crosser. It has been clear for some time that the book—or at least pages or segments of the book—circulated in Cuba in the 1970s. Whereas it will remain for some time unclear to what extent it circulated, it *is* clear that when the government gradually allowed urban Afro-Cuban religion to be practiced openly in the late 1980s and early 1990s, Cuban anthropologists in Havana were surprised by the extent of the popular knowledge about the various plants used in religious practices that had been proscribed for over twenty years. They pointed to the clandestine circulation of copies of Cabrera's *El monte,* either as a complete book or in fragments—for many *yerberos* possessed copies of certain pages of the book, particularly sections of the glossary.

It is important that we keep in mind this sense of localized praxis when approaching Lydia Cabrera's texts. This practice does not entail hiding or "closeting" something; rather, it is a form of speech that is transparent in different terms for different members of the reading audience, who have been initiated into one of its many circuits of meaning. As I explored in the essay on Villaurrutia, and as I will again take up in the one on Piñera, circuitousness, evasion, avoidance are all modes of praxis and not necessarily forms of denial. They do not imply failures of utterance but rather particular ways of *saying*.

Cabrera wreaked havoc with other people's confusions. During her long exile in Miami after the revolution, she was revered as an ethnographer, but also as a fiction writer. She compiled dictionaries of Cuban medicinal plants. She painted magical stones and regaled visitors with tales of avant-garde Paris and prerevolutionary Havana. She was a symbol but also a cipher. In one episode in Reinaldo Arenas's memoirs *Before Night Falls*, she appears as the example of all that Cuba lost after the revolution, but also of all that Cuba could still convey:

I saw an old lady sitting at a small table under a mango tree, signing books: it was Lydia Cabrera. She had left behind all of her past, her huge country estate in Havana, her extensive library, and was now trying to make ends meet in a small Miami apartment. When I saw this blind old lady signing her books under a mango tree, I understood that she represented a greatness and a spirit of rebellion that perhaps no longer existed in any of our writers, either in Cuba or in exile. One of the greatest women in our history, she was completely forsaken and forgotten, or else surrounded by people who had never read a single one of her books and were now just looking for a quick news story, taking advantage of the splendor that old lady still radiated.[4]

For Arenas, she is an emblem of the relationship between the writer and the state, an emblem of the tragic situation of Cuban writers, condemned to exile unless they acquiesce to dictatorship. In her radiant exile, Cabrera became something more than an anthropologist; for Arenas, she represented Cuba itself: destitute but proud, Havana in Wim Wenders's *Buena Vista Social Club*, refusing to die even in the midst of absolute decay.

Queer Evanescence

Lydia Cabrera's life up until her later exile was marked by class privilege. Her father was a prominent writer associated with the struggle for Cuban independence, and the publisher of a magazine titled *Cuba y América*, where Cabrera published her first pieces when she was fourteen.[5] Although her father did not allow her to attend high school or university, it seems that he did encourage her literary and artistic talents. She traveled as a young girl to New York and, by the age of twenty, threatened to commit suicide if she were not permitted to study at the Sorbonne in Paris. Her father acquiesced to her wishes, although he died in 1923, before he could fulfill his promise.[6]

The autobiographical account in most of Cabrera's interviews leads directly to two of the most important events in her life: her relationship with Teresa de la Parra and her interest in ethnography as a career. Both aspects, as we shall see, are linked. Parra made a stop in Havana on her way back to Venezuela in either 1924 or 1925,[7] traveling on the ship *Miguel Arnús*. One evening, Cabrera was invited to eat on deck and immediately noticed Teresa dressed in black and cutting an impressive figure against the backdrop of one of the most dramatic harbors in the Caribbean. Parra was mourning the death of her friend Emilia Barrios, who was, according to Cabrera, one of the most important figures in Parra's life, "a second mother and an understanding and stimulating friend."[8]

The question of mourning is important in this tale, not only for the degree of social convention that it entailed, but also because mourning was part of a codified ritual. There were degrees of mourning depending on whether the deceased was a family member, a spouse, or a friend. Social convention and codes in Parra's case dictated that the mourned person be seen as a family member. It would have been too strange for a woman to mourn another to the degree that Parra mourned Barrios, had the latter not been thus identified: "She followed the rigorous mourning that one then followed for a mother. On her nighttable she kept Emilia's picture, which she carried everywhere."[9] This coded motherhood permitted a certain degree of social freedom: it allowed Parra to travel with Barrios's picture, and to insist that the picture itself be put in her (Parra's) tomb when she died—a wish that Cabrera says Parra's sister fulfilled.[10]

In Havana that afternoon, Cabrera gave Parra a small presentation card, on which she wrote, "please do not forget me" (favor de no olvidarme).[11] A year or so later, while in Paris in 1927, Cabrera encountered Parra at the Hotel Vernet. This time she did not seem to be in mourning, the two women struck up a conversation, and Cabrera found out, to her surprise, that Parra still kept the presentation card she had given her in that meeting at the Havana harbor. At this point, Parra and Cabrera started a relationship referenced by the previous one between Parra and Barrios.

In both cases, these relationships were coded as the meeting between an acolyte and a mentor. Parra was ten years older than Cabrera and, at that time, already well known for her novel *Ifigenia*, a book that was seen as "immoral" in the Venezuelan society of the time, and that had been banned by the Catholic Church.[12] According to Cabrera, Emilia Barrios prompted Parra to write the novel, just as Parra herself later encouraged Cabrera to write her collection of stories, *Cuentos negros de Cuba*.[13] Even if the Parisian fascination with the exotic beckoned Cabrera as a modern woman, her becoming "merely" a compiler of Afro-Cuban tales is similar to the role chosen by her friend Teresa. Parra's writing was all about creating an "autobiographical" effect, for example in *Ifigenia (o diario de una señorita que se fatiga)* (1924), which she published before she met Cabrera, and in her *Memorias de Mamá Blanca* (1929), where she underscores secrets that pass from one person to the other.[14] There are elements of this in Cabrera's tales, as well as in her ethnographical work proper, as we shall see.

Cabrera's tales are fascinating and complicated because of their morphological twists and turns; they give the impression that they have been *deployed* instead of prepared. The tales of *Cuentos negros* seem at certain points improvised. The narrative moves randomly from place to place, it has the same kind of improvisatory effect or "spontaneity" that was also part of Teresa de la Parra's work.[15] As Sylvia Molloy has observed, the circuits of resistance and complicity between Parra and Cabrera were mediated by literature and art.[16] As in Parra's work, the origin of Cabrera's tales belongs to a context where the autobiographical meets the literary.

Cabrera said by her own account (and we must underscore how important this narrative was for the author) that she listened in her Havana childhood to the stories later published as *Cuentos negros*. But it was only when she lived in Paris in 1928 with Teresa de la Parra that Cabrera developed an interest in Cuban black culture.[17] "While still in Paris," as Ana María Simo explains, "Lydia had started to remember the world of her childhood, a world dominated by the inventions of Black nannies, cooks and seamstresses."[18]

The circuits of death that surround the publication of *Cuentos negros* in 1936 are related to the appearance of voices from a past that refuses to die. In 1932 Lydia Cabrera's mother died in Cuba, and that same year Teresa de la Parra was diagnosed with tuberculosis. As Cabrera has explained in her interviews, she started writing at least a first version of her tales as entertainment for her friend, convalescing in a Swiss sanatorium. At some point during Parra's illness, Cabrera traveled to Paris, wrote and assembled the tales as a collection, and gave them to Francis de Miomandre. He translated them into French and published them as *Contes nègres de Cuba* at Gallimard.[19] The book is dedicated to Teresa de la Parra. According to Cabrera, Parra saw and read the book a month and a half before her death from tuberculosis in Madrid in 1936.[20]

This turn to anthropology or ethnography should be underscored, since it would always be directly related to Cabrera's relationship to Teresa, as well as to her understanding of death.[21] Cabrera herself recalled that when the *Contes nègres* were published, she was in distress: "I was, I remember, very worried; I was the witness to an agony (Teresa de la Parra's) and I was thinking on how evanescent life is."[22] Evanescence speaks of a tendency to vanish, to pass away like vapor; it connotes a vision of impermanence, of things that are fleeting, or of extreme delicacy. For those who read Cabrera's recollections of Teresa de la Parra, these are the words that best describe not only Cabrera's act of remembrance, but also the context of those years. Even forty years later, when Cabrera gives her interviews in her modest house in Miami, she makes us notice how painful this context must have been: Cabrera laments Parra's death while also recalling the fact that she met Parra at the moment Parra herself was mourning another woman.

The prolonged circuits of death surrounding these tales are painful when we consider them closely: Barrios died with Parra at her side, and Parra died with Cabrera at her side.[23] Memory and recollection in *Cuentos negros* are a way of reclaiming the dead, even if it is clear from Cabrera's words that the dead are something more than just memories. Life as evanescence is directly related to Cabrera's scene of writing and her pursuit of ethnography. Indeed, the very *personal* sensation of evanescence (over and beyond the evanescence implied by ethnography itself—the spectacle of dying cultures) is important not only to her work as an anthropologist but also to her *mode* of work, her position as a *female* anthropologist, and the invisible or visible threads of that link with her sexuality.[24]

Cabrera intervenes as a writer by manipulating—or orchestrating—her own understanding of presence and absence, of what is physically tangible at the moment it starts to fade out. This fading is the work of desire in her tales and in her anthropology. In biographical terms, after all, we owe Cabrera's work as an anthropologist not only to a relationship, but to its very literal death. Presence and evanescence are desires that accompany the text, and they define the mode of authorship Cabrera chose for herself—the way she intervened in Cuban letters. This collecting of African tales was all about liminality, about the self that is also an other, or about a sense of otherness within. It is also about the relationship between death and homosexuality—in short, this is a work about desire.

Queer Methodology

In *El monte*, we have indirect access to situations in which the native informants seem to be observing the observers. Cabrera never questions her informants' visions of *her*, although her *otherness* is remarked or talked about throughout the text. First, Cabrera underscores that she does not examine the rituals with racist intentions, and the disclaimer reinforces her status as a white woman from the Cuban upper classes who decides to study the Afro-Cuban religious universe of the lower classes. It is clear that this class and race dynamic produces a very specific situation, and the moments where it seems that her observers are observing her are like scars in the text, events that are left in the narrative for another perceptive reader to examine. Take, for example, the whole question of lesbianism in Afro-Cuban religious practices—the way Cabrera (not necessarily her informants) limns the situation. In the second chapter, called "Bilongo," Cabrera says that:

*From very far back one registers the nefarious sin as something that is very frequent in the Lucumí Regla. However, many babalochas, omó-Changó, died punished by an orisha as manly and womanizing as Changó, who repudiates this vice. At this point, the proportion of pederasts [pederastas] in Ocha (not so in the sects that claim to be Congos, where they are profoundly despised and from which they are expelled) seems to be so numerous that it is constantly cause for indignation for the old santeros and devouts. "At every step one bumps into a sissy [*partido*] who swishes about like a piece of meringue!"*[25]

There is really no context at all for this statement, which appears in a paragraph by itself. The chapter in question does not talk about homosexuality but rather about *bilongos* (spells), and the story that precedes this paragraph is about Papá Colás, a man who mistreats his *santos*. Cabrera says she has heard the story of Papá Colás from many sources,[26] and at various points throughout the story she quotes directly from them, although at other points she does not. It seems she has threaded some sort of coherent narrative out of all the stories she has heard, but the last sentence of the story that I will quote below comes with no attribution whatsoever. We do not know whether it is common knowledge, hearsay, or one version among many. I am quoting Cabrera at this point and not one of her informants:

This Papá Colás, who has left so many memories among the old, was a famous invert, and taking advantage of the simpleness of a priest, he married dressed up as a woman, with another invert, thus motivating the scandal that you may imagine.[27]

This detail is what provokes the paragraph quoted above, as well as the next story, where an informant named Sandoval claims that many male homosexuals are sons of Yemayá. And it produces still one other story, whose source is not given, about two *santeros*, named simply R. and Ch., where the latter was fond of dressing up in women's clothes. The story is then inexplicably followed by still another homosexual account—this time a lesbian one. This in turn prompts Cabrera to remark on the irony that lesbianism is associated with Inlé, a very chaste saint (actually, an adolescent), and with Yewá:

Yewá, "Our Lady of the Dispossessed," virgin prohibits her daughters all sexual commerce; that is why her servers are always old women, virgins, or sterile, and Inlé, "as severe," as powerful and delicate as Yewá, perhaps demanded the same from his santeras, who abstained from having sexual relationships with men.[28]

Cabrera does not allow us to reconstruct the scene where this information is being gathered. Her text may mix the story of her informants with her own gloss of their statements, but what is more important is that there is nothing in this chapter that pertains per se to the role of homosexuality in santería. The story of Papá Colás is brought into the text as an example of how not to forget or mistreat the saints, and only secondarily in order to show the relationship between homosexuality [pederastia] and santería. Of these two—in a chapter dedicated to *bilongos*—it is the first that provokes Cabrera's interest and allows her to indulge, in her performative text, in the quite lengthy aside on the question of homosexuality quoted above.

Homosexuality, it must be pointed out, does not appear in the book's glossary. Cabrera registers the different names for homosexuals—Addóddis, Obini-Toyo, Obini-ñaña, Erón Kibá, Wassicúndi, Diánkune (p. 58)—but does not say where or at what point she heard those names or who she heard them from. It seems that the key figure here is the informant Sandoval, and that he is the source for this information, although he does not appear as one of the major informants named by Cabrera at the beginning. It would be too easy to say that Cabrera has been adding this information in order to inform her readers about homosexuality. The more interesting option (and one I prefer) is to think that Sandoval or another informant is actually reading Cabrera, and that she may or may not realize this.[29]

El monte hides as much as it reveals; it uncovers but it also keeps its secrets well below the surface. It is a moving text that is threaded with voices, comments, and even signs of anthropological surprise. Cabrera is present as an ethnographer—she does leave the trace of her own comments and observations on site—but she is more concerned with openly weaving the record of her interviews into the text itself. She is relatively unconcerned with the veracity of some of the tales that she recounts, and leaves it up to the reader to decide whether the information is credible or not. She *does* note when one of her sources does not appear to be particularly believable: "The source of this story may not merit much trust," but then she says, "At least I feigned not to doubt its veracity" (Yo al menos fingí que no dudaba de su veracidad).[30]

The scene from which these statements are taken is particularly interesting. Cabrera is here talking with two black women who are *themselves* doubting the truthfulness of another informant's tale. Although Cabrera has not been initiated in the mysteries of the religion (she never says whether she was ever initiated), she keeps for herself a guarded distance that does not preclude her *performance* of the informant's believability. As for the reader, she adds,

The reader, fully aware of where the tale comes from, is at complete liberty, as always, to believe whatever he wants [lo que mejor le parezca]. As for me, I am inclined to accept it as veridical, since I have witnessed other events that would appear equally or more unbelievable.[31]

The act of feigning to believe and then proclaiming her belief is an interesting one. Cabrera always argues for her—and her informants'—own sense of coherence in terms of practices and beliefs that, in a wider context, seem to be incoherent in themselves. And she frames the question of incoherence by relating it to the question of race. Coherence already appears in the introduction to *El monte*. Cabrera warns that "One will not understand our people without understanding blacks. . . . We cannot immerse ourselves in Cuban life without meeting that African presence *that is not manifested exclusively in the coloration of the skin.*"[32] She clarifies that the material in *El monte* "has not gone through the dangerous filter of interpretation,"[33] because in order to understand fully what is being talked about, the (white) readers need to "aprender a pensar como ellos" (learn how to think like them—meaning blacks).[34] *El monte* is a study of Afro-Cuban religions and cultures, but it is also about Cabrera's understanding of how that form of knowledge assumes its own coherence and its own sense of intelligibility.

Cabrera's method demands a certain degree of distance from the reader, and Cabrera manipulates this distance by writing a text full of jarring temporal dislocations. This creates its own particular effect, as if *El monte* were created with some sense of urgency, meant to register an impending absence. Cabrera gives her information in a style that resembles a pastiche of the oral histories of her informants and her science. In the introduction she allows that the method, the very methodology of the work, is in a sense *queer*—full of repetitions and digressions, at times difficult to follow. She indulges her readers by participating in the text—by presenting herself—but she gives us very little in terms of how the book itself was organized, or what ethnographical method she used. When she does, it is generally in an indirect fashion, as in the following example:

> *At the entrance to el monte, where ideally we have paid our tribute accompanying it with some kernels of corn and lighting a candle, or, to be more truthful,* in front of the pile of index cards where I jot down information on those who know *how to propitiate the god Osaín and in effect buy the intelligent will of the plants, as was told to me gravely by the grandson of a lucumí—"When the godfather realizes that the godchild calls each plant by its name knowing what they can do, without confusing them, then he sends him off to walk by himself in the world." (My emphasis)*[35]

This aside sends readers to the anthropological scene (Cabrera asking questions and jotting down answers on index cards) and also allows for the direct quotation of an informant to be included in the paragraph. She will not reproduce the questions that provoked these interventions, and it is not clear whether she has selected certain informants to speak on particular subjects. The book, in this case, is an echo chamber, where Cabrera not only speaks, but also indirectly weaves her informants' accounts into the interview, while at the same time copying their information word for word.

This queer method of writing allows *El monte* to mimetically reproduce what the author means to show. In the passage quoted above, the entrance to "el monte" is also equated to the scene of research, and the relation between one and the other seems to promise secrets that will be unveiled in the book. This queerness marks the status of the book as a hybrid that in turn comments on the very queer position of Cuba within Western discourse and Western modernity. Cabrera tells us that her informants "do not know the speed that undermines modern life and that sickens white people's spirits." Her almost third-person–like reference to whiteness is interesting in this regard.[36]

El monte is an "open system": a rhizomatic work of multiple, ever expanding, deterritorializing and reterritorializing gestures—gestures that have no apparent beginning or end, but are apprehended at a determinate point in the mapped coordinates of time and space.[37] Cabrera's subtitle (*Notes*) points to the logic by means of which the book operates. It does not necessarily profit from a linear (patriarchal) reading that works from beginning to end, but from one that notices underlying relationships between objects and themes, stories and practices. The book does not seem to follow a particular order, neither in terms of the chapters nor as a whole. In other words, there is no discernible sequence. *El monte* gives the appearance of something that is left uncompleted—a book that takes place in the present, instead of a book that has been structured according to a plan. Its queer method also befits Cabrera's self-presentation throughout the book. She will at times admit that she forgets or does not jot down things, she talks about what she has done for her informants ("Oddeddei, for whom I had the pleasure of paying the rent on a house during her last days"),[38] and she appeals directly to her readers ("let us have an old iyalocha explain this custom to us").[39]

El monte never clearly defines the separation between theoretical and practical knowledge. It is organized into ten chapters, a glossary of plants and herbs (along with descriptions and uses), a set of photographs, a subject index, and another index for the chapters as well as for the glossary.[40] The glossary can be better described as a compendium of herbs and different remedies concocted with them. The links between theory and praxis are there for the readers to uncover, as long as readers do not ask questions that take them on different routes, for some of these may be too queer to explain.

Queer Identity

The mechanics of authorship in Cabrera's text point to a mode of intervention that negotiates dialectical structures. The structural relationships between homosexuality and heterosexuality, between different races, cultures, and systems of belief are embedded one into the other. These embedded narratives are found in Cabrera's *Cuentos negros*, and they can also be found in the structural and formal dynamics of the chapters of *El monte*.

An apt emblem for the mechanics of authorship in Cabrera's work—her penchant for embedded narratives—can be seen in Cabrera's conversations with Rosario Hiriart. Hiriart remarks on a ring that Cabrera always wears, and that Hiriart knows was a present from Teresa de la Parra, so she asks whether Cabrera still wears the ring for good luck. Cabrera replies that it is an emerald ring that Parra always wore, and that Parra left her not only that ring, but also her entire library. She adds, with a smile, that she never reclaimed the library but she did keep the ring. Further along in the conversation, Cabrera explains that Parra wore the ring because it had been a gift from Parra's friend Emilia Barrios (Cabrera calls her again "su segunda madre" [her second mother]). The ring bears an inscription, which Cabrera discovered only after Parra's death. It simply says, "Au revoir." When Hiriart asks her how she felt when she received it, Cabrera says, "What can I tell you? Many different things. . . . People we love, we feel them present in some object that has been in contact with them."[41]

More than the fact that Cabrera is still wearing this ring so many years after Parra's death—while also living with another woman companion, María Teresa de Rojas—what I think we should pay attention to is signaled by the ring itself, by the circularity of its shape and the circuit it metonymizes: from Emilia Barrios to Teresa de la Parra, and then to Lydia Cabrera. It allows Cabrera to claim objects that are always already traces, mementos of an eternal departure more than an eternal presence.

If we want to speak of notions of identity in Cabrera's work, this is, metaphorically, the door we have to knock on. The first word in Cabrera's *El monte* already speaks about this in such open terms that the fact that it "passes" is important in and of itself. Cabrera here does not argue for identity but rather for "persistence": "Persiste en el negro cubano, con tenacidad asombrosa, la creencia en la espiritualidad del monte" (The belief in the spirituality of el monte persists in black Cubans with astonishing tenacity).[42]

Persistence implies a process-in-motion that is not necessarily oppositional, but relational—this relational structure can be compared to others in the text: the relationship between "monte" and "city," or between the civilized and the uncivilized. The *monte* is a magical space that needs to be approached cautiously, somewhat circuitously, and always with a sense of respect.[43] It is not, however, a space that is "out there" since it may be found in the very heart of the city—in a small, even minute, plot of land, on any piece of land that has not been covered with cement.[44] The growing urbanization of those empty plots of land condemns a nature that "speaks" to silence, but resourcefulness is the key here, and the initiates will find ways of overcoming this threat.

Cabrera's authorship entails relating things to each other, and the complexity of the web that she traces includes also dialectical relationships between gender and sexual identity, anthropology and race, exile and religion.

There is a female homosocial network in *El monte*, a network that is always spoken about in code. The reader has to search, look, recompose the fragments of the stories scattered throughout the volume. This is particularly true of the story of Omí-Tomí, which seems to be the foundation for the book, and displays the origin of a network of female homosocial contact disseminated throughout Cabrera's work. This network is embedded in the book; it is not outside of the book. It is like a plot of land (*monte*) within the city that is the text.

Omí-Tomí's story is part of the genealogical history of how Cabrera came to study Afro-Cuban religion.[45] It is found in the first chapter of *El monte*, though it is never told in a direct fashion. The story appears in order to illustrate the relationship and allegiance black Cubans have to their saints. At an early age, Omí-Tomí (at this point she is called Teresa M.) and her mother were emancipated, and Teresa was raised in the household of two older women, who are referred to as "spinsters." According to Cabrera, who is reproducing at this point Teresa M.'s narration, she not only was raised in the main household, but also served as a surrogate daughter for the two women:

*"I grew up in the living room like a white lady," with all the care and excessive tenderness that could be lavished on her by her nannies—two spinsters—to a daughter. And both took their love for the little black girl [*negrita*]—jet black, but who came to fill for them the void of their frustrated motherhood—to the extent that they named her their universal heir.*[46]

Omí-Tomí's statement, reproduced here in quotation marks, is qualified by Cabrera underscoring the child's blackness ("jet black" [negra como azabache]), while also adding a dramatic formula ("frustrated motherhood") to explain the love that these women had for this child. What brings Teresa into Cabrera's life is the question of inheritance. When the house became the object of a legal battle after the two women died, Teresa M. went to Cabrera's father's legal office to reclaim it. Cabrera's father took pity on the woman, and although he could do nothing to help her (she had been legally dispossessed) the woman became a presence in the household, particularly because she was an extremely talented seamstress.

At some point that is not registered in the tale of origins presented in the work, Teresa M. insisted that the two white women who raised her prevented her from learning about the rites of her ancestors. Her gradual "return" to the religion of her roots is recounted at *another* point in the text.

The web traced in the second part of this tale joins the question of "passing" and "coming out" to the issue of religion. It is not narrated, but rather *dissimulated* within the text. It is sewn and woven as if it were a secondary story to the primary anthropological narrative that Cabrera is constructing, a narrative about dissimulation: Cabrera asserts that the most faithful and religiously observant Afro-Cubans, the ones who always insist on going to mass and force young girls to observe the precepts of the Catholic Church, are also the ones who dissimulate the rules of the "other" pantheon of saints into the Catholic rites.[47]

The second part of Omí-Tomí's story concerns her "coming out" as a person well versed in santería. It is told in the context of Cabrera's explanation that "invisible" forces are always threatening Cuban blacks, and they see religion as a way of explaining many of life's misfortunes. If the first part of the story joined Cabrera and Omí-Tomí as two children raised in the codes of the other (Omí-Tomí is a black child in a white household, while Lydia is a white girl growing up among the black help), the second part of the story will show how Cabrera initially understands Afro-Cuban religion, since at this point Cabrera takes the modernizing stance and says that the majority of Cuban blacks live with the suspicion of hidden forces conspiring against them.[48]

Let us recall that Omí-Tomí explained that as a child she did not learn anything about the religion of her ancestors, since she was raised in the home of two white women. The story of how she came to understand these secrets, and how she understood who she *really* was, involves the loss of her own child. This child, named Belén, fell victim to a *bilongo* (spell) by María del Pilar, the best friend of a woman who used to go out with Omí-Tomí's husband (and who remained bitter about his marriage to Omí-Tomí). The baby for some reason no one could explain hated María del Pilar. One day, Omí-Tomí caught María del Pilar about to hit the baby, and because of that threw her out of the house. The baby fell ill and refused to eat, so Omí-Tomí took her to all the doctors she could find, but no doctor could treat little Belén. The baby died. Two or three hours after her death people witnessed a small reptile on the baby's stomach and confirmed the fact that she was the victim of a spell (*bilongo*).

From this point on, all those who wished the child harm came to a bad end. María del Pilar died nine days later. So did the spurned woman who started the whole *bilongo* (she died of colic) as well this woman's father, who felt such misgivings over what he had done with the baby's placenta and blood that he committed suicide. According to the *congo* that Omí-Tomí consulted, the reason they had all died was that she herself had been consecrated to Olokún-Yemayá at the moment of birth, and the principal author of this crime was also a daughter of Yemayá. The goddess does not like her daughters to wage war against each other.

This complicated tale is told at the beginning of *El monte*, but we should not see it simply as a tale that narrates Omí- Tomí's origins. It could illustrate a number of running threads in the book and in Cabrera's work. Questions of responsibility (and thus, authorship) are constantly displaced; the tale comes to us in an upside down manner, moving toward a past. The author of the *bilongo,* the spurned woman, never appears except at the moment of her death, at which time she is then displaced for the sake of another, more originary and "authentic" principle represented by Teresa's mother, who commended her to the saints before dying.

The past unfolds as the broader story progresses. Teresa M. is first presented as a woman who knows nothing of Afro-Cuban religion: a black woman supposedly raised as a white child in a white household, and her legal problems are not clarified in any clear temporal narrative line in relation to the issue of her daughter's death. That Cabrera's father employed her as a seamstress is significant, for she is the one who sews the visible (and invisible) links of the tale.

The issue of passing and instances in which someone or something "comes out" or is revealed as being *who they really are* recur many times in this work. The secrecy that surrounds the object of investigation and the webs of female homosocial desire embedded into it never quite coalesce into one narrative, but are threaded to each other and closed off at the same time by Cabrera's own interventions, which are always closing off the questions that identity may provoke.

Cabrera reveals the secrets of a religion, but then marks her own secret lesbianism as an open system in her work. The relationship between intervention and definition is not as clear- cut as the opposition between praxis and theory. One covers the other and bleeds onto the other. They hold each other at bay by serving as each other's foils. Different audiences may read the same tale and arrive at different conclusions. To trace the bloodline that Cabrera speaks about is partly a way of having access to the code. But it is clear that the code can be traced only if we enter into the space of the queer methodology that Cabrera deploys. The question here is not to arrive at some center of stability that will allow the secret to "come out," but to allow oneself to be seduced into the code as it traces its own figure and puzzles out its own dynamics.

Queer Intervention

Cabrera occupies a queer space in Cuban letters. Her mode of intervention was always coded, in one way or another, by her situation as a woman anthropologist, her relationship with Teresa de la Parra, her politics, and also her pursuit of two seemingly contradictory writing practices: anthropology and literature. The way her work was produced also conditioned its reception, as we can see in the introduction Fernando Ortiz, Cuba's foremost anthropologist, wrote for *Cuentos negros de Cuba*.

Ortiz explains that the book is the first written by a woman "whom we initiated in the taste for Afro-Cuban folklore."[49] For Ortiz, the distance marked by gender defines the author's work as a "taste," that is, a kind of "hobby" rather than science or even creative endeavor. In other words, Ortiz gently codes the information that Cabrera is a rich woman who has a taste for anthropology, and "taste" and, perhaps, money have produced this book.

"She penetrated," says Ortiz in the introduction, "into the forest of Havana's black legends out of sheer curiosity and then out of delight; finally, she started transcribing and collecting" these legends. Curiosity and delight for Ortiz are meant to be opposed to rigor and scientific distance, and in these terms we can already find the gesture that opposes male "science" to female "curiosity."

One may not demand much from an introductory essay, and my aim here is not to focus on what Ortiz did or did not say. But his words guide us into the dense and complicated forest of Lydia Cabrera's mode of lesbian authorship—one that deals with vanishing people, with traces, with the passage of time, and mostly with death. This bears a direct relationship to the questions of authorship that are at the foundation of these texts, as is clear in Ortiz's introduction when he focuses on the issue of translation:

One must not forget that these tales are the fruit of a collaboration, of black folklore with its white translator. Because the text in Spanish is also a translation, and strictly speaking a second translation. From the African language (Yoruba, Ewe, or Bantú) in which these fables were imagined, these were rendered in Cuba in the mestizo-ed and dialectical language of the creole blacks. Perhaps the old black woman who narrated these to Lydia had received them from her forebears in a creolized language. And from this form of speech the collector had to pass them into a legible form in Spanish, and from here on they will appear in this language.[50]

For Ortiz, these *Cuentos negros* represent what is left of a disaster: they are the *criollo* remains, the mulatto-ized fragments of a (linguistic and cultural) totality that exists no more. Ortiz insists on the inaccessibility of the original, while at the same time underscoring the permanence of the tradition. But this may not be, necessarily, the way Cabrera understands this issue.

In *El monte*, as well as in *Cuentos negros*, Cabrera is not necessarily concerned with presentation, but with what we should call the *performance* of the text: what can be said and what should not be said, how to embed life into the text, and how to represent representation itself. The method is very different from that of Fernando Ortiz, who was the author of the immensely influential *Cuban Counterpoint: Tobacco and Sugar* (1940) and to whom Cabrera dedicates *El monte*. As an anthropologist, Ortiz was more concerned with concepts like "transculturation" and grand historical narratives like the one he constructs for tobacco and sugar in the Cuban republic.[51] No such grand statements seem to be forthcoming from Lydia Cabrera. In relation to Ortiz's major work, Cabrera's is discreet. It even positions itself as ephemera (as can be seen in the subtitle *Notes* to *El monte*). Ortiz underscores this mode of authorship when he implicitly calls translation a "secondary operation," and this relates to his notions on gender: a rich, white *habanera* does not a scientist make. For Ortiz, Cabrera's work is all about translation or transcription: putting on paper an oral tradition that she saves from disaster.

One could start teasing out a different view of Cabrera's work, if one displaces the perspective that reads the original as the sign of plenitude and the translation as something secondary. This does not entail merely reversing the terms of the equation, but actually changing the structures of power that Ortiz participates in. In this context, translation becomes the reply to a demand made by the original, and the original then becomes subordinate to the plenitude achieved by translation. This postmodern deconstruction seeks to subvert translation as supplementary discourse, and it is voiced most openly by Jacques Derrida. As he explains in a "Roundtable on Translation" from the collection titled *The Ear of the Other*,

> *[The original] is in the situation of demand, that is, of a lack or exile. The original is indebted a priori to the translation. Its survival is a demand and a desire for translation, somewhat like the Babelian demand: Translate me. Babel is a man, or rather a male god, a god that is not full since he is full of resentment, jealousy, and so on. He calls out, he desires, he lacks, he calls for the complement or the supplement or, as Benjamin says, for that which will come along to enrich him. Translation does not come along in addition, like an accident added to a full substance; rather, it is what the original text demands—and not simply the signatory of the original text but the text itself. If the translation is indebted to the original (this is its task, its debt [Auf-*

gabe]), it is because already the original is indebted to the coming translation. This means that translation is also the law.[52]

Every text, if I follow Derrida on this point, is the partial apparition of a future text, just as prophets foretold the coming messiah. From this point of view, *Cuentos negros* allows us to peek at an abyss. Like a labyrinth, it leads not to an author but to a series of translators who repeat in turn an ancestral voice dissolved in an act of ambiguous authorship. In *Cuentos negros*, as in *El monte*, Lydia Cabrera's black informers appear here as voices inscribed within the text. As voices, they already beckon and ask for a text from the very depths of their ancestral nothingness. And this text, if we follow Derrida on this point, will turn into a text of plenitude when the translation is allowed to appear. Babel in this case is not the masculine god talked about by Derrida, but a phantom that *wants* to become a body, one that *becomes* a body in Cabrera's text. In other words, that text, from the very depths it inhabits, already repeated within its endless variants—from Africa to the colonies to the republic—is corporealized in the pages that Cabrera writes.

If we see translation in this way, the fact that Cabrera *transcribes* these tales in order to entertain another woman writer at the hour of her death is given added poignancy.[53] That the woman is Teresa de la Parra, Cabrera's companion, illustrates the threads that link identity to intervention in a mode of authorship that refuses the patriarchal gesture of authority and assumes the political praxis of the mask. As I have mentioned at other points in this book, the mask creates a network that allows different elements to come into contact with each other: Teresa de la Parra's absent body and Lydia Cabrera's present text; the invisible narrator and the visible translator; the anonymous voices of Afro-Cuban storytellers and the way they are turned into bodies and names. To defy Teresa de la Parra's evanescence, Cabrera assumes ethnography not in order to mask *Being* but rather as a way of giving herself over to an ethnographic work centered on the other.

In Cabrera's work there is an implicit analogy between body and text, an analogy where all visible marks—those of gender, of sex, of evanescence itself—confirm the profound identity of one text with another. These analogies also silently confirm that there are linkages that may be passed over in silence while others are inscribed on the page.

A homosexual text does not necessarily proclaim its own identity in words but in acts—in the coded secrets that it tells, and in the decoding that it *wants*. *El monte* is a scaffold for a network masked and revealed at the same time. There are two sides to every encounter: one point of view will say that Cabrera is only the translator and the transcriber of tales; the other, that she is an author who conjures the death of her lover. Some will say that there is chaos in *El monte,* where others will see method. On the one hand, she is a mere vehicle for the voices of others; on the other, she is the one who has always been destined to trace the passage of those voices into a text. What is clear is that Cabrera moves from the death of the body to the life of the text, marking its own figure with the figure of lesbian desire.

4 Outing Silence as Code

Virgilio Piñera

Homophilia

In Witold Gombrowicz's novel *Trans-Atlantyk* (1953), a Polish writer also named Gombrowicz is forced to stay in Buenos Aires when he learns that the German army has invaded his homeland. His progressive sense of exile—from his homeland, from the Polish émigré community in Argentina, from the mercantile classes because of his condition as a writer who does not glorify the nation—forms the basic plot of a tale written in a language that calls attention to its own code. Gombrowicz writes in "old" Polish forms, but makes it clear that the book is a roman à clef whose sense of antiquity is a foil for his acid comments on the present.[1] In Buenos Aires, Gombrowicz (the main character) meets a very mannered South American called Gonzalo at an embassy function. Gonzalo, as far as the reader understands, tries to cruise and pick up (in the book's code this is called "walking") the author and then the young son of a Polish businessman. When the businessman learns this, he challenges the fey Gonzalo to a duel. Verging on a state of hysteria, Gonzalo calls on Gombrowicz and asks him to be his second in a duel whose outcome they both seek to prearrange with false bullets. At this point, the Polish author is torn between the claims of allegiance to his invaded homeland, his Patria, the land of the Father (represented by the Polish businessman), and Gonzalo's demands for loyalty to a different concept, which he calls "Filistria":

Thereupon I cried: "Be still! Cease that Importuning of yours as 'tis impossible for me to be against the Father and the land of our father, against Pater and Patria, and what's more, in a moment such as the present!" Mutters he: "To the Devil with Pater and Patria! The son, the son's the thing, oh indeed! But wherefore need you Patria? Is not Filistria better? You exchange Patria for Filistria and then you'll see!"[2]

It is not clear what Filistria is meant to stand for, other than the concept that justifies the actions of the man the narrator calls the "Puto" Gonzalo. But what is clear is that the conflicting claims of a doubled male allegiance motivate a tale where both Patria and Filistria are seen in terms of both loss and gain. The narrator may lose a Patria toward which he was always skeptical and whose love he refuses to proclaim even at the hour of war, but he is also wary about his gaining Filistria as part of a new configuration of loyalties. Torn between what Gonzalo calls the claims of the Son (Filistria) and the claims of the Father (Patria), Gombrowicz writes his tale in a code whose language also speaks of both a gain and a loss—a particular form of male hysteria that seeks control precisely at the moment control is irremediably about to be lost.

Gombrowicz's "transatlantic" tale is meant to speak on many levels, and my aim is not to explicate or blur them all into one.[3] Gombrowicz's own struggles with homosexuality are written not only in the form of a disputation but also in way of a code, and at this point I want to highlight the importance of the code itself as a way of refusing the flattened-out language of simplified allegiances. Gombrowicz's struggle occurs on many levels—war, exile, ambivalent alliances, and even language—and to package all of these into one does a disservice to all the others. It is clear that Patria and Filistria each carries its own particular weight, and that Filistria resembles (or simulates) Patria as another form of male bonding. In this case, a rebelling against nationality implies dealing with the sexual bond between males, and the novel is split between the claims offered by the nationalist plot and those given in the homoerotic "'revolutionary' intrigue."[4] I think that substituting one for the other does not necessarily entail making the language or plot more transparent, for "cruising" as a word is as metaphorical as "walking" is. Patria and Filistria, then, are not meant to be oppositional, but rather *positional* terms, for the difference between the Father and the Son is merely a matter of position. Sons may turn out to be Fathers, and all Fathers and Sons may choose to act as if they belonged to Filistria.

Codes always expose their own sense of camouflage, and they call attention to the ways they seek to "pass" by denying their own passing, so that any unmasking of the code places the subject (in Gombrowicz's terms) at the level of the invader, the one who ruptures a fragile transparency that then needs to be reconstituted in exile. This is what Gombrowicz meant by writing his tale in old Polish, although this is also just a partial reading of an issue that can be rendered adequately only if we follow Gombrowicz step by step on this point, which is not my intention here. In spite of the many disclaimers by his wife and some of his friends, it is clear that Gombrowicz sustained long and meaningful relationships with men, and a cursory look at the volume *Gombrowicz en Argentine*—a series of homages collected by Rita Gombrowicz—will allow us to see many of them.[5] They appear in photographs that have a vague aura of Mitteleuropean cliché transported to Buenos Aires. The chalets have become *quintas*, but the same dogs appear in the hunting scenes. From the point of view of the observer it is clear that unmasking the code entails simplifying it. The coding calls attention to itself: it plays with the full spectacle of the disclosure. Paraphrasing Sandra Bernhard, without the code, we are nothing.

The Cuban writer Virgilio Piñera is one of those who appears coded in *Trans-Atlantyk*. His picture can be seen in *Gombrowicz en Argentine*, and his testimonial in that book is full of codes and innuendos.[6] Piñera coded his work on two conflictive levels: homosexuality and politics—or in Gombrowicz's terms, Filistria and Patria. What happens when you flatten the code? What are the consequences of being forcibly brought into visibility? This is what draws me to the work of Virgilio Piñera at this point. I will look at his work with the eyes of the voyeur, in order to notice the violence that erupts when the code is undone.

Book in Flight

"What he wrote," said Piñera's friend Guillermo Cabrera Infante, "are only the notes in the margin of his marginal life." And he adds: "Few people like him could say my life is an open book and then say in the same breath that his book is an open life."[7] But is the life truly an open book? And is the book truly the perfect imitation of life? Cabrera Infante can conceive of only one secret in Piñera's life/book, and this secret is, of course, the fact that Piñera liked men. But is this truly the only secret? Seen from a certain angle it is not a secret at all, for if we actually think that this is the most private inner sanctum of a life, then we are playing into Cabrera's heterosexist reading of a gay writer (of any gay writer) as one who is defined by his "condition." I would rather use a different anecdote to illustrate Piñera's situation in Cuban literary discourse. The place is Algiers, and the time is 1964. According to the Spanish writer Juan Goytisolo, and as recounted by Guillermo Cabrera Infante, when Ernesto "Ché" Guevara saw a volume of Virgilio Piñera's *Teatro completo* in the Cuban embassy, he hurled it against a wall. "How dare you have in our embassy a book by this foul faggot!" he shouted to an astonished (and, at that time, fairly closeted) Goytisolo.[8]

Why does El Ché react with such venom toward such an insignificant volume of plays? Let us pause and consider what it is that El Ché considers truly indecent, in order to trace the complicities involved in "gayness" and subversion: the fact that Piñera's book is found in an embassy (that this representative Cuban space outside Cuba contains this book as a representation of the *letras patrias*) and that the book in some way could be misconstrued as a model of what revolutionary Cuban literature is. The sin is compounded by having such a book by such a foul faggot within another revolutionary situation (Algiers), for the space of the faggot for El Ché is diametrically opposed to the very hygiene of the revolution.

I will have more to say on what it is that bothers El Ché so much, but for the moment I want to place this scene in an emblematic space, as a perverse model that responds to Cabrera Infante's notion of Piñera's life "as a book": it is not a book without secrets but an object that, presumably, everybody kicks around. And it is precisely because of this *lack* of a secret that the book is thrown about, from one corner of the room to the other—a gesture that the passive silence of the book seems to allow.

Rather than seeing Piñera as a book that has only one secret insistently proclaimed as a nonsecret, I think Piñera's volume is marked by reticence, and the "secret" is constructed and deconstructed by other people's voices and other people's memoirs. In this sense, Piñera's death in Havana in 1979 not only mobilizes Cabrera Infante's recollection of Piñera's books and life, but is also a prelude to a dispute on homosexuality in the Cuban revolution. What I would argue is that the main topic of this dispute is not secrecy, but silence—certainly an element that forces us to nuance the version of Piñera's life as an open book.

First, let's tease out what we can out of Virgilio Piñera's "life." The son of a working-class family, Piñera was born in Cárdenas in 1912 and before the revolution of 1959 left Cuba three times for Argentina (1946–47, 1950–54, 1955–58), where he met Borges and his circle, published in *Anales de Buenos Aires*, and established a friendship with Witold Gombrowicz, another expatriate living in Buenos Aires, whose novel *Ferdydurke* Piñera, among others, translated.[9] Piñera had already written a considerable body of work before the revolution of 1959: his novel *La carne de René* (published in English as *René's Flesh*), a collection of stories, *Cuentos fríos,* and plays like *Electra Garrigó, Jesús,* and *Aire frío*. After 1959 Piñera wrote for the journal *Revolución* and the literary supplement *Lunes*. He was arrested on October 11, 1961, and spent a brief period in jail. He was not sent to the notorious UMAP (Unidades Militares de Ayuda a la Producción) camps, where from 1965 to 1967 the revolution imprisoned homosexuals and other "antisocial" elements. But he was, according to most accounts, internally ostracized, a writer who was seldom published, and whose immense output still trickles out of Havana in piecemeal fashion after his death.[10]

It is Piñera's silence during the more or less ten years before his death what I would like to examine at this point, while keeping in mind El Ché's gratuitous outburst.[11] This was a heroic silence and the silence of fear, a silence of repression and the silence of inner exile, the silence of the literary closet and of the refusal to respond to the mechanisms that created that closet. Depending on your political point of view, this silence was all of the above and something more. For me, it completes the arc of the book that El Ché throws from one corner of the room to the other in Algiers. It suspends the book in midair, in midflight, in a perfect seesawing motion: in one corner of the room, the book signifies total outness, in the other corner, the book is consigned to the realm of the totally closeted. In one corner Cuba, in the other corner Algiers, in one corner the hero, and in the other, the coward. Leaving aside for the moment the implications of this opposition (and the notions of masculinity deployed by that very opposition), I want to leave this book flying in the air, *volando.* I want to arrest the motion of this flying object. What I would like to do is read this silence as a kind of cipher that becomes, over time, an intricate weapon.

Silence

What kind of weapon can silence ever be, especially when a society such as that of revolutionary Cuba was and still is bent on a theatrical demonstration of what it means to defy all possible odds for the sake of revolutionary social justice? Before we explore this paradox, we should consider this scene from Piñera's best novel, *René's Flesh,* an erotic tale of masculine desire, a tropical version of Witold Gombrowicz's *Ferdydurke,* an account of the nightmares of masculinity that climax in a school scene where the attentive pupils of Dr. Marblo patiently lick René's body in order to initiate it into a bizarre cult of the flesh. "It's necessary that René's flesh be licked systematically.

What I mean is, licked from the top of his head to the tips of his toes," says Swyne, one of the instructors:

Just as we test the point of a pen once or twice and, assured of its quality, move it from left to right over the sheet of paper, and now and then the hand pauses as the brain vacillates between one thought and another, so too Roger stuck out his tongue and taking René's toes, applied his tongue to it once or twice to assure himself of the quality of its point. . . . Roger resembled one of those calligraphers who makes a few strokes in the margin of the page with his pen. He let go of the toe and moved over to the face. He slipped one hand under René's head and leaned the other on his chest. Then he looked at Swyne.

He was indicating the tongues that were to second Roger's. One for each part of the body: two legs, two arms. . . .

"Roger, please open the session," he said.

Roger licked René's forehead profoundly. He shook his head in doubt. He passed his tongue over the rebel's lips. He shook his head again.

"What's wrong, Roger?" Swyne asked.

"Hard as a rock," was all he said.[12]

This has to be one of the more erotically charged moments in Cuban literature. The equation between Roger's tongue and a pen, and René's flesh and the surface of paper, is the most transparent exposition of the erotics of writing itself. René's flesh is like the surface of paper, and Roger's tongue resembles the tip of a pen, the contact between tongue and flesh doubling the charged eroticism of a writing inscribed as licking the hardened flesh of the allegorical René. Why is René's flesh so hard? And why does it have to be "softened"? Hardness is not the phallic mark of raging sexuality—or maybe it is, and we could see this book as a fable of how René is desexualized. But I think Piñera has much more complex notions in mind.

As part of the school's program of instruction, students initiated in the cult of the flesh are made to contemplate, when they first come into the school, strange pictures of themselves as gleefully suffering, crucified Christs. The scenes of instruction create a pliable surface out of the flesh, a surface where the students realize the weakness of the flesh, so that in turn those same students can be recruited for a political cause, which in Piñera's novel is absurdly centered on chocolate. Flesh and politics are the two foci of Piñera's allegory, which loyal readers are treated to lick with their tongues in order to soften their deliberate hardness. In this allegory, Piñera is a voyeur—inscribing, examining the fissures within heterosexuality, opening them up, licking them. The voyeur is the silent one, the one who is content that others actually speak. In a context in which everybody screams out their own suffering, the most destabilizing member of the polity is the one who remains silent. If the theater of cruelty demands confession, René will make every attempt not to participate. He will not reject the demand—he will be, rather, indifferent to it.

Ramón, René's father, opens *René's Flesh* with a demand for self-observation: "Look: your body, mine, your mother's body—everyone's body is made of meat. This is very important, and because it is often forgotten, many people fall victim to the knife."[13] The father's demand is in itself a literary critique of Piñera's literature, for Piñera's stories and novels are outbursts of energy whose convoluted plots are written with no attention to style—as a matter of fact, with a deliberate flatness of style. Piñera is not the careful writer inscribed in the neo-baroque Cuban tradition of Lezama or Carpentier. He does not allow the reader to stop and look, he more often turns readers away from themselves. Indeed, one can say that the point of *René's Flesh* and of much of Piñera's work is to prevent the inner gaze. All of Piñera's plots are elaborate, masturbatory foils for something that the reader must not stop to contemplate. Our eyes are fixed on the shape and contours of reflections that try to overcome a certain kind of heaviness, against which all the characters complain. This avoidance of the self, of observation, is what leads to Piñera's collapsing of text into flesh. But in this complex textual realm the flesh does not reveal the true essence of a self but is actually a shield that prevents readers from gazing into their very selves.

Piñera's story "El enemigo," for example, starts with a man asking his shoe shiner whether he is not afraid of himself. The man responds that he does not know what fear is, which prompts the narrator to explain how the prime mover of his life is precisely fear. This is not a fear that comes from the outside, or that even goes outside, but a fear that is constantly inside: "My fear is my own self and no revolution, no stroke of adverse luck would be able to defeat it."[14] He knows that the origin of this fear is guilt, but he does not know what it is that he feels guilty about, and feels guilty for not knowing the origins of his guilt. The narrator understands that the only shield that he has left in terms of his guilt is literature, since authors do not only write what they live, but also write what they do not live. Literature is always, as the narrator says, a shield that is perforated, traversed by the wounds of a battle. In Piñera's words, "the immense perforation that it shows is none other than the work."[15] So Piñera collapses text into flesh in order to show a certain kind of wound: the flesh is the shield that the author uses to cover himself, in order to engage in the battle against fear. The work, *la obra,* is the perforation of that shield.

Piñera's flesh is not just any flesh, but one that exists in order to be wounded, that demands sacrifice as the site of observation. The book that we have been trying to read is one that Piñera writes on flesh in order to expose the wounds of the flesh, one that allows the flesh to be wounded. The writer avoids the wounds, but the wounds are inevitably there, a result of the very kind of avoidance that the author seeks by means of writing. In this constantly moving universe of resistance and repression, readers are not necessarily asked to perforate the flesh, but to uncover a common space, as readers and writers, where pain and humiliation coexist. One is to accomplish this without looking at the self, without the inner gaze that literature seems to demand.

No critic should violate the space where a writer like Piñera avoids self-observation without understanding, first of all, the subtleties of the system. My intention, then, is not to have Piñera look at himself, but to fill in the gaps to be found within his silence, and at the same time try not to betray its profoundly conflictive gesture. Sometimes texts need to be read in terms of the context of their creator's lives; but sometimes the state provides the context of those lives to neutralize how gay texts may dangerously and unwittingly collide with the power of the state.

Stigmata

Virgilio Piñera deliriously wanted, desired, ached to be canonized—but canonized, of course, as irreverence itself. In "Testamento," the final poem of his collection *La vida entera,* he claims not to want to be a statue in death: "Since I have been an iconoclast / I refuse to be made into a statue; / if in life I have been flesh / in death I do not want to be marble."[16] But this desire needs to be contrasted to another, where Piñera drags himself into a woman's voice. The poem is titled "Solicitud de canonización de Rosa Cagí" and it is the confession of a woman who desires to be canonized "as a laic saint / with every right to figure in the altars of Horror."[17]

Canonization stands at the very border of Piñera's text, where his terrible sense of beauty blooms with particular demands. The stigmata of the flesh are an answer but also the point of departure for another question; revelation may be a sign, but it is always a sign of itself as something else—a mode of bearing witness to a power beyond comprehension. Indelible, inexplicable, but also immanently present, the signs by means of which the canonized finally achieve sainthood imply attempts at reading and uncovering what ultimately cannot be explained.

Piñera knew—particularly, I think, after the revolution—that all attempts to read him would carry the mark of canonization as a kind of vacuous homage, that is, he would become a martyr for art, a sacrificial victim because of his iconoclasm. He appears as all of these in recent Cuban discourse. But no attempt at inscribing Piñera within the canon of the saints can overlook the particularly terrifying aspects of his religion, a religion where sainthood entails the passive act of humiliation—a debasement that cannot be glossed over, or smoothed, in the process of reading critically (or canonizing) the author. The work appears already with the mark of silence—a silence whose immediate cause was a homosexuality lived, in one of its many forms, as a literary strategy. This strategy needs to be seen step by step.

First, there is the space of deliberate avoidance, the refusal to look at oneself. Piñera's stories do not begin and end; in dramatic terms their heroes do not trace the outlines of Aristotelian drama. Their first lines take great pains to be accidental: "Last Tuesday, at three in the afternoon, Damian called me on the phone."[18] Characters emerge totally formed, voices whose anterior history does not occupy the weight of the page, but are created at the moment of utterance by the addition of details whose very insignificance turns the narrative into a sort of stuttering, an accumulation of details: "When I turned fifteen—the age when I would begin my first job as a humble employee—my father gave me an unusual present."[19] The beginning is always a nothing, an utterance meant to put a mechanism in motion, as in the beginning of "Hot and Cold: "Well, here I am. . . . Since there's no one to introduce me, I'll do it myself. My name is Rafael Sanchez Tevejo (Rafa to my wife, Rosita, my family and friends)."[20] Everything is circumstance: characters are constantly moving, continually changing places or situations; they are involved in the most accidental or incidental events, and these events are moved by means of a seemingly aimless plot.[21] There is no way to foresee where the situation will lead, or how the characters will end.

The stories often have convoluted plots where there is sometimes no climax (therefore no exit), but a constant seesawing motion. For Piñera, to tell a story is already to allow the Book to fall, in order to avoid the fall of the subject and seek a space where the subject itself is suspended: "The book falls from my hands, the music I'm listening to seems a dense and viscous substance that stops up my ears; I speak with my mother and feel the words congeal in the tip of my tongue; I write a letter to M—I have a lot to tell him—but after two lines, I break off writing."[22] This mental and physical stuttering on the page is the incidental beginning of a story called "The Great Staircase of the Legislative Palace" (La gran escalera del Palacio Legislativo) and it concludes with a more incidental obsession: the protagonist has fallen in love with the marble staircase that leads to the legislative palace, and because he ascends and descends it all the time, he never pays the taxes that he needed to pay, which had prompted him to go to the legislative palace in the first place.

This avoidance of self-observation can be linked to repression, to the formation of a "phobia proper" or the series of avoidances that are intended "to prevent a release of the anxiety."[23] The accidental nature of the tale turns it into a spectacle, but also gives it the impression, as Freud says, of a "mechanism of flight." The convoluted plots, the paradoxical plays on words turn the narratives into spectacular creations where the mirror reflects its own avoidance as a mechanism. This avoidance is linked to the collapsing of text and flesh, where the work is like a scar demanding attention.

In Piñera's constantly moving universe, readers are asked to touch the scar, to perforate the flesh, to uncover a common space where pain and humiliation coexist in us all. As the professor says in a scene of instruction in *Rene's Flesh*:

So, pain is our star and it will guide us over this tempestuous sea. You'll say to me: but why do they put muzzles on us when one is supposed to give free rein to pain? We put them on because we stand for pain that is contained, concentrated and reconcentrated. The mouth that opens in order to cry out automatically displaces a precious amount of pain. If I were to express myself in psychological terminology, I would call it a discharge. And we are wholly and completely against discharges.[24]

The fantastic regulations imposed in Dr. Marblo's school allow for pain to be transmitted in the most ritualistic manner, by means of a series of rules that resemble the permutations of Piñera's plots. Once pain appears, it must not be let out, but it also must not be kept in. One must think about pain, and another rule demands its particular expression: it cannot be kept in, but it also cannot be put out.

In *Rene's Flesh*, as soon as the text is tortured (or read), it flings its mute tongue back out to us as if producing the image of pure transparency. Dr. Marblo's class at the School of Pain is an example of this. Since a number of chapters of this novel take place at the school, the scenes of instruction are examples of a twisted morality of education, a mode of passing on knowledge from one generation to the next. Students are seated on electric chairs whose charge is controlled by the professor. The professor reads a text that cannot be heard or understood by the students in the class, since they are too concerned with suffering due to the electrical discharges he administers. The text he reads appears in the midst of this carnival of suffering. We do not know if the ritualistic suffering always demands the same text (if it is part of the "canonical" texts used by the school) or if the text has been produced at random. What is important is that the text is a distant, classical one. It narrates the story of Lena, involved in a conspiracy during the fourth century before Christ, and forced by Hipias to confess the names of others involved. Because Lena refuses, the text continues, "Hipias, impatient and bloodthirsty, had her tortured."[25]

At this point the text is perforated by the narrator of the novel: "Here the professor pressed slowly down on button B, spit to his right and his left, and proceeded in a nasal voice."[26] Once the text resumes, after this perforation that only allows for further pain to be administered, Lena is seated on a chair that resembles the students'. The baroque punishment also demands that she not be tied, but on the contrary left free to leave her martyrdom when she is ready to confess. The terrible beauty of Lena's torture, in effect, also allows us to see and hear the voice of the translator (Piñera himself), who has in effect also perforated this text: "From his table, Hipias contemplated her in silence. A little later Lena's flesh began to roast. The smell was unbearable; Lena was being suffocated by her own fumes."[27] It is at this point that Lena, condemned to sacrifice, but also refusing to pronounce the names of the conspirators, bites her tongue so hard that the tongue comes flying out of her mouth: "[she] stuck her tongue between her ivory teeth squeezing it with such fury that the enemy left her mouth, mortally wounded."[28]

The text that is presented to the students in Marblo's school and the tongue that Lena bites at the moment of most intense pain are silent witnesses to something that can never be uttered except by silence. The silence is already given in the fact that the tongue represents itself. One should not interpret the tongue as offering up the secret of homosexuality, or any other secret at all, except that of its own materiality. It is the mark of its own transparency. The translator's inscription appears in the text as a mute presence that passes itself off in silence to all readers except the professor, who warns the students not to pay attention to what he calls "the picturesque style of the chronicler and that ending that speaks of the enemy leaving her mouth mortally wounded."[29] This "enemy," the professor clarifies, is the tongue, and he further adds that he sees expelling it as a defeat, since, if Lena had been in this school, "[h]er beautiful tongue would have gone with the rest of her body into the bosom of the earth."[30]

In this fable, Lena brings out the part of the body that is her enemy, and she offers her enemy as a substitution: if the torturer demands confession, Lena will fling out her tongue. It is a tongue that says nothing except for its own being, a silent and mute mark of an offering—like the text that is not heard, not read, but only felt with the piercing sensation inscribed within the very muteness of its apparition in the novel. This quoted text of Lena's torture perforates the very structure of the novel. But Piñera passes it off without further thought, with no explanation, as if telling us, "I don't want to explain why this text is here but it seems that it should be here." The inclusion of the text does not respond to naïveté; it is a deliberate act. We are not meant to question where this text is coming from, and there is no reason for the text appearing as it does. It is a text that does not want to think about itself; it wants *suffering*.

What this suffering proclaims is that canonization merely freezes the horror, gives it a higher purpose. Hence the silence that this kind of writing entails, for it does not speak of liberation, it does not give a moral to the story, but arrests itself at the moment when what can only be seen is the image of suffering. What Piñera asks is no less than for us to become the perforators of a text that we do not understand, while becoming aware of our own pain in the process of perforation. The readers should offer their own flesh so that other readers might perforate it, and thus create the community of beings, not of ghosts like René.[31]

Blood

Piñera was no amateur when it came to homosexual politics, and this is important considering his own position on outing. Since the 1950s in the Cuban magazine *Ciclón*, Piñera wanted Cubans to appreciate the complex and sometimes baroque codes authors use in order to talk about their homosexuality. In his article "Ballagas en persona," Piñera tackled the work of Emilio Ballagas, one of Cuba's foremost poets, who had recently died. Introducing the essay with a quote from Roland Barthes, Piñera decries the whitewashing of Ballagas's life. He complains that all traces of Ballagas's complex and tormented homosexuality have been cast aside by his friends. He attacks the Cuban poet Cintio Vitier's somewhat ecumenical reading of Ballagas—one that merely alludes to, but does not face up to, what Piñera seems to term Ballagas's very human imperfections.

If the French write about Gide taking as a point of departure this writer's homosexuality, if the English do the same with Wilde, I don't see why we Cubans cannot speak of Ballagas as homosexual. Is it that the French and the English have the exclusive rights to that theme? Of course not; there are no exclusive themes nor would they pretend that there are, it's just that the French and the British would never be prone to turn their writers into that source of Immortality that so seduces our critics.[32]

Piñera uses the French or the British, of course, for a complex rhetorical jab, telling Vitier that in spite of all his cultural baggage, Cubans still belong to a provincial milieu. But apart from being the choices *de rigueur* for the male gay culture of the 1950s, Gide and Wilde stand at two dialectical poles of male homosexuality: Wilde, the celebratory writer who poses and thereby assumes consciously his own "perversion," and Gide, the writer who uses it as the starting point for self-knowledge.[33] In expressing the "unitary center" of Ballagas's poetry, Piñera is still opting for Gide's model—homosexuality as a key to an exploration of the self.

In order to appreciate the revolutionary character of this essay one should recall, as Piñera does in the essay, that Ballagas was deeply religious, and that he married and fathered a child, while still writing some of the more erotically charged poems that passed into the canon of Cuban literature.[34] In retrospect, it is still difficult to conceive how this poetry could have been heterosexually gendered. It is possible that Ballagas would have argued, in a particular context, that he was not a "gay" poet. After all—and this is no minor irony—he is mostly known as a poet who excelled in what used to be called *poesía negra,* poetry that attempted to "represent" Afro-Cuban tradition. In fact, that he was not a "black" poet—meaning an Afro-Cuban poet—had been pointed out by the black poet Nicolás Guillén, who rightly complained about the "folkloric" representation of blacks in the poetry of Ballagas and others of his generation. But for Piñera Ballagas, over and above the claims of "thematics," has to be read in reference to his homosexuality: "All his acts, including in these acts his work as a whole, are the reflection of a fight against sin. What is this work but a long and reiterated *De profundis* from which Ballagas perhaps would have emerged victorious had he not died so young?"[35] For Piñera, Ballagas's tortured homosexuality structures the entire work; it endows its open silences with a particular weight; it soils the page with its notion of homosexuality as pleasure and as sin.

Piñera names Wilde's prison letter because he wants us to read Ballagas's work a memoir, a work that is a pure expression of the subject and not of a particular "project" or "politics." Its notion of homosexuality as sin does not allow for the facile distance of the literary critic. This lack of distance that male homosexuality gives to the work is a conscious rhetorical move on Piñera's part, and he is well aware of the risks it entails. Hence, his deliberate outing of the writer as *tormented* being.

If sexuality is the real kernel of individuality, then Ballagas, by his consistent act of sublimation, merely repeats, compulsively, a cultural problem that Piñera wants to eliminate by undoing the very specificity of homosexual desire. In arguing for the public's confrontation with Ballagas's sexuality, Piñera is leveling the playing field: that the object of desire is male should be foregrounded so that we see the universality of desire itself.

The political ramifications of this outing can be understood better when we contextualize the essay. It was written for *Ciclón*, a journal financed by the wealthy gay patron José Rodríguez Feo after his rift with José Lezama Lima (whose journal *Orígenes* Rodríguez Feo also financed, as I explained in the introduction and in chapter 1). The rift in particular entailed a running dispute between one male homosexual poet (Vicente Aleixandre) and the irascible and openly homophobic Spanish Nobel Prize winner Juan Ramón Jiménez. Lezama's decision to side with Jiménez over Aleixandre was one of the reasons for Rodríguez Feo's impatience with the secretive and somewhat whitewashed atmosphere of *Orígenes,* whose publisher, editor, and many of its writers were "closeted" homosexuals. The new journal, *Ciclón,* was meant to be the antithesis of *Orígenes.* It valued scandal and openness, publishing excerpts from Sade's *120 Days of Sodom* as well as essays on Oscar Wilde, Freud, Gide, and pornography. As members of a self-conscious cultural elite, the writers of *Ciclón* wanted to open up Cuban art in the waning days of Batista's dictatorship. These writers continued their sense of irreverence after the Cuban revolution of 1959. Most of them, including Guillermo Cabrera Infante, Antón Arrufat, Pablo Armando Fernández, and the recently diseased Severo Sarduy, went on to write for the even more anarchic *Lunes de revolución,* with Virgilio Piñera as their guiding mentor, until *Lunes* itself was closed down by the revolutionary government and most of its members either chose exile (as Cabrera Infante did) or tempered their irreverence in view of the more complex cultural politics that followed.

Piñera's essay, then, was a landmark in many ways. For the first time in Cuba and in the late 1950s, it inscribed homosexuality in the canon by calling for a gay reading of a precursor. By doing so, it allowed not merely for a "different" reading of Ballagas, but for one that was also not to be inscribed within the teleology of the Cuban nation. In other words, Ballagas is not one more piece in the history of Cuban poetry, but rather a complex subject whose subjectivity needed to be examined on its own. The essay saw Ballagas as a *unified* figure. For Piñera, homosexuality gave Ballagas's work its *raison d'être,* and Piñera was always interested in writers who maintained a degree of "sustained concentration," writers who did not create just "poems" but "books," not works of literature but a "Work."[36] For Piñera, what sustained Ballagas was a struggle against sin. If the *Orígenes* generation criticized Ballagas and other immediate precursors as being merely concerned with questions of "inner life" and having no concerns for aesthetics, philosophy, or the nation, Piñera turned this upside down—for him, Ballagas's interior life was "political" to the extent that it dealt with issues of morality that were at the center of social life.[37] At the same time, the essay itself was a coded riposte to many in the Cuban cultural circuit who continued to sublimate homosexuality with culture. One can say that Piñera's piece exchanges one idea of national identity for another—this time, and in a subtle rhetorical shift, Ballagas becomes not solely a Cuban poet, but part of a transnational network of male homosexual writers like Gide and Wilde.

"Ballagas en persona" signaled the open expression of a homosexuality that was everywhere on paper but nowhere to be seen. But it was also the opening shot of a much more dramatic chapter in Cuban culture. The openly homosexual gaze under which Piñera claimed that Ballagas should be read was, in retrospect, but the prelude to a period in which Piñera's terms were used as a weapon against authors, in a context where nationality took precedence over subjectivity, and where in many cases—Piñera's in particular—homosexuality would be the cause for a generalized repression. Piñera's future in the revolution was going to be inversely proportional to Ballagas's past: Piñera decided to live his *life* openly as a homosexual while his *texts* only marginally dealt with homosexuality. His life and texts, in spite of their apparent simplicity, are densely textured within the inversely proportional relationship that they sustain with each other: open, crystalline life, that of the "faggot"; "simple" tales in a colloquial language that actually represses more than it says.

At the time Piñera wrote this essay, Ballagas was going to be an inverted image of Piñera himself. Piñera was going to refuse the space of the closet and offer perhaps his most "outed" works. It is an irony, then, that the social conditions after the revolution rendered him perhaps closer to Ballagas than what he intended to be. In a very "piñerian" way, he set out to be an "invert" to Ballagas's suffering and ended up being the silent witness to a decade of despair.

Six years after opening the issue of homosexuality in his strategic outing of Emilio Ballagas and all of his conflicting legacy, Piñera found himself silenced—as a writer and as a homosexual. He was pursued and harassed. The bureaucratic culture of the island demanded that he consider homosexuality a "deviation" from socially accepted norms, and revolutionary cultural institutions did not allow him to forget that homosexuality was not to be relegated to the space of the innocuous. This repression was not due to anything that may be overtly found in Piñera's text, but to the dangerous levity of those tales, and to the way he negotiated his life. For a writer known as a "flaming queen" before and after the revolution, one who defended Ballagas against his own acolytes, the repression of homosexuality in Piñera's texts has to be profoundly disturbing: there are homoerotic scenes but very little open expression of homosexuality—certainly none of the kind that Piñera's doppelganger Lezama flung out to an unsuspecting public as part of his public outing in *Paradiso*.

There is, in this sense, a rift in Piñera that is very much unlike the one mentioned by Cabrera Infante above, while it is also different from the one that Piñera himself saw in Ballagas. Critics generally have to look for Piñera's homosexuality in his life, and as friends like Antón Arrufat have mentioned, this life was lived as openly as possible:

Until death he exercised two parts of his body. One of them, his sex, and the other, his mind. He went to bed two or three times a week with one of his regulars, to whom he paid small amounts of money. He called this "sexuating." Paying was another way of defending his liberty. In this case, his sentimental liberty. Paying his "regulars" did not compromise him or link him sentimentally. It was like paying for a service.[38]

According to Arrufat, Piñera was very clear as to the distinctions between sex and mind. Piñera flings his own sexuality to the critic-to-come in statements such as the following, taken from several published fragments of his autobiography "Of course I could not know at such an early age that the price to pay for these three gorgons—misery, homosexuality and art—was a terrible Void."[39] The critic who tries to approach the gorgon's head of homosexuality will find himself or herself squarely in the realm of a homosexuality written in terms of agon and sin, and the resolution that Arrufat talks about can only have come out of this context: accepted homosexuality, openly lived, but certainly not the stuff of "gay marriage" or even "virtual normality."

Flesh

Piñera was venerated in Cuba by a small circle of disciples even as he was ostracized by the revolutionary state after the revolution of 1959. The pain this caused can be seen in Antón Arrufat's recently published *Virgilio Piñera: Entre él y yo*. In this memoir of a literary relationship, Arrufat talks about the hardships the Cuban state had inflicted on Piñera and others during the 1970s:

During the seventies, classified by Piñera as the years of civil death, the bureaucracy had configured us in that "strange latitude" of being: life in death. . . . Our books were no longer published, those that had been published were taken away from bookstores and surreptitiously retired from library shelves. The plays we had written disappeared from the stage. Our names ceased to be pronounced in conferences and university classes, they were erased from the anthologies and histories of Cuban literature composed in that awful decade. Not only were we dead while alive, we seemed to have never been born and to have written nothing. New generations were taught to despise all that we had done, or rendered ignorant of our work. We were taken from our jobs and sent to work where no one would know us, in libraries far away from the cities, in primary school presses and in iron ore foundries.[40]

This was felt even more acutely because Piñera had specifically returned to Cuba from Argentina in the late 1950s in order to end his exile. Piñera never left Cuba after the revolution, although he felt its more repressive gestures, as is clear from Arrufat's memoir. Reinaldo Arenas, one of his most important protégés, was one of the first who publicly insisted that Piñera died a somewhat forgotten man, in a kind of "living death," unpublished for at least the last ten years of his life.[41] His name was presumed to have been erased from all histories of literature, his funeral barely noticed, the status of his papers a source of mystery. Only after the late 1980s, when the collapse of the Soviet Union caused a social and economic impasse in Cuba, were Piñera's works once again published on the island, and his plays performed, frequently to packed houses.[42] Piñera was "rehabilitated" by the government, and this rehabilitation has been followed by accounts such as Arrufat's. On the one hand, he has been rescued as a social satirist and absurdist writer; on the other, he has become a saint and martyr to those marginalized by revolutionary homophobia. These rereadings do not strictly flesh out the political divisions between writers outside and those inside Cuba.[43] For some, the fact that he was published during the sixties and remained in Cuba throughout the seventies until his death, while other writers left, proves that the revolution in its more Stalinist phase (what Cubans term "the gray five-year period," 1971–76) exercised a repressive, but not a silencing function.[44] For others, such as Arrufat and Arenas, the truth was much more perverse.

Piñera is a slippery signifier: a "cosmopolitan" writer who also managed to be profoundly Cuban. To add to the sense of dislocation, Piñera assumed an ironically mordant moral pose: that of the homosexual who never proclaimed his homosexuality in published works after the revolution but on the contrary, registered his opinions in code.

But Piñera's work not only speaks in code: it likes and seduces the code, and it encodes its own interventions. To rupture the complexity I have deployed in this essay for the sake of a politics of outing does not do justice to the particularities of the work itself: it neutralizes Piñera and confines him to a space that Piñera himself could not have foreseen when he wrote his essay on Ballagas. It turns him into the safe figure of a suffering homosexual, a moral example. At this point in time, when the competition over Piñera's body and legacy is part of a general "coming to terms" with the history of homosexualities and revolution, it is important to be aware of the gains and losses of visibility as it colludes with the designs of a state that can be repressive at one point, and proclaim liberation and "rectification" at another.

My skepticism about the consequences of such visibility, particularly when it entails unmasking a writer's code, prompts me to render the whole issue of *outing,* of unmasking a text, as densely as possible—not in an openly political manner as this is generally understood in the fractious Cuban context, but in an indirect, albeit not wholly apolitical, sense, in line with the polemics that I pursue at other points in this book. I much prefer validating the code as a mode of agency than flattening it out for the sake of an illusory freedom. If to celebrate the existence of a precursor entails assuming his or her particular legacy, then how do we negotiate this visibility when the legacy also speaks of silence, inner exile, and a sense of liberty that is fundamentally dependent on the existence of a code as a response to the arbitrariness of power? Does outing in this context (of canonized literary precursors) allow us merely to *gain* a certain kind of body—a collection of weightless lives on paper—and *lose* another kind of flesh? Does not excessive attention to this run the risk of collaborating with a homophobic cultural imaginary, one that consigns these authors to a specific *place* where they might be controlled and normatized and returned as stereotypes, emptied of their flesh and blood?

I am obviously not arguing for dividing, once again, the terrain of sexuality from the "work." What I am insisting on is noticing the complexity of the surface that the work deploys, for the way it speaks is related to the social reading that the work performs. Piñera's texts before the revolution argued for outing, for disrobing, for understanding an "essential" nakedness. Piñera opted initially to belong to the camp of those who "outed" writers, but after the revolution he was silenced in many ways because of that collusion between sexuality and the text. I think Piñera's silence in his later years is the silence of fear, but also the mark of a sense of damnation that he as homosexual poet flings to his heirs. It is as ambivalent a cipher as any I can think of in Cuba: an act of absolute passivity *and* power. To invoke the weightless body of the stereotype that Cabrera Infante invokes, with all the affection that he undoubtedly had for Piñera, does not do justice to the flesh that Piñera wanted us to pierce.

Who does the telling is important. Who does the outing, it seems to me, is an ancillary point. All citizens of the republic should do the telling but there should be, in theory, no telling to do. The narrative, as Piñera understood it, was going to be comic and tragic, for the mannequin sensibility of homophobia demands the tragic buffoon that can only be given a borrowed space—one that can easily be withheld. The "queen" could never again publish after the revolution, but she also opted not to risk banishment. As the picaresque tales of Piñera's life after the revolution multiply, and as the editions of his unpublished work find more and more of a space in Cuba and elsewhere after his death, we are forced to understand his legacy: writing a book on paper is not the same as writing a book on the very flesh of another.

In the case of Virgilio Piñera, we can think of paper itself as flesh, except that flesh does not render the book any more visible than it already is. On the contrary, flesh gives a false transparency to a book that should still be flying, suspended, in midair.

5 Revolution

Strawberry and Chocolate

What happens to a dream deferred?
Does it dry up
like a raisin in the sun?
Or fester like a sore—
And then run?
. . .
Maybe it just sags
like a heavy load.

Or does it explode?

—LANGSTON HUGHES, "Montage of a Dream Deferred"

Male Homosexual Montage

In post–Cold War Cuba, the male homosexual is a cipher. His body stands for an excess of signification, or for *the* Excessive as a category. He is, first of all, a sexual body; as such, at times he promises sex for sale. He foreshadows the impending consumer economy, but also recalls the remnants of revolutionary history. He stands for the precarious sense of the present but also for the untangling of the past—an unfolding that can only be partial, simulated, directed, and mediated by his past victimization and his future despair.

In principle, let us recall, the revolution has always defined the Homosexual (capitalized, of course) by attaching an inordinate amount of signifiers on him. No such meaning could be imposed at the outset on the lesbian. The lesbian was apparitional, nonexistent, inconceivable. The revolutionary dismantling of rigid gender roles meant that propaganda could produce female figures such as the exemplary female revolutionary, the platoon leader of the women's militia, or the architect of social engineering, but not, openly, the lesbian. The male homosexual, on the contrary, was always part of a baroque project, and he always promised the baroque as exemplary Cuban form. He did not produce meaning as an agent: meaning radiated from him in fragments, in circuits of cultural flints, in shards that voraciously consumed more culture. There was so much meaning attached to the male homosexual that he ended up becoming the absence of meaning as such: part of the *petit histoire* of gossip and innuendo, a useful *thing* that is ultimately worthless, unless he is being tolerated as exemplary cultural worker. If the male homosexual turned into a being with a history, he also became the means by which history can say absolutely nothing.

Intellectual thought after the 1960s in Latin America was fashioned out of the debates around the viability of the revolutionary Cuban model, and this model, we should recall, was also important for the fashioning of the New Left in the United States.[1] In the early 1960s, the revolution offered its North American sympathizers an intellectual mode of action that could be found in the triumphant interventions of Cuban journals such as *Lunes de revolución*—anarchic, nondogmatic, impatient with the procedures of the traditional Left, and always, first and foremost, situationist. The revolution swerved out of this model after the late sixties, and demanded from its intellectuals acquiescence to a new set of circumstances that pitted the needs of the individual against the wider demands of society. At this point, the revolution "betrayed" many intellectuals who had cheered its social processes in its beginning stages. Fidel's famous "Words to the intellectuals" have to be seen, in this regard, as the official government response to a moment of growing intellectual disaffection.

Already for Jean-Paul Sartre, one of the first European intellectual visitors to postrevolutionary Cuba, homosexuals were ready to become the "Jews" of the revolution even before Allen Ginsberg came to Havana and said he wanted to sleep with the comandantes. Ginsberg was summarily kicked out of the country, for reasons that have more to do with the absence of revolutionary humor and the dynamics of homosexual panic—the comandantes *were* handsome—than with any kind of socialist lack of commitment. In the work of Guillermo Cabrera Infante, the sissies and the writers were turned into victims of a revolutionary morality play that demanded absence where there used to be nightlife—destitute queens like Calvert Casey committing suicide in Rome, martyred ironists like Virgilio Piñera, or monstrous culture vultures like José Lezama Lima. In a give and take of heroic and horrific proportions, B. Ruby Rich and Lourdes Argüelles saw male homosexuals as pawns in a global effort to discredit the revolution—singled out as repressed entities by a discourse that was fundamentally unsympathetic and counterrevolutionary.

Historically, the term "homosexual" changed to "gay" after the Cuban revolution—and as a term it carries the mark of a New Left that existed alongside, but also outside, the revolution itself. Let us recall that the term "gay" was used mostly after the New York Stonewall rebellion of 1969, a rebellion that took place just as Cuba was about to enter its most bureaucratized and Stalinist period. More than a simple change in nomenclature, "gay" meant something that "homosexual" did not. The refashioning of the personal and the political after the Stonewall revolt would never find its way into the Cuban discourse. In fact, the years immediately following Stonewall were not liberatory at all for sexual (or even political) minorities in Cuba. These years were marked by the disastrous ten-million-ton sugar harvest, the First Congress on Education and Culture, and the Cuban family code of 1971, which heavily promoted the nuclear family. We should keep these historical markers in mind in order to account for the particularities of Cuban political discourse in its relations with the discourse of the New Left in Europe and the United States. At a time when young university students in the United States, Europe, or Latin America wore long hair, used drugs, and saw Che Guevara as their model for rebellion against authority, the Cuban government embarked on a wholesale repression of long-haired adolescents as dissatisfied members of society who did not belong in the transition to socialism. Even the growth of the nueva trova or the *canción protesta* was mediated by government intervention. While in the rest of Latin America or in the United States figures such as Joan Baez, Bob Dylan, Victor Jara, and even the Beatles personified the new spirit of revolutionary struggle, Cuban singers associated with the nueva trova insisted that there was nothing to protest in Cuba.[2]

These would be simply matters of social history were it not for the fact that the post-Stonewall gay intellectual was a creation of a New Left, and that the Cuban revolution, as the most visible of Third World liberation struggles, mobilized minority revolts in Europe and the United States at the time when those same minorities were being excluded from participation in Cuba itself.[3] The paradox of this situation is clear, at a thirty-year distance. The revolution was the litmus test for a revolutionary Latin American society, and at a time of external and internal threats it had to count on the support of disaffected communities outside Cuba that included, but were not limited to, feminists, gays, and lesbians—communities that also constituted segments of the New Left. At least in terms of state policy (we have no way of accounting for the distance between state policy and public opinion—except by means of testimonials produced later), this means that on paper, public policy had to respond to the progressive agenda, and when it did not, the revolution had to argue contextual and cultural differences in order to explain already obvious disparities.

The Cuban government put gay men and women at the center of a social discourse, but always in a negative light: the raids on members of an "underworld" of homosexual men in the early 1960s, and the policy of incarceration that took place from 1965 to 1967 in the infamous UMAP camps. Public policy at that point (and also later, in different ways) constructed a visibility that existed only in relation to the punishment meted out against it. Punishment turned behavior into crime, and the criminal had to be separated from the society as a whole. This, in turn, fragmented the incipient revolts.[4]

One of the reasons homosexuality was such an issue after the last vestiges of capitalism had been eradicated in the late 1960s was that the question of the homosexual was important to the debate around public loyalties and private space as these were understood in a revolutionary situation such as Cuba's. This was also important in Europe and the United States, though the very real siege mentality produced in Cuba as a result of the U.S. embargo gave an added impetus for new versions of this debate.[5] What the Cuban government defined as politics obviously did not allow personal choices as these were seen by the identity-based gay movement in the United States. If for "First World" gays and lesbians the personal was the political, and this meant fighting for individual rights, for a Cuban state that saw itself as externally and internally besieged by disaffection, the complete politization of every facet of the individual meant something different: "gay identity" was subsumed to the desires of the masses.[6]

Postrevolutionary Cuban culture on the island produced intellectuals who were gay or lesbian, but no lesbian or gay intellectuals, or none who would assume the centrality of homosexuality as the starting point for social politics. The revolution did not consider this a progressive response. It was read as a deviation from the norm, producing an individuality that entailed separation from the Cuban nation. This is also true for the rest of Latin America, though in the case of Cuba it seems more important given the fact that the country, at least on paper, always assumed progressive positions in terms of social policies. But this is also interesting given the fact that much of Cuban intellectual discourse before the revolution was carried on by gay men with a degree of openness that was perhaps unheard of in other parts of Latin America and the Caribbean. Indeed, the very question of gay intellectuals (as opposed to intellectuals who were gay) had surfaced in Cuban intellectual discourse at the outset of the revolution in the pages of *Ciclón*, the foremost Cuban journal of the immediate prerevolutionary time, founded by José Rodríguez Feo, an openly gay millionaire, and directed by Virgilio Piñera, an openly gay writer who was not part of a financial elite.[7]

The public theater of revolution had homosexuality as one of its closets. A social, revolutionary process that articulated a viable critique of all things Cuban in terms of class, culture, and gender could only confront the issue of sexuality by confining all difference to the realm of the private, unproductive, and theatrical. Difference was seen as disloyal and suspicious to the social solidarity entailed by revolution. As early as 1962, the revolutionary government had already categorized homosexuals as more or less part of the officially tolerated or officially repressed *gusanera* (the curious term, roughly translated as "worm-like," that the revolution gave to all its disaffected elements) or, in the same vein, as part of a lumpenproletariat that, in Marxist terms, was a nonproductive circulator of goods. This collusion already appears in Marx, as Andrew Parker has shown in an illuminating read of Marx's *Eighteenth Brumaire*.[8] There, the intersection of class and sex occurs at the expense of sex. While producing a sex-inflected analysis of class formation, Parker deconstructs Marx's equation of homosexuality with the lumpenproletariat, and hence with everything anal and excremental—what in Cuba has to be seen as the wider discourse of the *gusanera* as the parasitical class that the revolution discharges or dislodges from its midst. But the metonymy of *gusanera* in terms of homosexuality cannot merely be assimilated to or imposed on homosexuals as a class. *Gusanos,* or "worms," are the essence of the fecal discharge—feces and anality the metonymized referent by means of which the homosexual is always named. The *gusano* is the essence of the homosexual. It was this discourse, via Marx, and not a kind of cultural "atavism" of Cuban homophobia, that inflected the prevalent Cuban orthodoxy after the revolution, though at the same time one must nuance the act of laying homophobia at Marx's door. Certainly, this Marxist reading was resonant with the triumphant notions of heterosexual masculinity that the Cuban revolutionaries wanted to convey.

The libidinal colony turned male homosexuality into a representation of something other than sexual choice. Ana María Simo and Reinaldo García Ramos made a useful analysis of this in their piece "Hablemos claro," published in *Mariel* magazine. Simo and García Ramos do not deny that Cuban discourse was homophobic before the revolution. What they argue, convincingly in my view, is that homophobia after 1959 was institutionalized and politicized because of what the revolution called its general political considerations, namely, its growing militarization; its repressive and homogenizing general character; and its use of homosexuals as an outlet for the frustrations of the population at large, first, in 1961 with the sweep of homosexuals and prostitutes in Havana, then in 1965–67 during the period of UMAP camps, and finally in 1980, when homosexuality was a legitimate reason to be part of the revolution's *escoria* (trash) that left through the port of Mariel.[9] In all these events, homosexuals appear in social discourse as threat and menace to nationality and to production in terms that are roughly equivalent to Marx's in the *Eighteenth Brumaire*. If the containment of that threat can be narratized as cause for either mourning or celebration, over time it becomes essentialized as representing the fate of the revolution itself, particularly in the recent and extremely successful Cuban film *Fresa y chocolate* (Strawberry and chocolate).

Strawberry and Chocolate was a belated response to the actions of two men who in the 1980s used the history of the Homosexual in the revolution as the centerpiece of a political argument. I am referring, of course, to Néstor Almendros and Orlando Jiménez Leal, who exposed the fallacies of the internationalist Left precisely where it hurt most: by turning the personal into the political, and insisting that there should be no complicity between the Left and repression in Cuba. The film *Improper Conduct* sparked the analysis of revolution and homosexuality found in Argüelles and Rich, and then *Mariel* magazine, where the brightest young exiled Cuban writers—many of them gay—published. And that all begat *Before Night Falls*, Reinaldo Arenas's memoir, his revenge against the world and all its discourses, his final act of love.

The male homosexual was always the wildest flower in the revolutionary pantheon. In terms of the Cuban revolution, no other "figure"—and I must insist that in spite of the very real homosexual voices out of Cuba, we are talking about a "figure"—has a more contentious history, a more "dignified" past. In a context of lost illusions, failed promises, and despair, the Homosexual becomes an object of exchange: history becomes nostalgia, and the past is redeemed for the sake of a future where resistance, memory, and pleasure may motivate a new beginning.[10] All these cultural signs do not come in a specific order and there is no need to see them within the specificity of an ordered narrative. Rather, they are jumbled, layered, coded one upon the other. Understanding them entails understanding different cultural traditions, periods, references—manipulating a kind of dictionary of "failed" or "successful" homosexual interventions. *Strawberry and Chocolate*, as one of the most successful of these interventions, does not represent a society that has broken down but a dream that has become so far removed from the ruling class that, as a dream deferred, it could just as easily explode.

"A Necessary Tale"

The release in 1993 of Tomás Gutiérrez Alea's *Strawberry and Chocolate*, based on the short story "El bosque, el lobo y el hombre nuevo" by Senel Paz, highlights the apologias and condemnations that have pursued the Cuban revolution on the issue of male homosexuality. By officially sanctioning a film that zeroes in on one of the more polemical aspects of the revolution, one that gives credence to most of its "enemies" and threatens to put its apologists in a sort of no-man's-land, the Cuban film institute has sought to openly present a situation that plays on the allure of the forbidden for a certain part of the population, but that ultimately falls behind the social realities of the moment at hand. It is significant that Tomás Gutiérrez Alea, the world-famous director of *Memories of Underdevelopment* (Memorias del subdesarrollo) (1968), a portrait of early revolutionary intellectual angst, decided to film *Strawberry and Chocolate*. The film has a gay character who resembles Walter Benjamin's angel of history, looking back and forward at a ruin, taking us back to other moments of crisis where the homosexual appears and disappears from the Cuban scene.

In *Memories* and *Strawberry and Chocolate*, the central character is meant to stand for something at a given moment in revolutionary history. In the earlier film, the intellectual is jostled out of his petit bourgeois world, and forced to ponder his alienation in contrast with the growing class consciousness of the population. In *Strawberry and Chocolate* class consciousness is replaced by erotic liberation, as the homosexual argues for the right to live freely and openly in a revolutionary society. Together, the films may one day allow us to write a history of revolutionary intellectual discourse in Cuba—how it moves from the petit bourgeois intellectual to the cultured homosexual. If the intellectual in *Memories of Underdevelopment* walks the streets of Havana like a parasite vis-à-vis a thoroughly productive society, the homosexual character in *Strawberry and Chocolate* circulates culture as a good whose value is understood by some straight objects of affection and then recharged for the benefit of the revolutionary community at large. Homosexuals may have offered their own bodies only for the sake of nonreproductive sex, but they bear culture from one generation to the other—culture being something whose worth in and of itself can only be found outside the usual value-producing social mechanisms.

Like *Memories*, with its constant internal references to the revolutionary process, *Strawberry and Chocolate* is a compendium of the visible and invisible histories of Cuban culture. The film glosses homosexuality as a debate *within* the Cuban intellectual milieu that, like the bourgeoisie, serves as a guiding national force. The homosexual here is deracinated from a context: he has few friends, bears little relationship to society at large, and has no lovers to speak of. Culture in this film sodomizes class, while same-sex desire is no longer an issue of private behavior versus social mores. The film implies that homosexuality needs a space because, like culture, it falls outside the parameters of the normative and because it is critical and resistant.

The narrative is allegorical in the broader sense of the term. There are only two flavors in the ice cream palace of Coppelia, the site of most gay encounters in Havana, and the choice of flavors is part of a common Cuban or Caribbean way of signifying gender relations. Since only real men eat chocolate, the thirty-year-old gay queen Diego partakes of strawberry as he sits next to David, a budding writer who follows all the Party dictates. The boy-meets-boy plotline is motivated by the political distance between the two men. Diego has found in David a real strawberry in his dish, and he savors it with the only topping he can find: banned books, including, one by Mario Vargas Llosa. Culture, as something that is at the same time possessed and shared, forms the most visible subplot of a sentimental tale that can only end with the unjust banishment of the suffering homosexual.

This is the legacy of the injustice the film seeks to address, but not before we viewers are treated to a tour of life in, supposedly, late 1970s Havana—its buildings and poor tenements, and the people's efforts to live from day to day. The story is told by the young David, and the cinematic gaze belongs to his (and the audience's, we presume) ambivalence toward a very effeminate Diego. By the end of the film David has turned from Party protégé to a critical voice—not quite a dissident, but a committed revolutionary who learns that being critical of the revolution is a very revolutionary thing. In other words, he has become a heterosexual who is not threatened by the open flirtations of gay men on the prowl. In the course of this process of self-awareness, David has also been marked by gay melancholia, and he is able to look at his city and his world with new eyes.

If my account of the film is too cynical, then perhaps it is because the gaze of the homosexual cynic is totally absent from the syrupy *Strawberry and Chocolate*. Its characters are stock characters, and its plot is lifted straight out of an after-school special. Diego, who as the film's gay icon is given ample credit for presenting gays in a "positive light," turns out to be a conservative culture queen.[11] On all accounts *Strawberry and Chocolate* is an official film that is also an official statement, what Gutiérrez Alea has called a necessary tale: "from its first reading, it revealed itself as a necessary story, something that all of us surely wanted to hear."[12] Since it has been hailed as opening up the complex issue of homosexuals in Cuba, any critique of the film has been accused of being blind to the very real problems entailed in making a film like this in Cuba. A number of years back, in a conference on postmodern discourse at Yale, a famous Cuban writer still residing on the island addressed foreigners' concerns that the film portrayed a stereotypical view of gay men with the following line: "In a homophobic country, I pray for us to at least appear as stereotypes."

All discussion about the film ends in a political cul-de-sac where visibility collides with desire. In other words, this might not be the film we want, but it is the film we have, and that is enough. The film is faithful to Senel Paz's "El lobo, el bosque y el hombre nuevo," the story on which it is based,

Diego and David confront each other with the truth. Videocapture from *Strawberry and Chocolate.*

although it gives more importance to David's attempts at informing on the suspicious Diego, and has added a heterosexual subplot: Diego's female next-door neighbor, who survives by dealing in the black market, constantly threatens to commit suicide, sleeps with David, and then consoles him after Diego's departure.

Style, Control, Visibility

Visibility is always, in and of itself, constructed and even fabricated. As Paul Julian Smith has remarked in reference to Néstor Almendros's *Improper Conduct,* even what is visibly self- evident may be subject to competing interpretations.[13] Where Almendros decided to give the illusion of transparency by immensely complex technical means, Gutiérrez Alea wants to provide the illusion of authenticity to a film that is, on all accounts, a game of illusion. The critical problem here has to do with the tension arising from the demands for authenticity coming out of an allegorical narrative. The characters here represent much more than their individual selves, not only by virtue of the dense context in which they live, but also because their representation exceeds (or is a surplus to) the given investment.

Gutiérrez Alea solves the tension between visibility and allegory by consciously assuming compromises and trade-offs between the allegorical character of the story (what made it necessary in the first place) and the fabrication or illusion of film. Throughout *Strawberry and Chocolate,* Gutiérrez Alea balances illusion and play. For example, as he stated in an interview, they had decided against a certain locale because it was too perfect, and the viewer might think that the locale was the set designer's brainchild.[14] Gutiérrez Alea's cinematic language creates the illusion of truth, while also rendering truth into a spectacle. He composes in a careful and lyrical language whose style limns cinema verité and staged acting. He explained that in *Strawberry and Chocolate* he did not want to impede the flow of the mise-en-scène, so he put the camera at the service of the actors instead of the other way around. Here, the aim of technical proficiency was to give the illusion that there is no foul play. Because of the parameters he sets, what is natural—the jerky camera movements—would seem in this context to be a contrivance. Gutiérrez Alea is interested in a different kind of illusion, where authenticity is a matter of technique. This is why he would rather err on the side of technique (formal sophistication) in order not to disturb the viewer with the intrusion of the real. In *Strawberry and Chocolate,* as he explained, he tried to reduce technical flourishes to a minimum, without at the same time compromising the quality of the mise-en- scène. He opted for natural light and tried to incorporate elements that accidentally appeared in the process of filming, aiming toward a mise-en-scène that, he said, would be as "organic" as possible.[15]

The key word for Gutiérrez Alea is organicness, and by that he seems to mean a kind of film practice born out of the particular situation filmed. What he has in mind is a degree of technical proficiency respectful of the "organic" relationship between scene and film. No effort is spared, no rational decision can be taken outside the demands of such contrivance. Gutiérrez Alea said that he challenged his actors in rehearsals to improvise, to move with total liberty so that the technical placement of the cameras could be determined from the actors' movements themselves. With the camera subservient to the actors and not the other way around, Gutiérrez Alea explained how Mario García Joya developed a system by means of which they could arrive at the same effects as those produced by a steadycam, a piece of equipment they did not have during filming.[16] When a director is working with limited resources and budget, the imprimatur of style demands a border where sophistication and spontaneity meet.

This question of style is so important because it bears directly on the film's representation of homosexuality. *Strawberry and Chocolate* ignores the standard debate of essentialism versus social construction. Its aim is to examine Cubans'—as well as the revolution's—social intolerance of homosexuality. Questions of origin are pushed aside: it is less socially relevant to ask *why* Diego is homosexual than to ask *how* society will treat him. The claims of spontaneity collide with those of fabrication because questions of representation take precedence over issues of origin. In talking about the way he selected the actors, Gutiérrez Alea explained the trade-offs he had to make in casting Jorge Perugorría as Diego, since he was much younger than the character they had in mind.[17] But this problem was also related to the question of the degree of effeminacy the actor should embody. The question that haunts Gutiérrez Alea does not seem to be political, but rather a question of *how* to represent homosexuality so that it is not offensive, disgusting, or crass.

What emerges out of these technical decisions is a thoroughly controlled environment, based on a series of collaborations that reproduce, albeit unintentionally, the given constraints and controls of the society as a whole. Diego's portrayal is an exercise in control; he needs to rein in a sense of besieged melancholia:

In terms of his mannerisms, we were not sure what degree of effeminacy the character should manifest. Senel's story described him with markedly effeminate traits, in fact at certain moments, deliberately provocative. We worked with the actor to see up to what point he could manifest himself at that level without being shocking, and above all, without turning the character into a caricature. The actor did a delicate and rigorous job to achieve an effeminate air that came from an internal attitude, more than from an imported mannerism.[18]

This is not a question of homosexuality; it is a question of how to represent a stylistic mark. For a film that purports to treat the question of homosexuality in a revolutionary manner within a revolutionary context, it is dominated by representation and style. It does not market itself as a film about homosexuality, but rather as a film about difference. But instead of exploring difference, the question is, how can it be *represented*?

In this sense, *Strawberry and Chocolate* can be seen as the Cuban counterpart to the Hollywood movie *Philadelphia*—necessary to the extent that it gives official voice to a situation, but utterly redundant given the realities at hand. The film does not portray the situation of homosexuals in Cuba in the 1990s, particularly after the loss of Soviet subsidies, and thus—unlike *Philadelphia*—it does not address the question of AIDS. Although at the time the film was made AIDS had not become a crisis in Cuba, the question of disease and treatment presented problems that would have taken the director outside the cultural sphere.

Control in terms of the representation of homosexuality involves anticipating the audience's response: what is going to be let out of the closet and represented, and what is not going to be represented, and why. There were at least eleven drafts of the script, not including the final version, according to Gilda Santana, who served as the script consultant.[19] Each version of the script was subjected to delicate and painstaking analyses that furnished the action with the criteria of believability and motivation. Each scene—for example, and particularly, the one in which David goes into Diego's private space—is the result of a rational decision that needs to be explained on the basis of what would be, at any given point, the essential behavior of the characters.[20] These drafts of the script debated at all points not only the form, but also the content of the tale (whether it was going to be told, as in Paz's story, as a flashback, for example). A minute examination of the characters takes place, a sort of microscopic analysis that cannot help normatizing and completely colonizing all illusions of personal freedom:

But it is only in these cases of difficult scenes with resolutions that are transcendental for the characters where it is necessary to examine up to the minutest detail the model of each micro-sequence. This examination will tell us, in the most direct manner, why the character acted like he did, or what are the reasons for the apparent delay in the action. We will then have a vision of the script that goes from the most general (the story that is told) to its most recondite particulars (the movement and inner behavior of the actions by means of which the story is told).[21]

What is invisible in terms of the seamless narration of the filmic discourse is the series of questions on every aspect of the characters in the film. Thus, for the sake of balance, the subplot of the hysterical neighbor is attached, in order to give David (and, presumably, the heterosexual viewers) some release throughout the film; a plotline involving the repression of Diego's sculptor friend is fleshed out; and David's conflicts with Miguel, his Communist Party friend, are given more prominence.

Visibility was the reason Senel Paz wrote the tale on which the film is based. It focused on a dark chapter in revolutionary history that needed to be taken into account at some point. But what the film does is turn the story's project of visibility into an aesthetics. Because the choice of material already dictates the way the story is to be filmed, we have to see Gutiérrez Alea's constraints as issues that he already registers in the story itself. This was always, in essence, a story about visibility. It was, moreover, a story about the relationship between visibility and culture—two of the most important spaces for revolutionary social engineering. As such, this was a necessary tale that the homosexual also needed to enact.

Culture Vultures

The importance of culture in *Strawberry and Chocolate* relates directly to social taxonomies and forms of classifying deployed by revolutionary politics.

It is also deeply involved with the deployment of power and its assertion as truth in the story on which the film is based. In other words, faced with a notion of power that asserts itself as truth, the discourse of power is voiced from the position of marginality, and this serves as a mask, or foil, for its profoundly conservative stance. In spite of all the radical pretensions Paz has given him, Diego is a profoundly conservative character not only in terms of culture but, more importantly, in his assessment of how sexual politics should be inscribed in the revolution.

Diego's range of knowledge disrupts local and global categories by making no distinctions between national and foreign. He can discourse on Mario Vargas Llosa and contemporary Latin American literature, John Donne and Cavafys, Maria Callas and *Giselle,* along with studies on Cuban nineteenth-century women poets, treatises on Havana architecture, and an incomplete study of male active same-sex partners (*bugarrones*) and their language in different parts of the city. What seems to be radical here is the combination of areas of knowledge, not the spheres of knowledge themselves. In the movie, Diego's research interests are suspicious to the authorities. It is not that his equation of the foreign and the local is radical, but that the class markers tamper with well-defined boundaries. Diego's cultural stew is meant to correspond to his understanding of marginality and commitment since neither one nor the other is as absolute as the authorities and the revolution want it to be. This is why Diego also presents himself, in spite of his exceptional style and his uncommon choice of sex objects, as totally committed to Havana, to its people, to Cuban social problems, and above all, to Cuban culture. At one point, he says that were he forced to choose between a penis and his sense of "Cubanness," his national pride would be more important ("Entre una picha y la cubanía, la cubanía"). These choices already belie the context in which Diego articulates his own situation as one that opposes sexual choice to national duty. The problems inscribed within his sexual desire are always placed in this structure.

In a remarkable passage that has been excised in the translation from story to film, Diego explains to David the different kinds of homosexual desire that exist in the revolutionary context. Diego becomes at this point a modern-day Virgil guiding a young Dante through the labyrinths of passion, or a Petronius voicing the varieties of sexual experience to be found in a tropical Rome:

We homosexuals fall into a more elaborate and interesting classification than I told you the other day. That is, homosexuals, *properly termed—this word is used because even at its worst it retains some degree of respect;* faggots*—also popular—and queens, for whom the lowest expression is the* drag queens. *This scale reflects the subject's degree of disposition to social responsibility or queerness. When the balance inclines to social responsibility, we are in the presence of a homosexual. There are those—I count myself among them—for whom sex occupies* a *place in their life but not* the *place in their life. Like heroes or political activists, we balance Duty and Sex. The cause to which we dedicate ourselves comes first. My cause is our nation's culture, to which I dedicate the better part of my intellect and my time. . . . Homosexuals of this category don't waste time on sex, nothing can sway us from our work. . . . Our intelligence and productivity warrant a respect we are always denied. . . . Faggots don't require any special explanation, since they occupy the midpoint between the two extremes: you'll see if you consider* queens, *who are easy to understand. They always have a phallus on their mind, and it's behind all their actions. Wasting time is their basic characteristic. If the time they devoted to flirting in parks and public baths were dedicated to socially useful work we could achieve what you call Communism and we paradise. The most wayward of all are the ones called drag queens. I loathe them for their fatuity and vacuity, and because their lack of discretion and tact has made such simple and necessary things as painting one's toenails into acts of rebellion. . . . The typology can also be applied to heterosexuals of either sex. Straight men of the lowest type, corresponding to the drag queens whose chief characteristic is wasting time and lust for perpetual fornication, are the lechers, who on their way to mail a letter, say, can even lay their hands on one of us without a loss of virility, just because they can't contain themselves."*[22]

Diego's taxonomies of sexual desire clearly demarcate the issue of borders and boundaries in terms of a hierarchy that depends on sex and productivity, on the net worth of sex. Sex is normatized in terms of its social worth, and thus colludes with productivity. The subjects that form part of Diego's exact and exacting taxonomies are fixed even within their apparently fluid construction, which runs the gamut crowned by the culture queen, and ends by categorizing members of society as a whole according to their apparent interest or disinterest in productive or nonproductive sex. The apparent neutrality of the taxonomical grid is, as a matter of fact, quite rigid—no trashy queen can belong to the cultured realm—while producing its own biases for the sake of the reader's pleasure (the more obvious reactionary effects of which are that Diego critiques and participates in the queens' painting of their toenails, implying that he does the same thing and wants to do it with impunity, and he constantly refers to himself in the feminine gender).

The reader understands that the whole discourse is meant to instruct but also to seduce the young David with the blatant existence of a sexuality that does not appear in traditional Cuban manuals.[23] Rendering all these men into visible categories turns visibility into the most radical weapon wielded by the master sociologist. Diego also includes himself in the definition, as that type of gay man who is properly called a "homosexual" (as opposed to faggots, queens, and the like, Diego explains), who should give the revolution no problem.

It is, as Diego would have it, a question of style, of the demeanor assumed by homosexuality. The cultured homosexual believes, or fools himself into believing, that given a choice between a good lay and serious, disciplined research, he would choose the latter. This discourse achieves the validation of truth—of *social* truth—because of who is recounting it. It is apparently not subject to interpretation or disputation, given that it is uttered precisely by a member of the tribal category at hand. Diego already speaks from the standpoint of *power*, and as such, it makes no sense to negate the discourse in terms of *ideology* in order to oppose other taxonomies to his. Precisely because he is the one uttering the discourse, and including himself in it, the whole section can be seen as one more example of the pernicious effect of ideology (thus excised from the script as unnecessary, irrelevant, gratuitous). The taxonomy is meant to allow us to participate in and identify a conspiratorial network of affection. Definitions and identifications are the key to Diego's discourse. From the space of his repression, he is able to proffer ideology and refer it back to himself as subject. It is from this perverse instrumentalizing of power that Diego can fling back to his own society the repression that he suffered, even as he flings it back as the sheer pleasure in perverting the categories of Marxist production for his own benefit.

The more perverse reading of the passage concerns whether this is a visibility wanted by the gay population, whether it responds to a desire. None of these types of men ever appear in the story. Their being mentioned does not clarify whether this is a space that they want. I am not merely referring to the fact that all of Diego's public and private, visible and invisible behavior differs from the "morally reprehensible" categories that he lists. What I am questioning is how this paragraph functions within the imperative of visibility that guides not only Senel Paz's story but *Strawberry and Chocolate*. In spite of all arguments to the contrary, *Strawberry and Chocolate* and "El lobo, el bosque y el hombre nuevo" show that all behaviors must be normatized, analyzed, and finally subjected to taxonomy as a categorical imperative. Sex can only be something that is permanently *other*.

A film such as *Strawberry and Chocolate* can only produce an anticipated kind of nostalgia for a time and a possibility that never were. Who is this nostalgia addressed to and what is it directed toward? It is an allegory that has been financed, filmed, and distributed by the state. At the same time, it is also an allegory where the state points the accusatory finger at itself, and accepts the social and political costs of repressing some of its most loyal members solely because of their "flaw" or "difference." *Strawberry and Chocolate* places the viewer in the same kind of nostalgic present that was seen in its forerunner, *Memorias del subdesarrollo*. It is, to refer back to Langston Hughes, a kind of montage of a dream deferred. It allows the state and the illustrated intellectual class some possibility of self-redemption at a moment in which the social and political situation on the island has gotten too complex and too out of hand for that same literate class to manage. In *Strawberry and Chocolate,* ideology and repression always have a way of bringing the discourse back to the subject and not to the state; they serve as sentimental pointers that repeat the melodramatic narrative of the subject. The film wants to speak to those subjects like Diego lost in the midst of revolutionary contradictions, and also to those whose sense of certainty is lost and confused in troubled times. Gutiérrez Alea wants to redeem the innate goodness of the revolution, the rightness of revolutionary struggle, and provoke a sense of faith in its potential to rectify the course. That the reality has been considerably messier, bloodier and infinitely sadder, that the lost dreams and illusions have completely shattered lives, is more than simply hinted at in the film.[24] That revolutions can be cruel and bloody no one will dispute. But when revolutionary artists start apologizing for the state's cruelties by essentializing themselves as true revolutionaries, the situation is as volatile and delicate as the one that sparked the struggle in the first place.

In the same way that it is the prerogative of the powerful to be magnanimous, one could say that only in the realm of power could power apologize for its own misdeeds. Power, Foucault warned, cannot simply be explained away as repressive:

If power were never anything but repressive, if it never did anything but to say no, do you really think one would be brought to obey it? What makes power hold good, what makes it accepted, is simply the fact that it doesn't only weigh on us as a force that says no, but that it traverses and produces things, it induces pleasure, forms knowledge, produces discourse. It needs to be considered as a productive network which runs through the whole social body, much more than as a negative instance whose function is repression.[25]

It is clear that the film gave voice to those who had no voice; it is also clear that it disrupted the state of Cuban discourse to the extent that it allowed the homosexual as a new social actor on the stage. It spawned acts of solidarity; it allowed for the creation of Web pages and books and television debate throughout the Cuban social fabric. Its opening weeks in the Havana theater where it played were a spectacle of open cruising, an outdoor theater registered by the stories it spawned and the narratives it created. I first saw the film as a semi-clandestine copy at a conference at New York University. It was not subtitled and it was introduced by a Cuban academic who had recently arrived in Florida, who explained the extent to which the movie had crossed borders already (copies had been smuggled out to Miami and could be rented at video stores, he said). He told anthropologically fascinating tales (later confirmed by others) of how the gays among the movie audience whistled and cajoled not Diego or David, but David's dour, dogmatic friend. He recounted how all the queens in the audience went crazy over a shower scene where the camera discreetly shows their naked bodies, how they taunted the character, and how this budding Party functionary was the real object of desire for the queens who improvised their fashion statements and their makeup to attend the screenings, and also for the ones who roamed outside.

As one of those who had no access to the event itself, I found that the tale of the event was also part of the melodramatic circuit that made me shed some tears for the sake of melodrama. Other viewers who saw the film with me were not as moved; they were certainly more cynical. In very personal terms, I can only question the tears that I shed and regret the fact that I *do* question them. The question of the dream deferred that Langston Hughes described is still a haunting one, and it is a disturbing thing that there seems to be no clear denouement for these tales except within the space of allegory.

6 Tears at the Nightclub

> If the romantic spirit is waning, the passion for the memory of passion remains. In kitchens, at sowing [*sic*] circles, during leisure time (when the television is turned off), in tired postcoital moments, to listen to one's idol is to go from the loss of innocence to the recapture of candour.
>
> —CARLOS MONSIVÁIS, "Bolero: A History"

The Queen of Bolero

It is an early evening in May 1998 in Madrid, and a friend has given me tickets to see Olga Guillot celebrating her sixty years as the queen of the sentimental genre known in the Latino world as *bolero*, in the Centro Cultural de la Villa, an auditorium partly hidden beneath the gushing fountains of a monument to Christopher Columbus. La Guillot herself carries all the tracks and marks of a musical history on her body and soul. The poster that advertises the concert and that has been plastered all over the city for weeks includes snapshots of all her incarnations at different points in time.

Born in Cuba, Olga Guillot has never returned after the 1959 revolution. She has become, in fact, the standard-bearer of antirevolutionary fervor ever since. But she does not sing political songs; her trademark has always been the sentimental, slow musical genre of the bolero. Her specialty, in particular, has been the bolero of despair and eros, the song that produces the erotic charge of steamy sex under a red lightbulb, or the one sung by the woman after the man has left her panting, and she hides a knife under the pillow on a creaking bed where the sheets are wet.

Olga Guillot, *Sabor a Mi,* Alma Latina ALCD 017, 1995.

For years, La Guillot has made a career out of expressing those volcanic urges that consume the flesh. Love, affection, desire are here rendered as bodily urges: desire is erotomania, love always seems carnal bliss. Even her trademark gestures are all coital reminiscences: the trembling lips, fingers of both hands moving as if caressing pearly beads in front of her face, and then moving down to trace circles in front of her stomach, down to her sex. Her voice has always been unique in its register: one cannot call it melodious or even soothing. It is ill-suited to the sense of caress, but also not as defiant as that of La Lupe, the other diva who is her more obvious point of contrast. It is an unmistakable voice: deep but not exuberant, all timbre and no inflection, embodied rather than ethereal. During the sixties she always knew how to provoke a sense of scandal, and the audience could expect her to deliver what it paid for: the faux elegance of the quivering organic flesh trapped in a rococo chamber that had become degraded from a pleasure that had to be assumed to be forbidden in order for it to be enjoyed.

La Guillot was innovative as a singer but more important as a product: she knew how to export herself as the voice of an invented time and space. Her life was one long pursuit of nightclubs where the ice always clinked in a half-empty glass: Mexico—where she resided after the Cuban revolution—Spain, Miami, New York. In fact, before the revolution she already had a career that exported a piece of Cuba wherever she went. After the revolution, her concerts served as points of contact where a certain sector of the Cuban diaspora could recognize itself in a Havana remembered as a form of quasi-elegant trash: she could create the sense of a past that had no need of being inhabited by anyone. It was, rather, a past that was absent of everything except herself as referent, with the geographical space of any concert as substitution, an emblem of the cities where she triumphed.

Tonight, the demands of her return to Madrid produce an expectant audience—one that knows that Olga, the object to be consumed, is just that: an object fit for consumption. The audience at the Centro Cultural in Madrid includes at least three kinds of expectant listeners: old heterosexual couples, Spanish or Cuban, who have come to remember the excess of yore (she will sigh, at some point in the concert, "Ah, those were great times"); the young homosexual couples or groups, who have come to listen to the excessive simulacra of the past (she will interpellate them with a sigh: "Ah, the new generation"); and here and there, the faithful members of the diaspora: the recently arrived who have come to listen to a living legend, and those who have been here for a long time and perform the rites of a *cubanía* forged outside the island for the past forty years. One never quite knows to what extent these three groups communicate with each other, except and insofar as the three are linked by La Guillot herself and by Cuba-as-absence.

The lights are dimmed and the bandmembers assume their places with an air of rehearsed boredom. The audience wildly claps and rises to its feet when La Guillot takes the stage, before she has even had the chance to belt out a tune. Her pink dress hardly conceals a frame that has grown enormous in the last decades. She does not hide the fact that she is touched by this reception—as a matter of fact, she wipes away tears and decides not so much to *sing* as to *speak*. She knows she does not have to work this audience, because the audience will rise to its feet no matter what she does. In mid-concert, she forgets the lyrics to her trademark song, and the audience cheers wildly. She barely sings, and she sings off-key. Nobody is really listening, and nobody really cares. She does not need to sing; she just has to be there, adored by the audience that talks to her, that talks *back* to her, that screams, "Don't leave, Olga, don't ever leave" while she appeals to the melodrama of impending death, of silence, of disaster. The spectacle is that of known degeneration: a voice that is no more. *That* is what we want: melodrama as willed parody, the trembling lips as trademark, as quotation, a stable center where confusion can be apprehended as such, without the requisite protocols of drama. There are moments when she stops singing in order to sob—sobs performed as a way of performing a sob—and these moments produce vaguely concealed chuckles from the audience. We all know that she is representing herself: this is, after all, La Guillot, and she can make a comeback only by refusing the sense of dignity entailed in retirement.

There is no performance of absence in this career, nothing like Greta Garbo hiding her aging body and face. She is more similar to the Cuban prima ballerina Alicia Alonso performing *Giselle* in spite of her blindness and advanced age. But then again, this is something else, and one can apprehend it only by following the gestural game played by La Guillot, with her trembling hands in front of her face and the quivering fingers that seem to caress an invisible necklace. Like necklaces, like constellations, the elements of this aesthetics are linked by an invisible thread—these rhinestones, these invisible pearls that her hands caress. They are what is left of illusion but they are also Illusion itself. The success of that illusion is not measured by any degree of open collaboration with Olga's performance of a disaster: we all understand to what extent we are laughing in the midst of this sentimental performance. We are part of a sentimental community, constructed around La Guillot as signifier, wrapped in that huge pink dress like a meringue about to collapse.

Neocapitalism, globalization, the millennial threats to democracy, armed insurrection, the possibility of a market crash—all of these are joined to La Guillot as a complex hieroglyph. One knows the form it traces, and one also understands the impossibility of reading it. La Guillot joins different publics, distant communities, just as boleros allow the links between different things to come together. Time and space, sexualities and capitalism collapse and coalesce. One can live the 1980s and 1990s as if they were the 1940s without wishing that they were the 1940s. It is a present constructed as a bricolage of past and present.

Bolero Publics

The fantasies and intimacies of the tropical night have always been the space for yearning. The landscape is simple: one demands only the clinking of the ice in the glass and the open balcony with the palm tree and the crescent moon. There is love and there is sexual abandon; there is love as a tragedy; infidelities are legion; one may be married and have a lover; there may be a razor blade somewhere for the suicide or the murder. And if these are sung by voices that validate desire as the ruling passion of the man or the woman, there is also a politics of gender involved.

Boleros appear as a point of reference in the work of artists who are not necessarily gay or lesbian, but who voice boleros in the 1990s via the melancholic homosexual as a polemical figure of mourning and celebration. The gay man turns into the most visible emblem of a modern paradox, posing a question that stops short of eroticizing the possible dissolution of the nation.

The question this figure poses can be articulated as follows: what part of Latin American identity is in flux and what part of it remains, in spite of changes over time? Because the very ambivalence of the question is embodied in the figure of the gay man as the consumer, it is important to understand that behind the revival of the bolero, there is something at stake other than merely nostalgia or "camp" sensibility. It is also important to understand that the nostalgia has chosen to represent its very ambivalence, at this time, through the gay man.

What is the cultural context for the reappearance of the bolero in the 1990s? I will attempt to give an answer to this question in the course of this essay, but I think it is important to quote first of all the theoretical answer given by the Venezuelan writer Rafael Castillo Zapata in his brilliant *Fenomenología del bolero.* Castillo Zapata names as mentors Roland Barthes (particularly *A Lover's Discourse*) and then Werther, Proust, Adorno, and psychoanalysis as part of the psychological baggage of a certain (left) aesthetics that any inhabitant of Latin American urban centers would recognize. He explains the origins of his own phenomenological gaze:

[O]bserving the textual milieu around which the book had come into being, and being myself, furthermore, in a period where listening to boleros had become an adventure of cultural self-recognition during the passionate period of the Grupo Trafico and of street poetry, of conversationalism and sentimentality recuperated for the sake of reflection and writing—that Latin American sentimentality that has been beaten down by disdainful modernizing, draped in an anachronism that, in the end result, has been beneficial, for it has saved, in spite of the barbarism of certain kinds of progress, in this area of the world, that uninhibited milieu of passion whose increasing deflation European modernity is now lamenting—slowly I realized that Barthes had never in his life heard a bolero, that he died without the experience of listening to Olga Guillot singing Luis Demetrio's "Bravo," in a recital, and that this lack of knowledge—crucial, without a doubt—was reflected, whether he wanted it or not, in his extraordinary book.[1]

What is interesting in this passage is not simply that it names the particular milieu for bolero's revival, or that it does so by positioning itself as the addendum, the supplement to Barthes's discourse—a supplement, furthermore, that in true Derridean fashion decenters the privileged status of the original. What is more interesting is that this supplement (the anachronistic bolero) is presented as part of a kind of "virginal" space (as Castillo Zapata names it at a later point) that European postmodernity does not have access to. The excess reenacted by the bolero accounts for Castillo Zapata's reluctance to theorize it, as if theory will immediately undo the magic, will disrupt "the stability of a free zone of the world."[2] Castillo Zapata's mode of theorizing, engaged in a battle whose most visible emblems are given in the opposition between authenticity on the one hand and intellectualism and theory on the other, teases out the context for the representation of the homosexual within the genre. On the one hand homosexuals, like boleros, are voices resistant to theorizing; but on the other, they also beckon the theoretical gesture.

Bolero as a genre had already appeared before the 1990s in a nongay context—in Guillermo Cabrera Infante's novel *Tres tristes tigres*, and in Pedro Vergés's *Sólo cenizas hallarás*, among others. But it is sung in a different register in the tropical settings devised by the Argentinean Manuel Puig, and in Luis Rafael Sánchez's *La importancia de llamarse Daniel Santos*. These works recuperate a mode, a time and a place, they bridge the tangible borders between high and low culture, in order to voice a certain dislocation for a time past. If Cabrera Infante had mourned a lost Cuba by focusing on La Estrella, in Puig or in Sanchez the bolero signals the beginning of a new voice that reappears from the past in order to seduce readers again into a transnational (and even a meta-Caribbean) space. Because the bolero as a recuperated genre demands that we break the tenuous border between the self and the other, between objective and subjective discourse, I will mimic Castillo Zapata's appeal to a Barthesian theorizing of the personal, but I will do so in order to remotivate the discussion along different lines. Since the issue here is the link between the public performance of the bolero and private and public sexual and erotic choices, let us at the outset confirm a link in the 1990s between bolero and gay men. One need only look at that mega-hit of 1991 that was Luis Miguel's *Romance,* a rehashed collection of boleros (the oldest, "Inolvidable," from 1944) heard not only in Mexico City and San Juan, but also in Buenos Aires, Montevideo, and Santiago during those years. Luis Miguel's North American tour was advertised with paid, full-page ads for three consecutive weeks in the very gay and very open and very Anglo *Washington Blade*. Something other than the quite evident sex appeal of Luis Miguel is at play here. In retrospect, Luis Miguel interpellated the audience that, years later, stood up to dance and jive while Ricky Martin swayed his hips.

Counterdiscourse

Boleros are all about erasure. What other musical genre can be so invested in its own sense of disappearance that it seeks to proclaim absence by belting out songs claiming that the only thing that remains is disappearance itself? Bolero refuses all that exists by mourning all that has been; its temporal mode is always the past or the future seen from the point of view of the ruins of the past—or of the past as a ruin. It works on the registers of defiance, nostalgia, anger, and lust; its geographical referents are a mental constellation of tropics that can be invented at will. These emblematic spaces can exist only by erasing other tropics, those where poverty is the norm and not the exception, where the panache and romance of the nightclub are available only to a few.

Boleros always have to be measured within the space of desire—desire, of course, not as an index of the real but as a mental construction *imposed* on the real. Boleros exchange reality for something else: they erase what is and create what could be. Because it is a discourse of the fantastic, bolero has to proclaim itself insistently, underscoring an all or nothing. Samba may invoke the sadness that accompanies the morning after a night of reckless abandon, but boleros insist on remaining *in* that night, *in* that space. They do not prepare you for inevitable disaster: they want and beckon the constant reappearance of disaster. Boleros proclaim denial as a mode of affirmation. They exist in this space of contradiction, which is what gives them their erotic tension: the voice always wants to annihilate Voice itself.

The bolero crooners and singers are ciphers. Daniel Santos, Carmen Delia Dipiní, Freddy, Olga Guillot, La Lupe—they all seem like incarnations of something in the realm of the unintelligible that can only be expressed in shorthand by means of a picture. Their rough edges are smoothed over for the sake of representation: the suave gentleman, la Reina del Bolero, La Yiyiyi, el Caballero de la Canción. They appeal to the elementary constructions of what remains uncomplicated—a universe of trademark gestures and emptied costumes. This emptiness relishes its own demise, its own fatuous embrace of the nothingness that seems to pursue the genre: affectation and illusion mingled into one. Neither nostalgic nor camp, bolero needs to be apprehended from the space of a performance, or from the scene of a nightclub.

An audience member who hears those old 1950s boleros in the 1990s participates in a unique temporal construction that speaks in two registers, with a double voice. The constant interplay between the text of one period and the context of another creates a new and different—but always necessary—text for the present. The context of Latin American neoliberalism in the 1990s creates this comeback—it insists on it. It deploys a text that refuses stabilities and seeks a degree of comfort in instability itself. Every bolero of old that comes back to us at this time is in a sense quoting itself, speaking of its own incomplete disappearance. It revels in its own opulent performance, an opulence not of the signified or the signifier, but of the act itself.

The act of belting out the song is part of this context, because that desperate longing comes back to us precisely so we don't feel the need to return to the time and place where boleros reigned. The starlit nights in Veracruz where the bandleader is dressed in an impeccable white tuxedo are understood as a fiction, the second time around. The content of the songs may seem to elicit the reactions of camp, but content is less of an issue here if we see these acts as interventions that do not refuse the failures implicit in their recuperation. This is ascertained by Carlos Monsiváis's comments on the Mexican Agustín Lara, one of bolero's foremost composers:

Without the context that made him necessary, Agustín Lara reveals himself progressively as anachronistic and pathetic. His isolated ridiculousness is a catastrophe that can be recuperated only by means of imported techniques such as camp. But these techniques or tricks bury him more than redeem him . . . the literary defenselessness of Agustín Lara's improvisations are essentialized if camp vision is applied to them. [Lara does not stand for] the opulence of form at the expense of the ridiculousness of content, but the last defense of a primitive context that sees in exaggeration its access to the sublime. It is a passion not for form, but for expressive urges, for the love that will become "Silver cradle in the morning / that will turn into song in the mountain!"[3]

Monsiváis argues against the recycling of Lara as camp—camp understood not only as an imported aesthetics, but also as a defensive posture against the very sense of *sublime* given in the lines of his songs. For Monsiváis, the regressive mode of camp merely prolongs the catastrophe of Agustín Lara's absence, since recuperating Lara as camp masquerades some kind of essentialism that is being implicitly exhibited only in the form of its revival. Monsiváis understands camp as the glorification of opulent form, whereas Lara himself was a believer: he understood seriousness of content as what allowed for access to sentimentality. For Monsiváis, until we understand the very content and idealism of Lara's work, we will keep returning to him with a paternalistic and nostalgic sentimentalism, with a nostalgia for an old time and place that has been transformed into almost a premodern essentialist "sensibility." This is why, for Monsiváis, this return falsifies: it blurs the sense of reality that accompanied Lara's words, a sense of reality that was tied to a context, one that provoked the urgent expression of its lyrics.

It bears insisting on the implications of Monsiváis's statement: boleros at this point do not seek the return of something that was there before. Imitation is not the issue when the copy makes no attempt to rescue the earlier time and place but seeks to control and have power over it. Boleros in the 1990s attempt to demolish the original context that the genre created in the first place. It is an ambivalent demolishing, and it is overdetermined by desire. Desire wants sentimentality back, but not the context; it seeks the expression, but wants to pick and choose among the rest.

If we imagine the context as canvas, then bolero is a gash; if any love song taps the vein of sentimentality, bolero cuts that vein with a razor blade. By the time the chorus makes its appearance, the curtains have been ripped and the apartment is in shambles. At the point in which the telling moves over to the realm of action, that red lightbulb has been hit by a baseball bat and you need to put on your Chinese sandals so as not to bleed.

Borders

The gash of sentiment is always a question of borders, and it works by turning every point of breakdown into a moment of reconstitution. Bolero performances deploy and reconstruct borders. The first border is that of the stage. To sing a bolero (always at the moment of despair) implies erasing the subject: the abandoned, plaintive, destitute, defiant, rebellious, or intransigent subject, always engaging in the shared memory of a loss, reconstructed because of its very sense of ruin. Arias may tap into the virtuosity of the throat and flesh out the mimicry of possibility for the one who lip-synchs. In boleros, the subject and the public position themselves within a complex web of indirectness in which the audience overhears a confession. Boleros are sung to no one in particular, or to someone always on the outside: they are voiced to a subject beyond the public, so that he or she can take stock of the afflictions of the present and offer redemption.

Boleros play with a border where masculinities and femininities are to be seen in ways that do not necessarily correspond to the ways gender acts out in the public sphere. In the personalized world of boleros, divas like La Guillot will always appeal to bolero as an entity whose sex is normatively masculine, and whose acquaintance one has made a long time ago. La Lupe talked to her man who was out there, though he was also the song itself. There is a feeling that bolero as a genre makes its own demands—one lives within the genre, one seduces it, one extracts the plaintive sentiment from it as if it were a kind of platonic body whose incarnation one assumes. Thus, one may speak, as La Guillot does, of the sixtieth anniversary of her wedding with the bolero, or one can claim a relationship with it by using, as Luis Miguel did on the cover of his first bolero compilations from 1991 (*Romance*), the phallic image of an antique microphone.

In Luis Miguel's collection, the microphone is meant to stand as a synecdoche for bolero itself. It is the phallic referent submitted to a series of poses that create a narrative in the CD booklet: Luis Miguel sings to it on the cover, bends his head to it, grabs it by the base until finally, the back cover

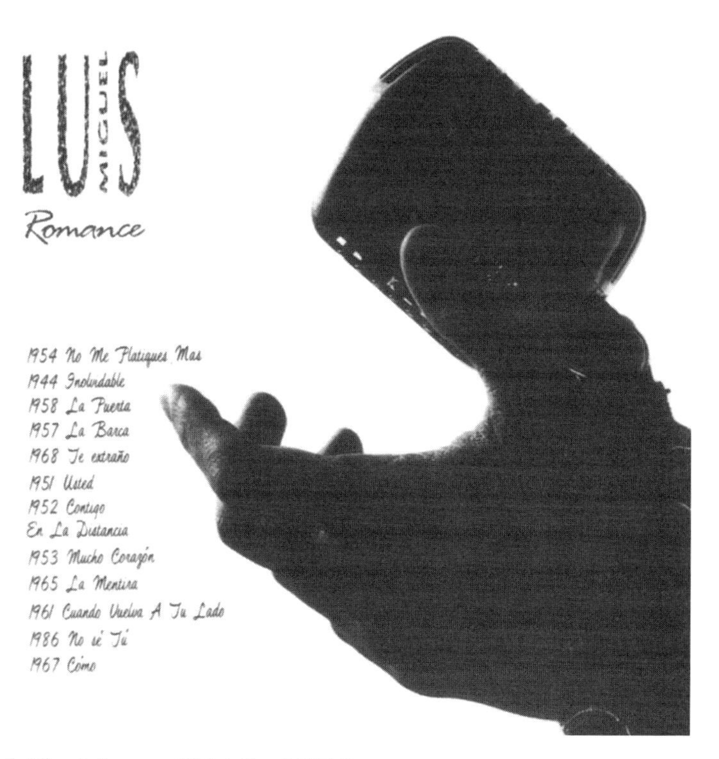

Luis Miguel, *Romance*, WEA Latina 75805-2.

of the CD is devoted to the sole image of the microphone with a hand assuming a plaintive yet caressing gesture. Luis Miguel here uses history (the antique microphone as well as a songlist that gives the dates of the original recordings) as a way of sublimating homosexual undertones that are barely under the surface. But he is also relating to a space that is external and openly phallic in terms of association.

In performing boleros, social roles may flip: women may be defiant or aggressive, and men may be forlorn, destitute, or disinterested. This does not mean that boleros are radical in terms of gender roles, for they never question their existence—as a matter of fact, they depend on the social fabric that these roles create. Gender roles can never be put into doubt, though boleros will use them as the point of departure for endless renegotiation. Once the theatrical mask has been ripped away, what we have is essential gender forms. The simulacrum, of course, was to believe that there was no essence to gender. Bolero is all about deceit.

This stage where dialectics are created and undone and where gender is renegotiated leads critics to analyze the genre's relationship to Latino American culture. Contrary to the at least presumed versatility of gender, bolero could only position itself within the space of its own creation, as long as it was firmly anchored in a cultural territory that it created for itself by virtue of language. This was so because boleros originally appeared during that golden age of mambos, danzones, and cha-cha-chá that was also part of a transnationalized Latin American urban popular culture. The primary locales here were the bar and the bedroom. As Carlos Monsiváis has acutely perceived, boleros recirculated the word *romántico* and gave it a prestige no longer to be had by the word *modernista*, which in Spanish entailed the anachronisms of the fin de siècle. Boleros created the possibility of a marginal nightlife; they gave Latin Americans a sense of modernity by making it possible to live "in sin" just like those fashionable urban denizens of great foreign cities, and without the strictures of Catholic moral condemnation.[4] Hence, the *mauditisme* associated at times with the genre. This sense of sin-as-modernity contrasts with how nature is embodied in the almost contemporary mambos, rumbas, and cha-cha-chá. Boleros were all about rhinestones; they had nothing to do with real pearls.

Boleros are almost conscious of the fact that they are ill-suited for translation—among other reasons, because they are too dependent on a sense of poetry and lyric that, even when translated, shows its obvious debts to the sentimentality of the fin de siècle space. In the sixties, for example, when aggressive salsa moved from the barrios of San Juan and Venezuela to the barrios of New York, boleristas never quite made it in the United States. New York was a city that could guarantee the survival of jazz players or salsa singers, and in moments of financial despair it had them go back to the boleros as a way of tempering the aggressive ferocity that their salsa already did not have. None of the "historical" boleristas like Vicentico Valdez or Santitos Colón could triumph in this medium; only Tito Rodríguez, Cheo Feliciano, or La Lupe occupied this space, and they could do so precisely because they had the salsa link. It was not that boleros could not be translated—it's just that they got lost in translation.

Sentimental Gash

At the end of the twentieth century the globalized ideology masks the rigid positionalities of center and periphery; the new flexibilized economy does not change the rigid polarities between rich and poor, and the present democratic openings in Latin America are constantly undermined by the authoritarian infrastructure that sustains them. This is why boleros are genuinely popular in the marketing apparatus of nostalgia: they give a fairly accurate account of what is happening at the base. In this case, the neocapitalist context produces its own marketing of the past as an act of resistance that it sees as ultimately useless.

As I mentioned at the beginning of this essay, in the early 1990s a number of films and texts seemed to relate either the male homosexual or the transvestite to the bolero. They spoke about a context of uncertainty in Latin America at that moment, in which the narratives of the Cold War had ended and state devolution was already seen by governments as the political course to take. The conjunction of what was then read in Latin America as two forms of hybridity—the homosexual as male/female and the bolero as a kind of past/present—served to map out a particular "state of things." This state of things entailed the fateful coexistence of a past that had not ceased to be, but could already be mourned, and an uncertain future that did not offer any cause for celebration. In this context, the bolero and the male homosexual allowed disaster and uncertainty to be represented, while at the same time they could motivate the histories of the present toward more liberatory futures. This is ambivalent only at a surface level, as we shall see briefly in two recent Latino American films.

The first is Jaime Hermosillo's *Doña Herlinda y su hijo*, a film where Rodolfo, the protagonist, marries Olga, the woman chosen by his mother, Doña Herlinda, for her very gay son. Aware of the fact that for his honey-

Doña Herlinda discretely passes on a handkerchief to Ramon. Videocapture from *Doña Herlinda y su hijo.*

moon Rodolfo has left his lover Ramón behind, Doña Herlinda takes Ramón to a spectacle where a singer (female) sings a ranchera of spurned love. The ranchera is certainly more nationalistically inflected than the bolero, but I think in this context the *feeling* engages a relationship between the two genres. At this point in the film, listening to the ranchera, Ramón cries, and his tears are meant to provoke the laughter but also the silence of the viewing public, aware that what we are seeing is, in effect, a crying game. The implacable normality of Hermosillo's whole cinematic affair (son, lover, mother, wife) gives the film a kind of perverse strangeness but also a curious sense of *ananké,* as if what happens is simply what *should* happen in the best of all possible worlds, where the social conventions are repeated like the plot of a movie seen by an indifferent (and thoroughly entertained) public.

Hermosillo may be interested in alternative sexualities and uncommon behavior but, as Daniel Balderston has remarked, he does not deploy these within the conventions of a "coming out" film, but rather in a "bringing back in" film, where homosexuality is accommodated within the structure of family and nation.[5] This accommodation is felt particularly at this moment. Ramón cried while listening to the ranchera because the circulation of events beckoned some kind of catharsis, something that registered the difficult nature of the situation. At this musical point in the film the sequence of events had to stop for emotion to appear. Underscoring her role in the whole affair, Doña Herlinda works as the postmodern aesthete (à la Frederic Jameson) and simply takes out from her purse a white handkerchief to pass to Ramón, who wipes away his tears. The ranchera ruptures cinematic continuity for a minute. This rupture is not necessarily violent, but it serves to highlight that what is being talked about in the film is not simply a farce.

Hermosillo allows a form of authenticity to appear in order to express the very real drama that underlies the apparent normality of the situation. The song functions as a commentary, but it also allows for what is repressed to come to the surface. That it is controlled, and to a certain extent normatized, by Hermosillo (contained within a melodramatic scene that immediately switches back to the comedic farce of the film) expresses the limits of the commentary. There is no need to return to the drama sung in the ranchera—its appearance in this scene is a sufficient reminder of the interactions of past, present, and future. The situation serves to underscore the disruptive nature of the gay romance, but also the way these gay characters remotivate the category of sentimentality—one quality that Doña Herlinda does not seem to possess.

María Novaro's *Danzón* is paradigmatic for the way it articulates a living past within the uncertainties of the present. In this film, Julia's search for Carmelo is aided by a transvestite who lives in Veracruz—almost a postcard quotation from a 1950s Agustín Lara song as rendered by Toña la Negra. But the transvestite here is not just another element in Novaro's search for a new space. Nostalgia—for a particular order, for the universe of the danzón—reconfigures the characters in the film, even if nostalgia never obliterates the fact that they want to live within the safety of an order regulated by *them*, and not necessarily by a return to heterosexual male dominance. The movie implies that this past as present, and as possible future, will not silence women, will not deny the presence of gay men.

It is obvious that the recuperation of the boleros (or the affective space of the ranchera) that is announced in these two films arises from a reappropriation of the public sphere in Latin America. But these films also show that desire was always more than just aesthetics; it was always the desire for participation and for pleasure. This pleasure includes the appearance of those who belong to the bolero archive: the succinct elegance of Tito Rodríguez, the allure of Carmen Delia Dipiní, the perturbed desire of Bola de Nieve, and a pantheon that certainly includes, and is not limited to, the bolero as a form, but rather to a time and a space: Chavela Vargas, Toña la Negra, the self-conscious (almost ridiculous) sublime of Agustín Lara, the portly elegance of Lucho Gatica, the epidermic *frisson* of the composer Lolita de la Colina, and the melancholic, bohemian moods of Silvia Rexach. This pantheon is crowned, of course, by La Lupe, the queen of them all, with her renditions of Tite Curet Alonso's "La tirana" and "Puro teatro."

These artists mobilized different audiences that understood the code in which they spoke. They joined these audiences by using their own bodies and voices as zones of contact. Lucho Gatica always played the sentimental, suave, elegant gentleman of the night. His hair was always overladen with brilliantine to the point where the very blackness of his hair would reflect the lights of the cabaret. His voice was always compared to a silky surface—it was not falsetto, but it was almost feminine in its command of the high registers. There was no doubt as to Gatica's masculinity, but it was clear that the performance of his masculinity was contingent on the almost feminine delicacy of his voice. In his own time and place, Gatica could interpellate the romantic men in his audience, the yearning females, as well as all the homosexuals who could tap into that dissonant performance of body and voice. By himself, this "Gentleman of Song" was a border crosser, his very figure symbolizing the constant reshifting of those limits between voice and maleness.

In the context of the early 1990s, previously invisible members of that imagined community that was the audience for the bolero could come to the surface. They wanted to recuperate the time that is gone but also to silently critique it for the absences contained in it. Bolero permitted some kind of tragedy, represented as an echo of the past, to fissure the postmodern canvas, or to rescue and remotivate a lost and forgotten tradition. The site where the whole notion of border was played out was now queer.

The use of the genre by gay men exposes the very marginalization given within borders staked out by society. Boleros allow gay men to deploy and suspend the borders implicit in the genre, and to remotivate them according to their own wishes and desires. By mimicking the constitution of the borders, by erecting them again and again, gay men reveal that the only possible essentialism lies precisely in the hybrid arbitrariness of the border. By placing themselves on the border, they refuse marginalization.

Because this recuperation has to be seen in terms of positionality, a certain kind of indirection is always at play, for in rescuing a voice, in taking over and subverting a space, the bolero will manipulate the very spaces that it puts under control. When Almodóvar uses Los Panchos and Bola de Nieve in *Law of Desire*, or La Lupe in *Women on the Verge of a Nervous Breakdown* this use implies, at least for certain Latino gay men, a kind of *validation* not given within the national space itself, as a quoted gesture of recognition sought after, delayed, displaced. The queer will use the borders employed by the bolero in order to jump out and appeal to other imagined communities for recognition.

Because the bolero involves some sort of inviolate space circled over and delimited by culture, performance, and gender, the essentialist gesture implied by camp turns into a performance of something else altogether. And in the context of a Latin America pursued and marginalized by its own sense of tenuous border, this act acquires a decidedly defiant mode, for the queer will not hesitate to manipulate the border, to attempt to be recognized by another space beyond the national, when the national does not offer the validation that queer people seek. In other words, the queer in the bolero house of essentialism will allow the house to collapse in order to gain the voice that is denied, and this position is predicated on the sadness that the bolero itself will perform. No heroics can be epically narrated at this point, but a dramatic sense of betrayal. Who is being betrayed? Family, culture, the imagined community of the nation? Logic would seem to dictate that the emergence of a suppressed group would create new forms of expression, a new aesthetics not necessarily conditioned by the catastrophes of the past. But the bolero implies a paradoxical desire to make the catastrophe whole once again. Only in manipulating this border may queers point out the tenuous construction under which we labor.

Puro Teatro

A final coda: La Lupe was having a nervous fit all the time. She wailed and pinched herself and pointed (to those in the know) to the needle marks on her arms. Anything that got in the way she just flung out at the audience: rings and earrings, bracelets and charms, fake eyelashes and wigs, and above all those high-heeled shoes. She had the best rendition of "Fever" in any language (she did it in both Spanish and English), and she was the biggest thing ever to happen to bolero, but also to pachanga and watusi and boogaloo. La Lupe was a phenomenon. Her fans were legion. Her piercing wails were a kind of existential flag.

She was a diva, but then again we like our divas taboo. To talk about La Lupe back in the 1960s was to code the housing projects and the knives without calling them by their names. It was a class thing—self-consciously so. It was all about the catfights before the bar was about to close. And it was about the men who cheated and expected dinner on the table after drinking out on Friday nights. The woman was no good for the collapsing middle class when she came out on TV. "She's just a low-class whore," they said. Some of this came out in the album covers. La Lupe could be defiant as the Queen of Latin Soul and pose in a Barbarella-like outfit made of a fabric that looks like tin foil. She could be dressed as a mysterious gypsy, as on the cover of *La Lupe's Era*, where she is bedecked in jewels, sitting on the floor holding a card, the Queen of Cups. In the first albums she was all exuberance: her tight blue

La Lupe record covers.

dress and all that sexy flesh next to Mongo Santamaría. As the sixties progressed her gaze was more defiant, more complex. In *Two Sides of La Lupe* the dialectical modes are fully fleshed out. She sits on the same chair but in two different poses and two different dresses. To the left, the impish singer of the boogaloo looks off to the side with a grin. It is not an innocent smile, though; she looks already high on something, or in some other space where sadness can be registered in those fake eyelashes and the enormous quantities of mascara. The right side of the cover is the bolero pose. Here, the back of the chair faces the viewer, and La Lupe uses it as a shield for the sexy vulnerability of sadness. Throughout her career, it was hard to shield oneself from her voice and her presence. La Lupe destroyed the walls that people put around their lives: the redlight bars with their rhinestone decorations, the one drink too many. There she was, venting her rage over the violins of an orchestra that couldn't tame her, with a sweeping gesture of defiance to the man who's left her. "According to your point of view," she said in one of her trademark songs, "I am the evil one."

Lupe Victoria Yoli, who later became known as La Lupe, and then later as La Yiyiyi because she screamed so much, was born in Cuba—but her origins are as hazy and confused as a rundown bar. It seems she was a schoolteacher before she started singing, and won a contest by imitating Olga Guillot. But La Lupe was out to create something different from Olga—she wanted to embody and inhabit the space of anger, longing, and desperation in song. She bit herself. She spoke foul language in those smoky Havana bars back in the lowlife days of the fifties and then in radio and on TV. She was a hit and she did whatever she wanted to do. She was part of a dream that was purely a dream of desire, because it could so easily turn into a nightmare.

As a dream, she expressed a time and a place: the late fifties and early sixties, that time when, as Guillermo Cabrera Infante said, all of Cuba wanted to do precisely what La Lupe was doing at that point: scream, cry, pinch, bite, take off the shoes, curse, do whatever, just break the tension of the old dictatorship and blow it out of existence. She sang "Tengo el diablo en el cuerpo" (I've got the devil in my body) and the vibrato in her voice barely controlled the devil within.

After 1959 she went to Mexico and then to New York. She was rediscovered by Mongo Santamaría and sang with Tito Puente. She tried to sing in English during the sixties as the Queen of Soul and recorded a version of "Yesterday" that is all her own—it is a goulash born out of a food processor of redemptive tears. Her version of "Unchained Melody" is a classic, and like everybody else in her time, she also recorded "My Life"—in Spanish and English, but ultimately in the kind of esperanto that was La Lupe's own: "This is my life and I don't give a damn for lost emotion." She sang this not in the plaintive Sinatra mode, but shouted out in the middle of the plaza for everyone to hear.

Her first husband tried to "discipline" her voice by forcing her to sing in one of those sugarcoated trios that she could never fit into. He said he left her for another singer who didn't feel the need to take her shoes off while she belted out a song. She did salsa and boogaloo but it didn't get her far, so she crossed over as the Queen of Soul. She smacked of anger and retribution. In one of her songs she says Tito Puente kicked her out of his band: "He kicked me out, kicked me out, Tito Puente kicked me out," she screamed. They all kicked her out, but it seems that what made her life into a nightmare was all those uppers and downers in a life that was, even back then, already lost to rumor. Her voice came out like tin foil, like shattered glass, like nails scratching on a blackboard. Some say it was drugs, though she denied it was drugs.

Her husband fell ill and she lost her life savings paying *santeros* and medical bills. And then, when he was cured, he left her.

Then one day, while putting up some curtains in her house, she fell and ended up in a wheelchair. They say she lost her house and had to sell everything she had. Another version (they may all be true) says her house went up in flames. And then La Lupe moved with her kids to a rundown hotel, and then to a New York City shelter.

It was at that point that the Queen of Soul turned to the only thing that could give her life some meaning: she walked again, she became a born-again

Christian, and spent the rest of her life proclaiming her love for Jesus. The songs she recorded after that were all religious hymns—or popular Latin American songs with the lyrics changed in order to proclaim her faith in redemption. She died in the faith, of a heart attack, in Lincoln Hospital in the Bronx in 1992. When the news came out, we all remembered how much we had missed her.

For many, La Lupe owes her comeback after death to Pedro Almodóvar, who gave the final coda to his *Women on the Verge of a Nervous Breakdown* to her trademark song "Puro teatro" (Pure theater). Almodóvar had it right: if you want to talk about how Latino queers like their divas controlling their nervous breakdowns while screaming that they're losing control, then La Lupe is the one. She was seen and heard in the houses of Latino queens who knew their divas, the ones who have hunted out her old gems in the forgotten barrios where old radio and TV stars live in a daze of memory and cheap bars and lost illusions.

There is ultimate sadness in La Lupe's version of "Yesterday." But she refried that song and turned it into the crying anthem of a Lady Macbeth with sunglasses, a silk turban, and a knife in her right hand. Her rendition speaks of a certain Caribbean *ananké*: it is all about migration from the past into a future that is faced with resignation. And she sings it with the kind of shattered voice given only to those who can possess no voice: in English, with a white handkerchief in her left hand to wipe eyeliner tears from her heavily made up cheeks.

La Lupe is the figure that contemplates the catastrophes of the past as the simulacra of a cabaret. The past is but an endless series of destroyed baccarat crystal piling up on satin sheets and lamé curtains, and the storm is a cheap perfume that blows from paradise, gets caught in her turban, and threatens to reveal her tousled, unmade hair. She is propelled "into the future" to which her back is turned, while the catastrophe of the cabaret keeps piling on, as she sings in an absolutely incomprehensible language, for another hand to rescue what the previous hand forsook.

And every time this angel of history tries to pick up the pieces from the cabaret, she allows us to understand that the curtains are always already ripped, but that the storm of progress may demand that we rip them once again. And if we did not have this figure to pick up the pieces, the storm would keep on blowing from paradise, and the angel would never be able to look back to the past or to the future, but always to the present. For the past that is related here seems to have been, and may be, always already retold.

7 Latino Dolls

Toy Stores

Celebrities are dolls animated by invisible sets of strings. Celebrity culture is always about size: the bigger-than-life mansion with the custom-made swimming pool, the oversized poster, the immense ad on Times Square, Antonio Sabato Jr.'s abs covering one side of a bus. The multiplex recasts Hollywood bygone dreams and makes New Age Gullivers of us all: the huge screens and the laid-back seats, the special effects and the movie ads. But when a doll takes on the franchised look of a celebrity, we are back in the land of Lilliput, with the sense of proportion inverted. The huge billboards turn out to be no bigger than your hand, the immense movie star palazzos are actually no taller than your waist, and we all become Alices playing with miniature teacups. That is why one of the best and most controversial films of recent times is Todd Haynes's *Superstar: The Karen Carpenter Story*. The dislocational universe of the dolls served Haynes as commentary on issues ranging from the star system to body worship, with bubble-gum songs as counterpoint to the very tragic story that needed to be told. The dolls were embodied abstractions—the Barbies had different faces and shapes but the Kens were all alike. One always plays with ideas when dolls are involved. The important thing to keep in mind is that the plaything is always the expression of play, but play itself may or may not depend on the plaything.

Todd Haynes could not have foreseen the gay toy store as the latest consumer fetish to hit the contemporary urban, mostly male, gay market. Gay toy stores can be found in almost every major U.S. metropolis these days, and one can also see them in major foreign cities, such as Paris, London, and Madrid, generally as a sign that gay consumers have finally occupied their place within the balkanized capitalist market, that the same hunger for spandex consumes the social fabric. The toy stores are generally made from the same mold: they are sleek, and their merchandise is uniformly vanilla. They seek to distinguish themselves from their raunchier variants, their poorer cousins that live next to them but toward which the gay toy store stands as if in a space of denial. Those poor relatives are of course the sex toy stores, which are not necessarily frequented solely by gay men or lesbians, but also by straight couples, and which not only sell sex toys but may also have one or a number of video booths for private consumption of doses of healthy pornography—straight, bi, or nonstraight.

The gay toy stores are different, and not only because they don't sell toys manufactured to add spice to a life of sin, but also because of their ambivalence toward the category they have defined as sin. This is a result of the gender-specific roles they are meant to assume. We associate gay toy stores mainly with white gay men. This is not only because the contemporary White Gay Male is the consumer par excellence—with the disposable income and sense of privilege and entitlement given to him since the whitewashing of Stonewall as a major event in White Gay Male History. It is also because the penchant for the trappings of overgrown childhood beckon the sense of besieged victimhood and Pride Appeal that are inherent to white gay males as a consumer category. The whole nostalgia for childhood doesn't seem to strike a lesbian chord in the same way that gay male Internet chatrooms are full of thirty-five-year-old "boys." The lesbian "rriot girrls" are more akin to the gay men of color's spelling of "boyz" than the white gay male normative use of the term.

The homosexual universe that the gender-specific gay toy store presents has the sleekness of smoked mirrors, plastic, and black-framed posters of winter scenes, carousing boys bathing in cascades, overblown magnolias, or tinted glass. It is not a question of reflection or narcissism in the broader sense of the term—there are few mirrors in the gay toy store but plenty of shiny surfaces. Consumers need only look at themselves with their own inner eye when they shop, because the merchandise they consume will reflect their gay selves better than any mirror. Where there are mirrors, these are the little pocket trinkets: the pearly drops that seem to fall from a lamp, as if they were tears that every gay man, on some Saturday night or another, has shed for a missed love. Or they are compact mirrors, fragments of reflections on glass, and they are not meant to assault the senses but to enjoin themselves to the bland consumerism that seems to permeate the site. The musical selections are soothing without lapsing into a New Age kind of spirituality. Some Holly Near perhaps (always for "gender parity") or Michael Callen. And there are tons of candles and enticing fragrances.

The toy store has its own genealogy; it came into being as a result of events, social discourses, and economic conditions. The gay and lesbian movement was born in the streets, in Stonewall, in the drag queens' and gay people of color's protest against police censorship, but it became—particularly in the seventies and eighties—a product of new reconfigurations of capital. It is unclear to me at this point whether bars created neighborhoods or if it was the other way around, but at some point in the 1970s the neighborhoods and the bars created bookstores and newspapers, and bookstores became places where the like-minded congregated and where political action could allow all the other disparate fragments to coalesce. In the 1980s and particularly the 1990s, gay politics changed as a result of the devastations of AIDS. With the growth of national gay and lesbian organizations, along with the relative manageability of the disease for certain sectors of mostly white, educated, middle-class gay men, the specifically gay commercial venues such as the bookstore lost much of their political import, to be replaced by the more openly commodified "lifestyle" commercial enterprise that maintained its links to the gay community, albeit with a "different" political language. The consumer base became fragmented, at some points it segregated into distinct parts of the urban landscape, and the center of the community moved in many cases from the bookstore to the café, and then to the specialty store, which sold products for its niche audience.

To pursue the cultural significance of the toy store, you need only look at what's available in order to refashion the collective histories of certain members of this tribe. It is a mixture of campiness and melancholia, historical markers and evanescence. There are picture frames for the loved ones—the sadly deceased and deeply missed, the present love interest, or the circuit of ex-lovers from which "we" derive a sense of gay kinship. There are bigger frames, but these are destined solely for the biological family, of course. Generally, close to the salesperson there are displays with the fancy stuff: rings for the commitment ceremony, elaborate rainbow rings for a chest necklace, rainbow cufflinks in eighteen-karat gold, and different studs for the varied piercings that may be done at another store, the one that also may function as a tattoo parlor. And then there are stacks of what can only be called tchotchkes. Keychains, bumper stickers, computer stickers or mousepads, writing blocks, pens—all of these with multiple, repeated, multilayered rainbow flags, or even leather flags, with their blue and black stripes and the red heart on a black upper-left-hand square.

There are only two natural fabrics allowed in the store: paper and cotton. The first is for the postcard bins, and the second is for the T-shirts or tank tops prominently displayed, undoubtedly the merchandise with the fastest turnover. The postcards run the gamut from the discreetly raunchy to the affably romantic, from the hunk who appears in a three-tiered card that unfolds to reveal the full-blown nude, to the summer sunsets and frosty landscapes that can be found in any card store. The T-shirts are equally varied, except that their version of "raunchiness" involves emblems that appeal to a certain history of gay male tartness: "I can't even march straight" or "I am not gay but my boyfriend is." The humor involved is snappy, but it is a wholesome kind of snappiness. It is a product of the neutralization of the drag queen, a product of her change in status from object of derision to princess in the costume ball. The laughter the T-shirts produce is a quick jab meant as a response to your gaze at the other gay man's perfectly defined chest.

The toy stores are the perfect breeding and mating grounds for the new millennium gay and lesbian. They are all about families and sappy songs. They are wonderfully communitarian in their sponsorship of the Gay Games or the AIDS ride. They relish in the gay version of the universe, which always means proving that you are gay enough to wear that T-shirt, and they provide the comfortable, homogeneous environment where you can buy those edible undies without lapsing back into the bad old times of furtive Times Square shopping, when homosexuals still had not turned into Gays, and then into Proud Gays who agreed with the ransacking of Times Square. And of course they have been crowned, in the evolutionary scale, by the picture-postcard bland normality promised by the 1999 Human Rights Campaign national dinner, titled "Honoring Our Families" with special guest stars Betty DeGeneres, Michael Feinstein, Nathan Lane, and Martina Navratilova, and sponsored by Shell (its Nigerian operations *must* be gay-friendly), American Airlines, IBM, Viacom, and Subaru ("The Beauty of All-Wheel Drive"). In fact, in anticipation of the Millennium March for Equality in Washington, D.C., in April 2000, the HRC opened its own toy store in the heart of the gay and lesbian Dupont Circle neighborhood, while the gay bars in the area are subject to stricter controls by the district. The HRC of course, has nothing to say in terms of the increasingly upscale corporate blandness that changes the area forever.

Toys

The gay male toy store was just another niche consumer venture until the arrival of the central figure in its pantheon—the figure that gave the toy store its *raison d'être* and defined it as something more than just a place that catered to fashionably cloned middle-brow gay apartment interiors. I am referring, of course, to the Billy doll, the perfectly correct, anatomically proper emblem of white gay manhood, and "his boyfriend" Carlos, another perfect anatomically correct (read: uncircumcised) doll.

Billy and Carlos made their entrance into the gay universe in the early 1990s. Billy was conceived by Jim McKitterick in 1992, and his first public appearance was at an AIDS benefit in London in November 1994.[1] This is referred to in the Billyworld Web site as Billy's first "coming out" party. By 1997 the manufacturing company Totem International was created, and the toy was launched at the New York International Gift Fair. First there was Billy—a lonely and isolated hunk of a man who found immediate acceptance among white gay male consumers of a "certain" socioeconomic class (the doll costs about fifty dollars). But Billy's lonely and presumably unsatisfied urban bachelorhood was too much to bear for some of his consumers, and they in turn asked Totem, the parent company, to give Billy a boyfriend. This boyfriend (and of course there is marketing genius here) could not be white. He had to be another fetish object for white gay male consumption. Since black would have been perhaps too risqué for the intended audience, and too full of connotations beyond the purview of the marketing itself, Totem opted for a Puerto Rican doll.

And this is how Carlos was born. Not really out of Billy's rib but out of some designer's brain. In the narrative created for the dolls, Billy is a native of Amsterdam. He met Carlos at one of Billy's "coming out parties" in Miami in 1997. The two realized that they both lived in New York, they exchanged phone numbers, and got together after that. Their love affair bloomed, and Billy and Carlos are now totally dedicated to each other. They live in separate apartments in New York, where Carlos has a schedule as hectic as Billy's.

A native of Puerto Rico, Carlos is described as an "up-and-coming fine artist" who paints and organizes gallery shows while also working for Totem International as a full-time Billy lover. This implies conveying a positive image of gayness, a positive image of Puerto Ricans, and a positive image of Latino manhood. His range of outfits is as varied as Billy's. There is Vacation Carlos (they spent Christmas in Puerto Rico and New Year's Eve in Amsterdam), New York Carlos, Fireman Carlos, and of course Cha-Cha Carlos ("complete with a hat adorned with the most exotic fruits and as a finishing touch she is drenched in fabulous bangles, baubles and beads"). Of course, there are problems in the relationship. One of them is the fact that Billy cannot emigrate to the United States to be permanently with Carlos, whereas Carlos could legally marry Billy in Amsterdam and maintain the same rights as any straight married couple. And Billy is scandalized by the fact that in the United States, their relationship can't enjoy the simple advantages of marriage, like being able to file joint tax returns and share insurance and benefits.

From the point of view of the company, Carlos allowed Totem to avoid the charge of a bland, uniformly boring sex-life-during-commercial-breaks while making perfectly clear, at least by implication, that Billy was an urban gay prowler who, within "certain" bounds, took "certain" kinds of risks in having a "different" taste in candy. The difference could be clearly marked in terms of ethnicity, but it still retained the sense of comfortable sameness that urban, majoritarian gay life supposedly needs in order to advance in its quest for equal rights for the "family." These equal rights, of course, are based on the tensions already built in to the Billy-Carlos binomial coupling. This is not only a result of the fact that Billy's whiteness exists in a space all by itself, but also a result of markers that scream out of these icons' bodies. First, in terms of the narrative construct, the one who had a tattoo proclaiming his love for Billy was Carlos until, more recently, both of them got tattoos proclaiming their love for each other. Billy still enjoys the broader wardrobe choices—Sailor Billy, Brunette Billy (he got tired of being blond), Master Billy, Cowboy Billy, and a limited-edition, one-hundred-dollar version of Billy with a Wall Street outfit. Carlos has a more restricted wardrobe range: he has the traditional gym outfit, but also a policeman uniform, and the obligatory jeans and tank top look.

Sure enough, Carlos is the prime example of budding Latino manhood.

And I use "budding" advisedly: Carlos is always the one trying to assimilate into Billy's fashionable lifestyle. He mimics Billy's costume but he can also gain a measure of control by putting out his own fetishized body as power, as a kind of riposte to Billy's clean-shaven ability to pass in settings as varied as the gym or Wall Street. Carlos, on the other hand, is more of the beauty slave: one presumes he needs to shave his perfectly rounded goatee in order not to look gruff, just as he has to clip his chest hair and perhaps undergo bothersome electrolysis sessions just so he can always be well presented—the sort of "Hispanic" guy you can take to your family. As a matter of fact, Carlos is the sort of "Hispanic" who may even give you a certain degree of status in the white spaces where the smoked mirrors and the candles beckon an intimate soiree with gourmet finger food, where talk veers from the circuit parties attended to the cute guys in the latest gay teen Hollywood romances.

It has been clear for some time that Billy and Carlos's appearance in the stratosphere of gay male lifestyle came at just the right time for queer cultural critics to turn that plastic into pulp, and then expose the pair for what it is and for what it pretends to be. In the magazine *ñ*, Eduardo Contreras rightly bemoans how Billy-Carlos reaffirmed the "color-crazed fascination" of white gay men at a point when anti-Latino sentiment in the United States was at an all-time high, and insists that "[i]f the dolls serve to promote gay rights, safe sex, and awareness about AIDS, shouldn't they also promote immigrant rights, equal access to education, and employment opportunities?"[2] Contreras exposes the controlled environment created by the ultimately fallacious combination of consumer culture with an activist or social agenda. The marriage of the market and social responsibility produces a universe limited in its scope, where the choices are always already made. This, of course, has been taken into account by the parent company, for now Billy, as we have seen, takes up broader causes like immigrant rights as these concern gay marriage.

The questions provoked by these dolls are broader than the act of attaching political meanings to a fantasy world. This must have been anticipated by the capitalist venture that produced them, and it is possible they decided the company could take the objections of certain radical members of the community precisely because the blatant merchandising of the fantasy precluded a number of embittered gay or lesbian talking heads from spoiling the show. It is also clear that the inclusion of Carlos as a boy toy entails at least a tacit recognition of the importance of the Latino presence in the United States, if not as a market (the steep doll price falls outside the spending allowance of many Latinos), then as objects of desire not fraught with the complicated histories that black and white relations have had in the United States.[3] But the question of the Billy-Carlos romance goes beyond all these issues. The fantasy involved here is a fetish but it is also more than that. To understand what *that* is, one has to distinguish between two different but very related issues here: the appearance of the dolls themselves and the interethnic pairing with a Latino.

Social history is the space where the concrete acquires meaning. The meaning involved in this case does not come from the object itself, but rather from the subject. A toy is not simply a toy, thrust out into the world, without any relation whatsoever to society in terms of its production, merchandising, or dissemination. The fantasy of toys in the traditional sense, as Walter Benjamin recalls, is not simply the act of dwelling in fantasy. Toys are "a site of conflict, less of the child with the adult, than of the adult with the child."[4] The psychology of the toy need not force us to look into the mind of a child. Children are not autonomous beings, and neither are the toys they play with. For Benjamin, toys represent "a silent signifying dialogue between them and their nation."[5] In this sense, as he clarifies, the more the toy imitates something in particular, the less useful it is, for imitation has no role in living play. It is the playing that imitates, not the plaything, as Benjamin recalls.[6]

Billy and Carlos are not meant as playthings in the traditional sense of the term. Nor are they aimed at children. In fact, Totem International explicitly warns that "Billy is not suitable for persons under the age of 21 years." As playthings, they imitate far too closely the modes of the urban gay male tribe. They leave nothing to the imagination—on the contrary, they seem to inhabit a world of repetition. Billy and Carlos talk about activist battles and parties—parties sponsored by major gay organizations and hosted by Paul Smith or Ingrid Casares. They even spawn creative artistic interventions, such as the one devised by the British artist Nigel Grimmer, who portrayed a battered and bruised Billy in a window installation in London, as a comment on gay bashing. As the artist explained, "Images like this reflect the real experiences that gays have, as distinct from images often presented about gay life."[7] The activist universe constructed around these dolls appears precisely at the point at which the future of white gay male activism seems to be foreclosed, and the battles that consumed the community in the past seem to have shifted without any clear center to supplant them. For the dolls' creator, Jim McKitterick, "Billy can be a political tool. . . . He can say a lot of things that people can't." It is not as if the battles have been won or lost—AIDS is still with us, civil rights have been only partially won, and there is still rampant homophobia in society at large—but it seems that the battles need to be remotivated in a different—perhaps even more fashionable—way for a segment of majoritarian gay and lesbian communities. The gay and lesbian community, so the narrative goes, has started to look like most of America: it is divided in terms of ethnicity, gender, and class. And the politics of the community is as fractured as the battles themselves: the struggle for equal rights in the military pits a left against a right wing of the gay-lesbian movement; so do the questions of sex, monogamy, marriage, and assimilation.

It would be too easy to say that it makes sense to merchandise childhood during a moment of cultural ambivalence, just as it would be too facile to explain the appearance of the Billy doll as a desire to return to a less conflicted universe than the one that surrounds those urban gay ghetto denizens. In this context, the question of meaning is not necessarily a question of the dolls themselves but of those who buy them. Of course, both Billy and Carlos come with their added quotient of campiness. There is an element of the ridiculous in the sight of grown men buying and giving each other dolls, and their creator as well as the company recognizes this by infusing the whole narrative found at the Web site with a happy, even campy tone. Those who buy the dolls, on the other hand, are recalling old battles and unhealed scars of all the rage and hostility felt in childhood, a point that is also cited on the Web page. For the dolls' owners, childhood is not necessarily something that is looked back on with affection. They remind the subject of all those dolls that were never given and never received, all those prohibitions that came with the expectations of gender within the territory of childhood. One can find real liberation in the act of having this doll only if its ownership is prefigured by all those prohibitions—not the Barbie or the Ken, but the boring GI Joe or the Hot Wheels.

Still, the Billy doll is not simply part of a desire to "go back," to repeat and recapture childhood. Freud, as well as Benjamin, pointed out that already in childhood repetition is the law that structures play. With the Billy and Carlos dolls the shattering experiences of childhood are now transformed into a habit. The dolls repeat our broken dreams with their own sense of tautology: the perfect relationship that one dreamt about within the space of idealism, two perfect bodies in a close match. If on the one hand, the dolls speak of a childhood not as it was, but as it should have been, they also soften previous traumas and signify the possibility of what could be and is not: Prince Charming, the perfect partner.

There is a sense of overdetermined meaning in these gestures. First, let us remark on the fact that these are not old toys put to new use. It is not a Ken dressed in combat fatigues, and it is not Barbie playing the part of Karen Carpenter. These are new toys, and their newness is marked by the narrative involved, one that gives the toy its raison d'être in a universe totally populated by gay male narratives—the narrative of coming out, the narrative of confessing HIV status, the narrative of the hideous or sweet ex-lovers, and then the queer subjectivity where one constantly asks oneself whether he or she knows or doesn't know that I am. Part of the merchandising coup is precisely having gay men play with the never-ending deployment of that narrative. Because Billy and Carlos are not remotivated in the sense that Bette Davis is refashioned by the drag queen who does her, their "naturalism" is contingent on the fact that they create a story that blurs the distinction between the child and the adult. When you own toys that have a sex life, those toys are meant to recall the sex life that the toys of childhood may or may not have had.

Gayness becomes a question of props, of stories that we share. And one of the stories concerns those lapses into the realm of the almost prohibited that one recounts with a wink. This is where Carlos comes in, that Latino guy endowed with a narrative as clear as his well-defined pecs. Was he ever the guy from the Bronx who hung around Christopher Street as a teen and then hustled his way to the Upper East Side bachelor suite? No, because he is foreign yet not foreign (Puerto Rican; therefore, a U.S. citizen), just as Billy is white yet in this context is "unprivileged" by the fact that he cannot claim citizenship. Was Carlos the product of affirmative action—the sweet and sensitive Latino with perfect grades who then becomes the investment banker? No, because he is an artist and as such, can always claim "raw" talent. The ethnic mark that is immediately branded on Carlos as part of the binomial Billy pair screams out for narrative. More often than not, because of that ethnic mark itself, that narrative is going to be hot.

Carlos is a product of context. It is hard to pinpoint exactly when all those personal ads in gay male publications started explicitly asking for GHM (gay Hispanic men) or GLM (gay Latino men). Some will say that this has always been part of the sex economy, the Latino Fan Club movies have been around for more than a decade, as well as the stroke magazines with the porno Latino gardener hosing down the Brentwood lawn. But something happened at some point in the late 1980s—something that had to do with the niche market for Latino men that produced Latin Inches or that whole uncircumcised penis fetish—this in turn produced the manuals for regaining your absent foreskin and it led straight (no pun intended) out of, or into, one of the periodic "Latin booms." Whatever it was that happened, it produced a different set of personal ads, for example. Now they were either asking not simply for the fetish object, but for the fetish object with class and brains. Now it was not simply the mute bottom or the mute masculine top, but the Latino with a job ready to set up house or go out to candlelit dinners.

That something had to do with a number of factors, among which, in random order, we can name the sheer population explosion of new generations of Latinos; the desire for a little kink and spice; Pedro Almodóvar movies and Antonio Banderas; increased tourism by middle-class, openly gay white men; Kristen Bjorn porno movies; the repackaging of the "natural" body while steroids rule; the "manageability" of AIDS and the search for presumably HIV-negative exotic locales; the dissatisfaction with gay politics; the repeated interventions of the United States in Latin America; the allure of drag queens doing Selena; the Cuban film *Strawberry and Chocolate*; the increasing numbers of Latino middle-class queers; the merchandising of South Beach; and Gloria and Emilio Estefan. All of these have some bearing on the sudden apparition of the Carlos doll—an apparition that is not, in retrospect, as sudden as it seems to be, and it reflects a number of cultural formations within the United States's real or imaginary constructions.

The fantasy of the brute young Latino boys in the Latino Fan Club was always the fantasy of money and sex for the white, somewhat aged, middle-class queens, who enjoy their kink and their spice. But the audience for this changed, since white gay men started liking their foreigners to keep their spice but not look too foreign. And this new market venue, supposedly insisted on by the very gauche and fashionable segments of the urban gay male milieu, could not have come at a more opportune moment, as it barely preceded the Latino explosion of the summer of 1999, spearheaded by none other than the Latino doll himself, Ricky Martin.

Ricky Rules

I would not be surprised if by the time you read this there is a Ricky doll on the market, though this is by no means an attempt to bash Ricky Martin. By the time you read this, he will probably have been bashed already and become another casualty of the white capitalist machine and its periodic ambivalence as to whether it really wants Latinos to share and destabilize the status quo, or whether it just wants Latinos for a short time as a way of remembering that we exist in order to forget about us with equal ease. To be sure, Carlos and Ricky inhabit very different and distinct universes, even though they both assume and play with—Ricky more than Carlos—their status as merchandise and as fetish objects. To put it differently, Carlos can't help but be a doll; Ricky, on the other hand, plays with his status as a presumed doll. His artist shoots are also fashion shoots, a move replicated by the salsa singer Marc Anthony posing in a fashion spread for the *New York Times* at the time when his crossover album was released. But Ricky's poses are meant to look unreal—a calculated aesthetic position meant to place the singer in a cultural space of his own, far, far away from the barrio but also separate from white America. The cover and the booklet to the U.S. CD show Ricky either in meditative trance gestures far removed from the boisterous exuberance of "Livin' La Vida Loca" or in a state of anxious expectation—the face photographed with a burgundy tint as he sits on a car, with lines from a song: "And if I could have one chance to have that / Moment back again / I'd never let it end." The backdrops either speak of stark simplicity as Ricky has a yoga moment or they look like the inside of corporate suites—dark paneled wood.

Ricky's most haunting moment is captured in the cover of the CD, mostly because of the angle of the face and the picture—tilting to the right, the face arrested as if about to say something or reveal something in spite of itself. The brightly scratched, metallic backdrop is where the light shines, a light in relation to which Ricky appears like a satellite that uses borrowed light. The head is not simply tilting to the right but actually moving toward the camera. The cover beckons the consumer to explore the secrets inside; Ricky wants to be explored, but he is not giving himself away. The interaction between the artist and the consumer takes place at this level, in that space between Ricky's desire for reluctant wanting and the unabashed grabbing by the consumer at the CD rack.

The force field that this creates between the singer and the audience reproduces the dynamic felt by the child who plays with the doll—or, in this case, by the adult gay male who buys the narrative product sold as Billy or

Ricky Martin. Cover of *Cristina.* Año 9, No. 8, 1999.

Carlos. It is a form of identification where the object becomes an other while at the same time coding the fact that he may be just like you, or that he is what you may want to be. This purely packaged construction collides with the Ricky pictures on, for example, the cover of *Cristina* magazine, aimed at a female Latina audience. Here Ricky is the sweet boy next door with an open smile, dressed in white, photographed from above as he almost lunges for the camera. He is less the doll and more of the overgrown kid with the sex appeal toned down. In spite of his more open approach to the camera, he is all the more distant. In the piece written for *Cristina*, Ricky is already the star who has crossed over, the one who is enjoying his fifteen minutes of fame out there in the world of the Anglo celebrities and the global market. It is a fluff piece created to push the magazine and sell copy.

Different audiences always read different meanings in the same cultural product. But in the case of Ricky, and also in the case of the Carlos doll, the play involved engages questions of homosexuality and ethnicity in different ways. There is no question as to Carlos's sexual choice—it seems to be a given for the narrative of ethnicity to unfold. His sexuality is taken for granted but not his origins or his class, which become part of a different narrative. The doll needs to make homosexuality safe for the fantasy to take place. This has nothing to do with sexual roles (Carlos may be the "bisexual" top who toys with women every once in a while, or he may be the active bottom to Billy's exercise routine), but it is related to the degree of assimilation that homosexuality allows Carlos to perform. Carlos is absorbed in the universe of circuit parties and designer drugs, he goes to the gym and takes care of his diet.

Ricky, on the other hand, is a more complex action figure. He may beckon your gaze as a gay male, but he also tells you that the gaze stops at the very moment when the issue of culture is addressed. When Maer Roshan from *New York* magazine asks Ricky about his generalized sex appeal, he is at first coy but accepting. He is unsure whether he likes being a sex object, since he insists he is a man at the same time: "I am a person too. A man that has feelings. And at the same time, I want respect from the audience, and in order for me to get respect, I have to have some quality in my music. Not just shake my ass."[8] At that point, the interviewer asks him about his sexuality. The question refers back to Gloria Estefan's *Interview tête-à-tête* with Ricky, where he stated, "What I say about sexuality is, I leave it for my room and lock the door." But the interviewer presses on: "Given the amazing success and the realities of modern media, do you really think you can keep the door locked for much longer?" At that point, Ricky responds with an appeal to the cultural values instilled in his family: "I've done it for fifteen years, and maybe it's going to be different now. But in the end, it's my space, it's my house, and it's not only for me, but also I have a mother, and I have a sister and brothers, and I have a father. And some people want to cause them pain. People are out there just wanting to destroy it."

What Ricky discusses in this context is of course a very real and deeply felt situation, even in spite of the fact that he may have constructed his whole appeal by coding different signs onto the gay male or lesbian audience. Still, his refusal of the coming-out narrative must be engaged on its own terms. Ricky's sexuality may be disturbing for a culture that needs to define it as fast as it can. Ricky may belong to any of the following merchandising categories: the Latin music pop phenomenon, the South Beach gay culture of high couture, or the urban New York and international sound. But the problem seems to be the fact that he belongs to all of these, and he joins them without exactly blending them or turning them into a seamless whole.

Ricky is a difficult doll to play with. The *Advocate*, a national magazine for lesbians and gays, had him on the cover of its July 6, 1999, issue, also in order to cash in on Rickymania. The whole question of Ricky here very obviously engages him as a play doll, with boxed asides titled "Oh Ricky!" where polls answer the question of whether it is such a terrible thing to come out of the closet, and small playful snippets like "Puerto Ricky" (!) or a review of the CD titled "La CD Loca," and then still another poll where readers are asked, "Are you surprised by the willingness of the mainstream media to talk about Ricky Martin's gay-fan appeal?" The contents page blurb on the article reads, "Gays are *muy loco* over pop wonder Ricky Martin, as the media will tell you. What does this gay-friendly spin mean for us—and Martin?" Of course, the *Advocate* piece intends to be a reflection that uses Ricky in order to comment on the state of homosexuality in the mainstream media ("Even lesbians are shaking their 'bon-bons' to the beat") and the media's relative willingness to talk about Ricky's gay appeal. Whether it's an issue or a nonissue, as many of the subjects interviewed for the article seem to insist, they all agree that some sort of reflection may be engaged by noticing how Ricky positions himself in different contexts. If it's not ethnicity, then the reason for the reluctance may lie in

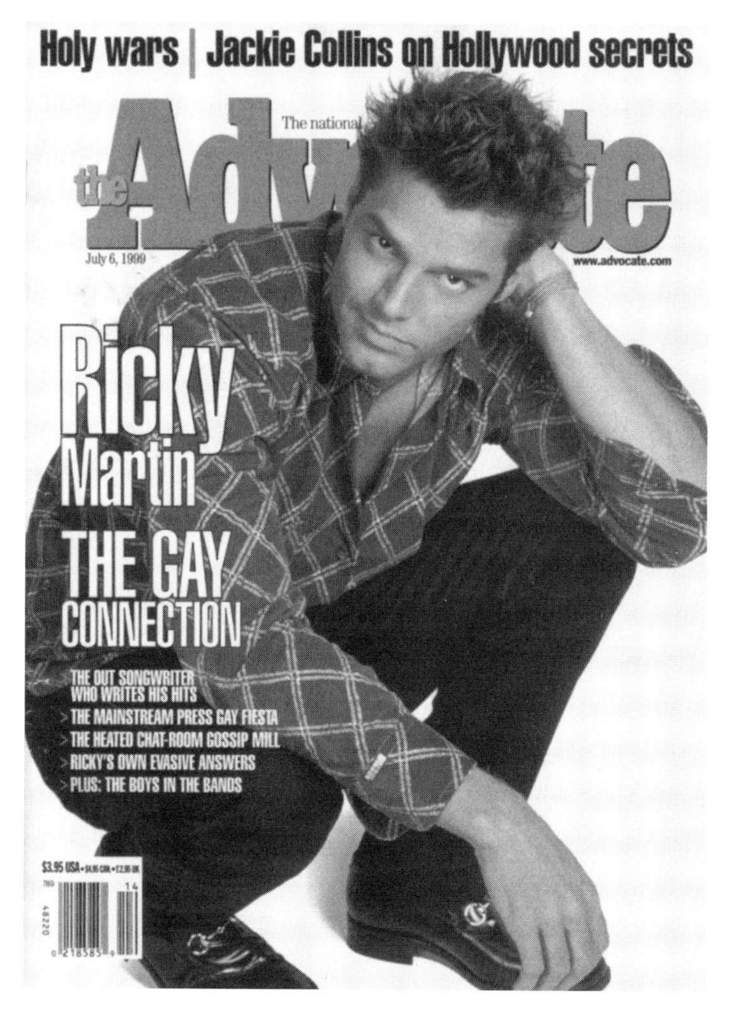

Ricky Martin. Cover of *The Advocate,* July 6, 1999.

other arenas: "Indeed, Martin's Catholic upbringing—he was even an altar boy in his hometown of San Juan, Puerto Rico—alone could explain his reluctance to discuss his personal life" (31).

What all this points out, of course, is not so much anything about the doll itself, but about the children who are playing with the toy. It is not simply a question of pegging onto Ricky a stable narrative so that we may then pursue the games we may want to play. The question here, as Benjamin recalled, concerns the nature of the relationship between the plaything and the play, as well as what both of these say about the links between the child and society. In the repressed and also seemingly "free" context of the United States, it is interesting that Ricky's sexuality as an issue was not allowed to stand out as one more element in a complex stew. One of the reasons for this, I think, had to do with the fact that Ricky looks *white*—that his ethnic appeal for whites is visibly constructed as a source of pride and also as a refusal of ethnic categories. Desi Arnaz could only come out on stage dressed in the *babalu* costume, but Ricky's costume was something different. It had the trappings of high fashion—there were *names* (Armani, Dolce and Gabbana) to back it up. There he was, performing and embodying the Latino craze, while he was also in some way performing whiteness with that supercool funky cat look in the David La Chapelle pictures taken for *Rolling Stone* magazine. The interviewer from *New York* magazine brought up the fact that Ricky looked white. At this point Ricky could not turn demure, coy, or flirtatious. He gave a bland response that nevertheless still managed to say something about the racial system in the United States, about the market itself and its manipulation:

I can't get any more Latin! It's so racist *to say that because you are dark-skinned you cannot make it in America. Whoever wrote that should go to jail or at least get sued. It makes me angry. People forget that there's a long list of artists who have been doing this for so many years, like José Feliciano, like Gloria Estefan. Santana played Woodstock! So this so-called Latin movement isn't new. There are a lot of artists in Latin America who have all the tools to cross over. It will happen. It's just not there yet.*

He was, in a sense, lecturing the interviewer, even if the lecture came out wrong, for I don't think the interviewer would have posed that question to Gloria Estefan, who has marketed entire albums in which she sings in Spanish, but only posed that question to Ricky because he was *Puerto Rican* and because the audience is at a loss to put him into some kind of category from which a conventional narrative may be constructed. After all, Ricky transformed himself into an image of what he wanted to be—Armani, Helmut

Lang, Dolce and Gabbana, South Beach, dyed hair. It is the kind of transnational *latinidad* that Americans never get to see but that is all over the place on Univision, or on CNN en Español, and it's been selling since 1998, when Ricky sang that same song from the Grammys at the closing ceremonies for the World Cup.

Ricky's reticent sexuality ultimately pushes the limits of "progressive" gay and lesbian politics and discourse at this point. Ricky's blend of Leonardo di Caprio and George Michael were elements of a stew that was out there, and he put them together in a smart cut-and-paste move. But a culture that receives the open codes emanating from the Carlos dolls is one that still hungers for approval in spite of the fact that it is able to look back and congratulate itself on the "enormous strides" it has been able to make. Its version of "normality" entails the colonizing gestures that rupture other carefully constructed representations. It demands the narrative of coming out even when it knows itself to be one of the communities interpellated by Ricky's swaying of the hips or choice of designer wear. Addressing the community in an oblique fashion along with other groups that choose to define themselves along ethnic, racial, or class lines is never enough, since for many sexuality should be the primary form of identification even at the risk of colonizing all others. The constant demands for Ricky to "come out," to proclaim his sexuality out in the open, are the clearest examples of how queer subjectivity can become an oppressive category that is always seeking validation to the extent of oppressing other choices and consigning the subtleties of sexual choice and play to a secondary status.

The most-often quoted rationale for outing Ricky and demanding a confession about his sexuality is that his "coming out" will give gays and lesbians—even Latino gays and lesbians—a source of pride in having another visible member of the tribe as spokesperson for the cause. At the same time, the opposite camp argues that Ricky is entitled to his private life and that sexuality is something negotiated between oneself and one's choice of sexual partner. Both positions are of course locked in the same structural dynamics of shame. As a public figure who sways his hips for the audience and uses his body as a means of expression, Ricky is bound to be the object of much speculation. At the same time, to perform the visible act of being turned on by it is no source of shame, regardless of the sexuality of the actor who provokes it. There is of course no need for Ricky to come out as gay in order to queer his persona. Particularly when it is clear that the trade-off for coming out entails further balkanizing the viewing public and losing the intersected communities that may go to his concerts.

Gay and lesbian culture in this way participates in the overall project of gay merchandising—the continuing atomization of an audience that needs to receive its messages in a clear-cut fashion, lest any ambiguity come to disrupt the party and spoil the obsessive penchant for an oppressive reenactment of self-affirmation. It is clear that at this point the culture intends to produce further replicas of the toy store: nonthreatening, nonambiguous, and ultimately sexually sanitized spaces where the subject can see himself or herself in the twisted reflections produced by the need for constant validation. It is one thing to out conservative politicians, morality-in-media junkies, FBI directors, and the like, but it is another thing altogether to push open doors that are open already, or at least sufficiently ajar for those in the know to come in and explore the merchandise.

Ricky may choose to claim his ethnic difference in order to gloss over details of his sexuality, but what he is doing, I think, is keeping alive the different constituencies that watch his performance. In this context, this is a more progressive project than the one presently entertained by the self-proclaimed engineers of the gay audience. To come out at this point, to rupture the diversity of the viewing public, is to participate in a project that, judging from the Carlos doll, may turn out to be a more insidious variant of capitalism than the one already in existence within a globalized economy. In this one, the oppressed become the oppressors, selling artifacts to the oppressed in order to entertain marginalization for the sake of profit. That Ricky chooses not to become the latest Latino doll for the already constituted moneyed gay and lesbian nomenklatura is something I applaud. There is much to be admired in his merchandising himself for the best and the brightest capitalists rather than for the ones who gloss their financial stakes with the received pieties of a noble cause that is not noble, with humanitarian gestures that keep the prison walls intact.

8 Latino Cultures, Imperial Sexualities

What kinds of domination are being imagined as forms of social good; what kinds of utopian desires are being tapped and translated into conservative worldviews; what means are being used to suppress the negative fallout of affirmative culture; what it might take to make linked kinds of knowledge, power and experience no longer seem separate.

—LAUREN BERLANT, *The Queen of America Goes to Washington City*

Global Jam

"Gay Is Global" was the title of the *Village Voice*'s celebration of Stonewall's thirtieth anniversary in 1999. Richard Goldstein introduced it by stating that "[j]ust as feminism has resonated around the world, gay liberation reverberates across wildly different cultures," noting also how many lesbians and gay men still suffer from persecution and discrimination.[1] The celebratory tone in all these pieces—they focused on a transvestite kickboxer in Thailand, the gay scene in Kenya and the Ivory Coast, the transsexual openness of the Israeli singer Dana International, the growing recognition of same-sex couples in South Africa, Canada, and Spain—speaks for the global reach of a movement that started in New York and has been exported to the world as a source of pride in identity. This celebration, however, is not without its cautionary notes. Martin Foreman's African sources contradict the simple celebration of identity: in the case of women, "some Africans warn against imposing a Western, sexual interpretation on what they argue is a series of social rather than sexual constructs." Charles Phiri, the chairperson of the Zambian Lesbian, Gay and Transgendered Persons Association (LEGATRA) denies any

Western influence in his organization. "'We are not white,' he says, 'We are indigenous Zambians, fighting without funds and without support for our right.'" Foreman closes his article with an almost nostalgic and ambivalent conclusion: "More and more African men will become 'gay,' with their sisters taking a longer, more difficult path to achieve acceptance as lesbians. Much will be gained—and much tradition lost."[2]

Foreman's cautionary note is echoed in the most unlikely place: New York. In Alisa Solomon's chronicle of the Queens Pride Festival in New York City she quotes Saeed Rahman, who gives a nuanced version of the global emergence of gay politics. This Pakistani native realized that "winning his asylum claim in 1997 meant demonizing his home," for he was forced to paint a picture of Pakistan as "a primitive place" while insisting, for the judges, that America was a wonderful country.[3] Solomon complicates the vision of what it means at this point to be an ethnic and queer minority, and she closes her piece with another disturbing source of conflict between the majoritarian white lesbian and gay movement and people of color: Caribbean Pride is openly defying white gay groups' intention to boycott some Caribbean countries because of their refusal to allow gay cruises to dock in their ports. "As immigrant groups continue to hold mainstream gay organizations accountable," Solomon explains, "they stand to change queer politics in New York as surely as immigrants have changed city politics in general."[4] Solomon names SALGA (Southeast Asian Lesbian and Gay Association) as one such organization, one that not only helps its immigrant members cope with the bureaucratic hassles of immigration, but has also developed what she calls a "sophisticated critique of mainstream gay culture."

Stonewall celebrates the emergence of the modern lesbian and gay movement, but the debate within the movement concerns whether the celebration is the starting point for a gradual assimilation of difference within society or a celebration of difference itself. These issues are all the more pertinent when we consider Stonewall from "the other side," when it becomes just one more piece of American culture exported for consumption, when lesbian and gay visibility collaborates in the imperialist project of making the world "just like us." From a left, or even radical, perspective, it is important for some of the *Voice* writers not to turn the social gains of the last thirty years into another exemplary argument for the essential superiority of U.S. democracy, since it has also been clear—in the past thirty years—that such arguments have global repercussions.

Two things stand out from the *Voice* issue: the future of gay and lesbian politics is not at this point simply a parochial concern limited to New York, the United States, and Western Europe, and the question of sexuality is and should be addressed along with ethnic and cultural issues. But the question of how to engage sexuality along with ethnicity and culture is difficult at a time when the major gay and lesbian organizations take increasingly conservative positions within a politics validated by money and increasing access to mainstream spheres of influence. One hopes that the "global" focus disrupts the normative U.S. view of gay and lesbian sexuality. It is more likely, however, that any possible disruption will be marginalized as fringe politics, while the "movement" furthers its collaboration with the U.S. government and a moneyed elite.

Bean Soup

Sometimes categories (sexual and ethnic) deserve to bleed onto each other like an inkspot that leaves a messy residue from one scrap of paper onto another. The stain, the spot that disseminates, is more interesting than the clear configuration of bounded spaces. The spaces themselves do not trace the boundaries from one thought to another, but rather allow some of us to see continuities where others see divisions.

In Frances Negrón's 1994 film *Brincando el charco: Portrait of a Puerto Rican* the main character (played by Negrón) struggles with the news of her father's death in her native Puerto Rico and negotiates her estrangement from family, land, and culture. Throughout the film, Claudia's decision on whether to go to her father's funeral is connected to questions relating to Puerto Rican culture on the island and on the mainland and, more broadly, to the different spaces where the politics of identity seems to collapse under the weight of multiple identifications. The film uses autobiography as a way of commenting on issues beyond the strictly personal, but it also reconfigures the meaning of the personal to include issues that are traditionally understood as social. Negrón piles up notions of identity and identification for the viewer to explore the relations between them. At what level does race communicate with lesbianism? And at what point can we relate lesbianism with Latino culture? There is a very open attempt to let these categories spread out from the space where they tend to be localized. There is also, in Negrón's project, a very clear desire not to make these categories "safe" in any way but to rescue their liberatory potentials.

In *Brincando el charco,* the body has multiple points of contact, but these do not turn it into the site where the American "melting pot" is reproduced. There is constant tension between the different zones that the body may inhabit, but its possible hybridity is not immediately the cause for celebration, for everything conspires to normatize and tame the disruptions produced by different vectors on one self. After watching a videotape of a Puerto Rican gay and lesbian parade, and wondering to what extent sexual liberation is contained within the colonial discourse that also sustains its possibility, Claudia can be seen combining different colored beans in a blender, while the film cuts to a list of dates of (mostly U.S.) imperial actions that have taken place throughout the world. The fiction of the melting pot is addressed as one of the "formidable fictions" that America has produced for itself, while the invasive actions that have sustained that myth are also clearly named. At the point in which the red and white beans have been pureed in the blender, Claudia's voice-over remarks, "I can't afford any purity," by which she also means that she cannot afford to flatten out complexity for the sake of comfort.

Like Negrón's *Brincando el charco,* the most interesting Latino American works do not remain in the localized space of an isolated identity world, but mobilize these identities. Manuel Puig put politics and sexuality in the same prison cell in *The Kiss of the Spider Woman* and addressed the question of rev-

Frances Negrón and blender. Videocapture from *Brincando el Charco,* directed by Frances Negrón, 1994.

olutionary politics by forced juxtaposition, at a time when a Latin American model for a revolutionary society would have wanted to eliminate gays from its utopian future. Pedro Almodóvar does not make "gay" films, but in *The Law of Desire* he cut across objects of affection in such a mode that the movie proclaimed its own truths as essential laws: desire and gender.[5] The question for these artists is not to present subjects negotiating a dialectical argument, but to notice the way the dialectic allows for confusion, for gray zones that in turn will open other spaces. None of these artists claim that Latinos and Anglo Americans differ in terms of behavior, or that culture entails simply difference. They are not interested in defining sexual behavior according to cultural models but in broadening the space of intervention by focusing on the sites where taxonomies don't quite fit. This political praxis does not originate necessarily out of more "closeted" contexts, or out of contexts that are more repressive than that of the United States, but rather from a different way of conducting social dialogue. Not content to remain within a world defined by categories, many Latino American works are not so interested in the violence of identity but in its negotiation. Confrontation is sometimes less interesting and more threatening than the messy residue that is left after different orders are juxtaposed. Impurity leads to progressive politics.

In Ela Troyano's *Latin Boys Go to Hell*, these politics as sites of dialogue and conflict are the creative mess produced by melodrama and farce. The movie is like a *telenovela* (soap opera) where different identity categories bleed into each other. Braulio is in love with Carlos, who believes himself to be an irresistible exemplar of Latino manhood. He plays around with Justin, whose negotiations between the Catholicism of Latinos and his own repressed homosexuality are put to the test when he receives a visit from Angel, a cousin from Chicago who has recently arrived in New York. But Angel, in fact, falls in love with Andrea, who is Braulio's best friend—and Braulio believes that Justin has taken Carlos away from him. The sentimental and passionate complications of this tale are compounded by the fact that Braulio and Justin are avid followers of a totally over-the-top *telenovela* where two sisters, Luz (Light) and Sombra (Shadow), compete for the affections of the same man. Transfixed by the passions of the tale they are watching on TV, the characters learn how to act by imitating the actions of the soap opera and incorporating them into their own lives.

Like Frances Negrón, Troyano shows how her characters move between two worlds that are not seen in opposition to each other (in spite of the tangled oppositions of the tale) but rather flow onto each other. The club where many of the scenes take place is, on the one hand, the space of homophobia (a "straight" Latino man insults Carlos as he is kissing Braulio), but as a Latino bar, it is also an arena that can progressively include gays and lesbians within varying degrees of contested marginality. Troyano's tale renders homage to a culture that she refashions as a space open enough to contain a parody of itself. In the evolving affections of Justin for his straight cousin Angel, the latter's masculinity is not threatened by the former's more open sexuality, just as Angel is able to negotiate a kind of "punk" white-boy American look with the proper modes of behavior that he understands need to be displayed in front of his deeply traditional aunt, resigned to her son's "strangeness." There is nothing typical in this film, except for the fact that all of it resonates with a degree of "typical" familiarity. This is, of course, part of Troyano's achievement. Confronted with their spectacular passions, the characters turn their own passions into a spectacle, and negotiate them as such. But the tale forecloses any anxious reading that pits one zone against the other. Homo- and heterosexualities, Latino and Anglo culture, culture itself and same-sex desire all coexist for the sake of multiple definitions that will in turn dismantle the normative definitions society has imposed.

Spanish makes a distinction between two forms of the English verb "to be": *ser* implies a permanent essence, whereas *estar* is a verb of position. It is the verb of position that interests me here. Spaces portrayed in Latino art such as Negrón's and Troyano's are not marked with their own specific borders—they are all (*están*) in constant interrelation with each other. Static definitions of culture clash with a sexuality mobilized by different positionalities. This negotiation allows us to see characters in a state of "becoming" similar to a Deleuzian *devenir*—possibilities and not fixed entities.

No account of Latinos' cultural situation can lose sight of the many different claims for allegiance that bisect minority subjects, and that allow for the possibility of dismantling dialectics rather than merely incarnating it. This may be a libertarian or even "utopic" stance similar to the one proposed by 1960s gay liberation theorists like Guy Hocquenghem (although Hocquenghem does not include women in his account).[6] Even if it is utopian, it conveys a sense of open political action, in contrast to the present discourse that defines the sexuality and positionality of the gay and lesbian Latino world. This discourse alienates and atomizes and does not take into account the way identities of a social and communal nature can also provide mechanisms for survival.[7] Latino communities do offer relative degrees of safety from which it is very difficult to disengage for the sake of upholding solely gay and lesbian identity categories. I think it is more interesting to destabilize identity categories for the sake of lateral identifications; to create new forms of relating across cultures, races, and ethnicities that negotiate aspects left unmarked by traditional white gay and lesbian politics; to inhabit the space of *estar* and not the pride in the complicities of the always essentialized *ser*.

Histories

Since at least the 1960s there has been a predominant model for minority access to power and representation in the United States: a particular group defines itself as such (it constitutes itself or *is constituted* after having been interpellated by discourses of power) and then challenges the system to change its legal, social, or economic situation. Feminism is the model that first comes to mind, but this model also holds for groups centered on race and ethnicity: the civil rights struggle and the Latino/Chicano movements, which shared the U. S. public sphere in the late 1960s and 1970s. The Puerto Rican Young Lords in New York, Chicago, and throughout the East Coast, for example, were the Latino "arm" of the Black Panther movement; MECHA (Movimiento Chicano de Aztlán) its Chicano or Mexican American counterpart.[8] MECHA and the Young Lords used lessons learned from the civil rights movement: they argued for recognition at a state or federal level, engaged in acts of civil disobedience, and staged rallies in order to keep their agenda in the public domain.

Out of this space where ethnicity and race first motivated the struggle, questions on gender and sexuality followed in the 1970s feminist and homosexual struggles for recognition. As Suzanne Oboler recalls, "the ideologies of the Puerto Rican and the Mexican-American/Chicano movements forced women to choose between nationalism and feminism in embracing La Raza" while they also glossed over issues of race and class.[9] Feminists and gay and lesbian activists initially used a model of social disobedience taken from the civil rights movement. However, these later movements were in part dominated by white activists, and they centralized issues of gender and sexuality while pushing aside questions on race and ethnicity as part of a tactical decision aimed at reaching broad segments of a population perceived as white and middle-class. Feminists articulated a critique of the patriarchal structures of power, but did not take into account the different forms of political struggle demanded by Afro-American or Latina women or lesbians. The homosexual rights movement critiqued generalized homophobia and claimed Stonewall as its originary moment, but it soon forgot that these events were initiated mostly by people of color—including Latino transvestites and poor lesbians and gays.

Lesbians and feminists of color were the first to feel alienated from the normative structures of the feminist movement. They created their own organizational models—based on previous collective work—in order to combat the implicit and explicit racism (and heterosexism) of white women. Latina lesbians as well as Latino gays also split off from the feminist and homosexual movements in order to rearticulate their struggles around ethnicity as well as sexuality. These groups initially understood that people bisecting different points along the grid of identity will see themselves in different ways according to where they decide to place themselves.[10] But the question of sexuality and ethnicity was never resolved—or it produced other issues perhaps not foreseen initially. Gay and lesbian movements structured along the grid of ethnicity found themselves isolated from both their own Latino communities and mainstream Latino organizations. The way these two categories were positioned within the economic structure (lesbian-gay/Latino) collaborated against political efficacy. Latino lesbian and gay national formations have always been ambivalent about the complexities of Latino organizing along multiple fronts. This is not simply the fault of these organizations, but of the economic and political structure in which they are forced to act. Instead of multiple identities, the disjunction between ethnicity and sexuality ultimately flattened out a degree of personal agency—what Lauren Berlant has named "the amputation of personal complexity into categories of simple identity."[11]

Bernardo García has remarked that "[a] better way of understanding the identity development process for Latino gay men is to view it as the management of multiple identities."[12] This is an important point, and I think it is the starting point for a more radical understanding of what a progressive

Latino movement should look like. At present, normative definitions of nationality collide with the question of sexual preference. Nationalism regulates, aestheticizes, and even "globalizes" ethnic differences without taking specificities into account.[13] When those specificities *are* taken into account, they are made to conform to specific gender notions that presume roles for heterosexual males or females in either a nation, a land, or a social polity that always should be pure, insofar as it is fantasized as feminine or maternal.[14] If this is a conflict on the level of "ethnicity" or national constructs, in the United States it is also reproduced as—and, in effect, related to—the issue of homosexuality. The nation of the queer—or the "queer nation"—is a world of mediated difference and forced assimilation; it reproduces ethnic purity on a different scale, in the comfortable self-isolation of gay Bantustans: suburbs of uniformity that would be terrifying were they not also distinctly American.

Chela Sandoval's remarks on the "racialization of theoretical domains" are useful in helping us understand the way gay and lesbian Latinos fall at the border zones of different discourses. For Sandoval, "queer," "Latin American," "postcolonial," and "Chicano" studies are different zones of inquiry that at this point engage in similar methodologies, yet never seem to transculturate each other.[15] Lesbian and gay Latinos embody some of these domains and others at the same time. The racialization and the compartmentalizing of these domains assure that they will never significantly radicalize those categories as they are constituted. These academic disciplines inhabit different spheres and speak with their own terminologies, thus forcing subjects to choose between different forms that are mutually, and not simply exclusively, oppressive. What Sandoval aims to restate, in my view, is that multiple identifications are meant to destabilize categories, not simply to assume them. What this illuminates is that in the present situation, and from the point of view of sexuality, gay and lesbian Latinos will always be arguing for their own specificity vis-à-vis white lesbian and gay organizations that have more visibility and more money and, consequently, more access. From the domain of ethnicity, Latinos who are gay or lesbian have to contend with social, racial, ethnic, and class forces within a community that is not homogeneous in terms of its politics, religion, or ethnic origins.

In spite of what U.S. gay and lesbian leaders seem to imply in most of their discursive statements, to "be" gay or lesbian is not a universal given. The word "gay," accepted as an anglicism in many other parts of the world, is consumed, cannibalized, digested, and reworked. These links between sexuality and culture—as well as links between sexuality and empire—have been questioned, problematized, and nuanced in queer studies, and they have been important in the political and activist discourses around Latino sexual identity in the United States.[16] But many of these discourses have to overcome not only generalized cultural homophobia, but most importantly, the homophobia ingrained in the hierarchical structures of minority politics.[17]

Political structures have been mostly set up to speak with either a patriarchal or a heterosexist voice. And here it is important to recall how the term "Latino" is one that defines broadly and imperfectly, conveniently lumping together individuals who belong to different communities. As with all terms that define a minority, there is always the nagging sense that the term "Latino" participates in the language of oppression—a language that speaks of categories that turn these very diverse communities into somewhat fixed and immutable entities defined by state taxonomical agencies.[18] "Hispanic" or "Latino" may appeal both to the government and to its citizens because of a certain "universality of experience," but it also glosses over the conflicting and interrelated claims of a wide array of groups that exercise their own sense of union or division along different lines. Many cultural, racial, or nationalist structures go completely unexplored in the broad generalizations used to refer to nationalities and ethnicities that originate from the white, black, or indigenous Caribbean, Central America, and South America.

Although "Latino" as a word may mark a certain imperfection, I have no desire to create a language of absolute plenitude. It is clear that in order to speak about "ourselves" "we" need recourse to a particular language that we then manipulate to suit our own needs. And taking the term as a mode of praxis, we can see that there is no more contested space for the "we" in the United States at this moment than in the multifaceted discourse around Latinos. The cliché says that it is the "fastest growing minority in the United States," but this cliché also turns the community into the object of much surveillance in terms of its growing power. Advertisers routinely question and poll Latinos on everything from their soda preferences to the language they speak at home and the degree to which it is spoken. Political organizations routinely survey the population to find out whether a candidate's Spanish word here and there will produce the expected results, or what segment of the Latino population will agree with conservative social positions.[19] Monique Wittig has stated that "[e]ach new class that fights for power must, to reach its goal, represent its interest as the common interest of all the members of the society." But this is also tempered by the fact that the "I" is always already a strategic construct: "[a]s an affirmation of subject status, the 'I' is strategic; the 'we' amplifies the same strategy, with a leap into the universal that allows the writer to speak for the culture."[20]

Advertisers know all too well that they must gauge the nuances of the distinction between the personal and the political, and the different tendencies and opinions manifested in different segments of the community. The tendency to homogenize Latinos is generally governmental, part of a "rhetorical and political" strategy that the state has used in order to "transform a series of diverse, primarily Spanish-speaking cultures into a single race." As a consequence, "when many Americans use the word Latino, they believe they are dealing with a race, equivalent to Asian or black."[21] Difference in this case is part of what creates a sense of commonality: many of us are different from each other and link sex to culture in different ways. These links mark not only our different points of origin but also the different forms of migration and exile that have brought us to the United States.[22]

There are at least three zones of inquiry that intersect with and interlope on each other within the term "Latino" itself. First, "Latino" defines the population of first-, second-, or even third- and fourth-generation individuals of Latin American origins who were born in the United States and who identify, over and beyond their possible use of the Spanish language, with that culture. Second, "Latino" describes all citizens or noncitizens of the United States who were born in Latin America and live in the United States. Third, "Latino" underscores a certain kind of positionality, by which I mean literally the place a subject inhabits at a given time. The term is predominantly used in the United States and not in Latin America, and in many ways the mere fact of crossing a political (though not necessarily an economic) border allows the subject to be part of the category.[23] "Latino" is a fluid and mobile identification in terms of concrete praxis. As a category, it may mask very different agendas that at this point have no common degree of political articulation; while at other times, it does name a population with a common political and socioeconomic goal. Who uses the word may be as important here as the context in which the word is used.

The problem has been articulated clearly by Robert Vázquez Pacheco. How do "we" take into account all of "our" differences, when the very notion of a "we" insists that "we" participate in what is at times a "fantasy discourse"?[24] The history of Latino organizing needs to be pluralized. Gender issues as well as issues relating to sexual orientation are part of these histories. These have at times coalesced into common projects, while at other historical moments they have splintered along gender, national, or racial lines. Latino discourse is all about positionality—about an understanding of where one is placed as a subject, an understanding that is also shared by other peoples of color in the United States. I would like to examine at this point the nature of this positionality as it relates to what Michael Warner has examined as the discourse of "shame," a zone left untouched by a politics defined according to identity.[25] In other words, I want to examine how the theoretical domains of ethnicity and sexuality bisect the figure of a Latino gay male. The choice of gender needs to be highlighted because of the sense of privilege contained in the category of the male. That I intend to examine this in the form of a narrative is also part of a procedural turn in this essay. It is meant to signal a switch in terms of discourse, a more "hybrid" way of understanding theory that also seeks to destabilize it as a theoretical domain in itself.

Narratives, Positionalities

Politics intersects with narrative at a border where the nature of the political is expanded. A man sat next to me at an outdoor café and ordered a "café latino." He was in his late twenties or early thirties, and his skin color was some shade of white that made his straight, jet-black hair even darker. He wore a tie and a fitted shirt, and he spoke to the waiter in Spanish. He then opened a book in Spanish on diplomatic exchanges between Mexico and the United States. I looked at his features carefully, at what he did, at how he looked at things. I had a somewhat vague knowledge of the publishing concern that had put out this particular book (a trade paperback), so there was some sort of identification there with what he read. But also I had seen him in this same café for a couple of days with this same book. And this café is frequented (not completely, but mostly) by lesbians and gay men. I not only presumed he was a gay man, I also indexed him as belonging to a certain class (the diplomatic milieu in Washington D.C.) and a certain level of culture.

Identity may be thought of in terms of essentialism and construction, but it should also be thought of in terms of the degrees of one's distance from categories that are normatively presented as such. The man's identity, I thought (I started inventing things to myself), was a category kept at a distance by the many identifications that he is able to make in the course of one day.[26] It is not a question of classifying oneself in one way or the other. In some contexts, I presumed, he thinks of himself as gay, and in other contexts he relishes the Latino side of him, and the times when he can take in both at the same time are few and far between.[27] That opposition becomes in these cases a question of *position*. It is not necessarily something that we can celebrate, since at no point do these operate nonproblematically, without some degree of hierarchy creeping in.[28]

Both sides of the equation, the gay side and the Latino side (and even to speak of them as "sides" does not do justice to what I seek to express), allow for certain degrees of comfort: the privilege, at times, to move in and out of them. The man may consider himself a subject who passes in some contexts, though not in others. On the *gay* side of the equation he is assimilated into the already known and normatized. He belongs to an urban lifestyle with wholly codified norms, institutions, practices, a language in which to express desires, and a history—Stonewall, gay marches, the *Washington Blade*. For him, the community of the "gay" allows for a transnational identification, but it gives him a "community" composed of people who are fundamentally the same.

The gay world will offer this man a lifestyle that he sees unmarked in terms of race, since for him "whiteness" means the ability to pass as unmarked. This lifestyle is as limited as his community—it consigns all others, including blacks, lesbians, and lower-class Latinos, to a space that is "other." From a class perspective, his vision of the gay male world is that of consumer culture. In this homosocial world there is little exchange with others who may be similar but also different. Like other white gay *male* subjects, he believes that the victimization he suffers from the society at large justifies his rendering others to the realm of the invisible. This is, in his view, part and parcel of his sense of privilege as part of a victimized minority. And he can constantly use that male privilege (he allows himself a privilege that is also allowed by others) in order to position himself. He knows when and in what situation it may be beneficial for him to insist on his gayness, and he also knows when more rewards will come if he defines himself as Latino.

As a Latino he privileges his ethnicity; as a gay man he understands things in terms of race (whiteness). Class is, of course, the way both of these categories relate to each other. To be Latino and gay (accent on the Latino) does not allow him to conceive of nights at the impeccably clean and classy white-boy gay bar in this neighborhood—it more certainly reminds him of cruising around the plaza. It does not include the openness or even the relative safety of a gay or mixed café such as this one, but the decidedly "unvirtuous" (he is ashamed to be a part of this) bathroom stalls in Mexico City or Buenos Aires coffeeshops. His positionality and mediated distance are fully ascertained in the *Latino* gay bar, where slumming whites mingle with what he considers to be low-class Latinos. And these Latinos are low-class because they do not necessarily participate in the lifestyle that he has adopted for himself. They don't entertain the narrative of "coming out"—a narrative that he also, in any case, uses discreetly. These are gang members, or dishwashers who have girlfriends. They may or may not like Madonna, they may also sleep with other men. They can be tops or bottoms, they can hustle for money, but they can also fall in love. In the Latino gay bar this man suffers some kind of cultural, ethnic, classist, linguistic, and personal crisis. He describes his own culture in anthropological terms to the slumming whites, while showing at the same time his Ralph Lauren (not Tommy Hilfiger) shirt. The Latinos speak to him in English but he answers them in the impeccable Spanish that he reserves for members of the working class.

My café neighbor, I imagine, has constructed his own vision of what being a Latino means, as well as what the culture entails. For him, the Latino side of the equation is where *meaning*—true meaning—lies. For this man, culture is lived as something to be preserved, protected, as a sign of difference that presumes, consciously and unconsciously, essentialist categories that he may or may not deconstruct. In terms of culture, he may not feel any conflict in calling himself Latino, although he may also think of himself along national lines, as Mexican, Chilean, or Guatemalan, for example. The gay lifestyle—parties at Velvet Nation and the packed crowds at Chaos—is echoed by the demands of culture (broadly understood). But the culture that he certainly identifies, invents, or constructs as Latino—*la familia*, the Catholic religion, the Spanish language (well-spoken or spoken embarrassingly), hierarchies of class, and rigid constructions of gender—does not really gel with the term "gay": Latino is what stabilizes an identity and fixes it within parameters at times more rigid than the ones found "south of the Rio Grande."

On the one hand, we have a constructed vision of the ethnic self that deals in essentials: a *cultura latina* that he reads according to the parameters that the U.S. media deploy. On the other, we have a gay culture to which he is drawn in order to escape from the minoritizing impasse to which the *cultura latina* consigns him. The two "identities" do not relate in any meaningful way, or they relate to each other as forms of "othering" the self. He is torn between the conflictive claims that keep these two groups distinct and separate from each other, while he also tries to negotiate these categories. More important, he has also believed in the arguments put forth by political powerbrokers from one community or the other. What this means is that the two identities are kept separate. We could say that these two "identities" are being lived "performatively"—that they actively translate each other. But let us recall how class intervenes whenever the body is called out, questioned, interrogated, or interpellated.

In all manners of dress, behavior, and self-identification, there is a consistent will that is here performed and that it would be unjust, for many reasons, to simply bracket as the internalization of a system of constraints arising from a hierarchical source of power. There is a sense of agency in all this. It is a system of constraints that the subject *voluntarily* participates in, not only because it is relatively easy and manageable, but also because of self-interest. It does provide certain tangible benefits, but they will fail (in a loose reading of Judith Butler's words) "to establish a radical commensurability between the terms it seeks to relate."[29] These identities are defined according to the discourses that have always already been given to him, that have interpellated him repeatedly, and that he has always already absorbed.

This image—this narrative, story line, or even fiction—seeks to establish what normative definitions of identity do for the subject who tries to accommodate himself or herself to them. What I wanted to express by means of this example and this anecdotal fiction is the fact that the politics of identity cannot address all the issues that pertain to an understanding of how people may classify themselves. It may address the issue of community, but not the broader issues of class. And when it does address the issue of class, it leaves aside gender. Ultimately, the politics of identity arises from the surveillance mechanisms that I myself have entertained in constructing this fable: a desire to classify that also belies a desire to normatize and fix people along preconceived axes. This whole story, of course, may end up saying more about who does the observing than about the observed subject. But even in this case, it unmasks the way defining people is a way of not taking into account our own politics of observation, a way of not marking ourselves for the sake of marking an other.

A politics of identity allows for a sense of bonding or even cultural pride, but it also defines both elements in negative terms and thus seeks to regulate the culture's own mechanisms for existence. I cannot see these negotiations as positive interventions, since their aim is not radically to question the categories as these have been given, but to assimilate those categories and marginalize and exclude those who fall outside a norm. It is not that I see my café neighbor as a victim of identity politics; I do understand that at many points he manipulates those same politics. I think, moreover, that he manipulates them for the sake of furthering divisions, rendering as "others" those who in another context would most certainly be counted as part of his "tribe."

Grassroots Blues

The narrative that I constructed above belongs to the wider context of Washington, D.C., the city where I live. I bring this geographical space into this text because it will be important in the sections that follow. It is no accident that these narratives of Latino sexual and ethnic conflicts are being played out in Washington, where gays and lesbians try to negotiate the links between national institutions of power and the grassroots base, between progressive social policy and institutional theory, or between forms of action better suited to the United States, and a social praxis more adequate to other national spaces.

One part of Washington, D.C., exists in order to oppress the other. One side is involved in national organizations: these are the people who represent other people and whose job it is to *represent* without ever coming into contact with them. Those people—those who represent other people—only come into contact with each other. It is a city of fundraisers and cocktail parties and more fundraisers. In order to have a cocktail party you need to call a catering company, and the people who set the food on the table are probably members of the community you represent, although they cannot possibly afford to pay the ten-dollar entry fee you charge, because the cost of food is extra, and this is certainly not an open bar event. So the people who end up coming to the event are the same people who represent other people, and they all mingle with the understanding that their act of representation is taking place because money is needed in order to *represent*. The people who are represented are called "clients" and they use the services you provide. And the system ensures the fact that the well-oiled machinery can function as long as you keep the clients as clients, and as long as you provide services they will use. The system guarantees that they will never control the means of production because that is what the national paradigm and the global paradigm are all about: huge institutions and huge corporations that exist in a discontinuous time, utterly incommensurate with each other.

This is not, of course, the whole picture. There are other spaces where something actually takes place, where the politics of the situation falls in line with the situational politics of the community. For example, there is a small bar on a second floor, frequented by Latino men whom nobody wants to classify as gay and who would never "use" the services of a gay organization. The bar has closed, reopened, and changed names a number of times, but it has always attracted the same clientele. In this neighborhood of upscale entertainment, it stands out like an open sore, like some remnant of a past that does not seem as "modern" as the Latino night at the white gay boy club. The perfume is different here, and the fashion is not Armani. But in the second-floor bathroom, next to the imitation cactus plants and the volcanoes painted on the walls, the drag queens are setting up their act as they strap their pads in place. They brought out a neighborhood kid to serve as the resident dj for the night, and when the sound of the violins announced the first ranchera by Ana Gabriel, one of them came out with a banana as a prop in one hand, and a rubber in the other. People here are not the ones who represent other people, and the drag queens make sure that the repertoire of fruits for the night includes the cantaloupe as well as the banana, the cucumber but also the papaya. The spoken portion of the show deals with facts of life that middle-class propriety would not talk about. The language is direct. The fruits are even—at the end of it all—consumed. The men in the audience applaud and jeer and scream "obscenities" and laugh. They walk out with rubbers in their pockets. It has been a brilliant intervention in terms of public health.

I put these two narratives at the beginning in order to reflect on another narrative that preceded it. This took place at a grassroots Latino gay, lesbian, bisexual, and transgender organization in Washington, D.C., and it demonstrates what happens when the corporate model of the national organizations is replicated at the grassroots level. Almost at the point of closing the business at hand, the board of this grassroots organization discussed two requests for money: one from a drag-queen Miss Gay Hispanidad contest, and the other from the U.S. Gay and Lesbian Military Services Organization. Miss Gay Hispanidad is a local event bringing together Latino drag queens from the D.C. area to perform in one nightclub one night of the year. The U.S. Gay and Lesbian Military Services Organization, on the other hand, is a national organization providing aid and legal counsel for gays and lesbians in all branches of the armed forces. The discussion opposed those two events first, in terms of gender politics and then in relation to sexual self-definition. First, two Latina women on the board (recent arrivals to the city and part of its urban transient population) complained that drag queen shows are always offensive to women; second, they argued that the audience that participates in the drag queen show does not define itself, in any way, shape, or form, as gay. In fact, they said, most of the men who attend the drag show are "straight" members of the community who hang around or sleep with the drag queens, and who will never use the services of a gay organization.

The question of drag, in this instance, created a divide along gender lines within an organization that was presumably balanced on gender terms. It is not that a discussion on gender should not take place in a Latino organization—as a matter of fact it should, since many Latino groups reproduce the male-centered norms of society as a whole. But the divide in this case concerned representations of Latino men borrowed from the worst stereotypes of white Anglo discourse: the men who went to this activity fell outside the parameters for social intervention that the grassroots organization had set for itself. And the question of gender inflected this discussion to the exclusion of the question of class, since the women who objected to funding this activity were recent middle-class arrivals to a city that has a considerable population of political or business transients. Their contact with the community itself was tangential, if not marginal.

The activity at the Latino bar that I recounted above was not funded, of course, by this Latino grassroots organization. Or it was funded by that organization back then, before it turned into the part-time job of people who had full-time jobs representing other people. Or it was funded by another Latino AIDS services organization in the city that set out to do whatever it could to stop the spread of the disease, with very little government funding and practically no help from the emerging class of Latino bureaucrats on Capitol Hill. In this context, I think it is important to state my own bias: I would have given no funds to the soldier and my total support to the drag queen. It is, surely, one position among many, and it marks me as belonging to a particular political, social, and class configuration. This was remarked upon at that meeting, but in less specific terms. I was the resident academic, disconnected from reality, or stuck in some space (the sixties) where I didn't really belong chronologically. They were established, seasoned bureaucrats. I should also say, in all bitterness, that for some of them the notion of a "board" and of an organization did not entail helping a Latino community that has almost no representation whatsoever in the racialized D.C. city political arena. It entailed a power grabbing mechanism that would inevitably collapse the minute the figurehead produced a vacuum by his or her departure.

What this discussion allowed me to perceive was that when a particular type of national organizing starts to appear in community-based organizations, the first thing that happens is a normative process of isolation that separates community members from their community. This separation uses notions of resistance not to create broad coalitions, but to particularize, atomize, and balkanize. It is profoundly conservative as a politics, and we should acknowledge that it is the result of a number of factors. These include, among others, a general history of neglect of issues concerning lesbian and gay Latinos within more traditional national minority organizations, as well as from members of the clergy in the predominantly Catholic—but increasingly Protestant—Latino community. Faced with ostracism from the Latino media because of sexuality issues, as well as with a lack of representation in the traditional white lesbian and gay movement, many Latino lesbian and gay grassroots organizations have opted to localize their fight in terms of sexuality rather than try to gain visibility in organizations centered on ethnicity or race. At the same time, and given the disastrous impact of AIDS in the Latino communities in the United States, community-based organizations are forced to devote themselves almost solely to the task of gaining funding to run AIDS-related programs, and these demand not only a growing professionalization of the movement, but also a series of compromises that further alienate lesbian and gay Latinos from many segments of the community.[30]

Internal colonizations always consign subjects to new forms of marginalization. In a universe where identities are supposed to be transparent and self-evident, not to take into account the opacity and contradictoriness of one's own negotiations between culture and sexuality will always collaborate against effective political work. Some of the more interesting work coming out of Latino community-based organizations entails creating zones of contact that allow for common goals to be pursued. These initiatives are constantly being fought over on two interrelated fronts, and they are not always successful (though some of them are). In terms of gay or lesbian politics, Latinos' attention to questions of ethnicity and race consigns them to a marginal space in the national white-identified movement. On the other hand, in terms of ethnic or racial organization, gay and lesbian Latinos become suspect because of their attention to questions of sexuality. Progressive politics *does* go on at the grassroots level, in spite of the fact that national organizations are at this point consistently producing and reproducing a politics of assimilation and exclusion that further marginalizes some members of the community in order to allow for others to become assimilated. While coalitions are formed in some quarters, certain grassroots organizations are following the national corporatist model and dismantling the possibility of progressive politics ever taking place.

Washington, D.C., is an exceptional space in its own right, and I do not intend to use it as an exemplary situation for other contexts. But the lackluster success of some community-based initiatives in this city can serve as a reminder of what happens when the politics of the national and of "representation" colonizes the politics of inclusion and voice. National politics is framed by a narrow space of choices that do not allow for new configurations—new forms of social polity and action—to take place. In fact, most of the more interesting forms of social dialogue take place at the level of interpersonal and interclass contact that follows the model of community organizing, though outside the terrain of institutional politics. We can say that progressive movements arise at the fringes of those national structures that purport to represent social agents. How this takes place, and how it relates to the national structure is the subject of my next intervention.

Imperial Sex Is Modern

> Tijuana, La Bella, just a short ride from San Diego, it is the welcome door to Mexico. Tijuana offers a very diverse and exiting [*sic*] night life, including bars, shopping centers and nightclubs of all types. Tijuana's Cultural Center is the space to see and experience a "mordidita"—a little bite of the flavors of Mexico. The Cultural Center has a theater that shows exciting films, such as El Pueblo del Sol, an incredible trip

> through Mexico via the magic of multimedia. While there, visit the museum that encapsulates the history of the country.
>
> —National Latina/o Lesbian, Gay, Bisexual and Transgender Organization, Web page materials on *Séptimo Encuentro: Creando un Mundo sin Fronteras*

Throughout the different stages of the AIDS epidemic, new ways of containing the disease as well as new forms of addressing populations affected by it started as dialogues and disputes with mainstream politics. Without the constant interactions where voices gradually and sometimes violently made themselves heard, the more open and frank discussions of sex and sexual acts demanded by the emergency would have never appeared. I think the same model obtains at some points in the relationship between United States–based discourses around sexuality and U.S. actions in other contexts. It is clear that in Latino America and in some parts of Europe, the motivation for a civil rights struggle in terms of sexual acts or identities receives support from actions that take place in the United States. The United States serves as a space of validation with which to confront the entrenched discourses of certain segments of Latino American societies. As I mentioned in the introduction to this book, activists in Latino America pick and choose the fights they are willing to fight, and quote the model of U.S. politics when it can be used to their benefit. In Mexico, for example, the case of Matthew Shepard served as an obligatory point of reference in discussions on violence against gays and lesbians. It is not that this question had not been addressed before, just that it could be redeployed in new and different ways given the response to the crime in the United States. When the news receives media coverage in the United States, the act of quoting the news and its response serves as a way of validating a particular struggle. Latino American activists show a remarkable knowledge of the national spaces they inhabit, and the politics of quotation is one of many ways of producing gains in social policy.[31]

The "mainstream" status of some gay and lesbian organizations demands an awareness of the marginal spaces created by their own compromises. "Mainstreaming" will always produce marginality. In the best of cases, the marginalized population will affect and radically change the center, but more often than not, the center will consign all critique to an ill-defined "fringe."

Issues of center and periphery were brought to light in debates that took place when LLEGO, the National Latino/a Lesbian and Gay Organization, sponsored its 1997 conference in San Juan, Puerto Rico, from October 9 to 13. From the outset, LLEGO's choice of Puerto Rico reflected its ambiguous relationship with the mainstream lesbian, gay, bisexual, and transgendered organizations in the United States. On the one hand, LLEGO participates in the politics of civil rights for sexual minorities in a U.S. context, but on the other hand, the organization sees its mandate and mission as "internationalist"—crossing the political boundaries of the United States. No other mainstream gay or lesbian organization, to my knowledge, funded solely by U.S. funds as well as the U.S. government, engages in this internationalist vision. This ambiguity is not necessarily a negative thing. It is interesting, however, that it generally goes unremarked. It is part of what LLEGO sees as its double mandate, and as a way of negotiating ethnicity in the United States with the sexual politics of nations seen at times as "home countries."

The fact that LLEGO does not open this internationalist component up for discursive analysis (I am not aware of the specifics of this political praxis other than the example I will discuss below) means that there has never been an open debate on how a national U.S. organization should interact with others outside the political U.S. arena. This is why the choice of Puerto Rico was significant. The appeal to "internationalism"—one that could also be performed safely within the confined spaces of a U.S. colony—enabled the organization to ally itself with the progressive politics of decolonization, although LLEGO did not take a stand (wisely, perhaps?) on the issue of colonial status except by implication, in the act of naming this an "international" conference. This rhetoric highlighted the many fault lines that bisect the issue of Puerto Rican identity. Puerto Ricans are citizens of the United States who do not possess the same rights as U.S. citizens—or at least only possess some of those rights depending on their geographic location. Officially residents of a commonwealth, Puerto Ricans are the only nonmainland Latin Americans automatically granted U.S. citizenship at birth, and because of this they are also eligible for military conscription (and have been conscripted en masse, particularly in Korea and Vietnam). At the same time, Puerto Ricans residing on the island do not vote directly in U.S. elections; Puerto Ricans can vote in federal elections if they reside in the continental United States. As residents of one of the fifty states they have representatives and senators; as island residents they have a representative in Congress who has voice but no vote.

The complex Puerto Rican political and colonial situation allowed LLEGO to conduct its conference as a test case for future interventions in Latin America. The question of the similarities and differences between mainland and island Puerto Ricans, or between Puerto Ricans and other U.S. Latinos was part of the political choice that turned Puerto Rico into a *necessary* choice. Puerto Ricans have retained a sense of difference in spite of over one hundred years of overt U.S. domination, and this sense of difference is not only a question of language or positionality, but also a matter of culture. These issues are similar to those faced by other Latino groups, but at the same time they are different, given the political status of Puerto Rican nationals. Even in the United States, and before identity discourses were deployed in force in the 1960s, Puerto Ricans insisted on the exceptionality of their separate culture, one that has been negotiated in difficult and creative ways. Language has been played with in the creative hybridities of Spanglish, and the standard narrative of migration has been supplanted by the realities of the round-trip ticket from the mainland to the island. At the same time, Puerto Ricans have assimilated culture into a creative stew where national pride thrives in a blatant colonial structure.

It seemed that by choosing Puerto Rico as the venue for its international convention, LLEGO attempted a progressive understanding of a thorny political and social problem. But after the conference was over, it was clear that LLEGO was not willing to think about how ethnicities and sexualities need to be constantly renegotiated in different political contexts. First, in spite of protests and without consulting its "local" affiliates in Puerto Rico, LLEGO chose as the venue for its conference a hotel that had consistently filed injunctions against Puerto Rican gay and lesbian organizations, and that tried to prevent the annual lesbian and gay rights march from passing in front of it—lest it upset the U.S. tourists who year after year find fun, solace, and frolic at the beach. According to some participants in Puerto Rico, the choice of this hotel was an act imposed from above (the national organization) and from the outside (the mainland). Other commentators differ as to the results of this intervention. Yes, they point out, this was an error in policy, though there is no need to see it wholly in negative terms: it can be seen as a symbolic "reappropriation" of a homophobic space. It could be that as a result of LLEGO's presence, the hotel has changed its position on gay and lesbian marches in Puerto Rico. But this does nothing to change the implicit structural dynamics of the situation, for the hotel will always host a "foreign" conference; the true test of acceptance would be if it allowed a Puerto Rican gay and lesbian conference to take place. Something may be gained, and this something is important to validate.

The choice of hotel in Puerto Rico highlights other issues and conflicts within Latino gay and lesbian organizing on a national or even international level. It is clear that LLEGO wants to be the organizational glue that binds disparate communities together in pan-Latino unity. The organization serves at one level as a clearinghouse where local affiliates—community-based organizations and the like—are able to talk *to* each other and *with* each other, under national sponsorship and guidance. The relationship is not unlike that of an organization's board and its staff: the board talks about the big picture and the vision, while the staff talks about how to implement that vision. This may not be the ideal model for organizing, but it is the prevailing one. LLEGO in many ways wants to be the board to the community-based organizations' staff—it seeks to give a sense of coherence to local efforts. But at the same time, it is at the service of those local organizations in order to insure their survival—it works as the "staff" (to flip it around) to the groups' needs.

The *afiliados*, or affiliated organizations, are the "vanguard" of the discourse—they are the ones that LLEGO serves, and its board carries out the mission as it is articulated from below.

As the case of Puerto Rico shows, there is a disconnect between the affiliates and national organizing that speaks of a blind spot in the organizational structure. Unaware of the cultural sensitivities involved in terms of language in a colonial situation, LLEGO chose to hire only English-to-Spanish translators for the conference, a decision that implicitly created the impression of English as the lingua franca of homosexuality. The issue of translation is one that has appeared in other organizational venues that attempt to include non-U.S. activists in the discourse. Translation is expensive and this expense does make a dent in an organization's budget. At the same time, it is clear that language is fraught with political meaning, and that choices regarding language are in many ways political choices. At the 1995 International Lesbian and Gay Association meeting in Brazil, for example, translation was provided in the plenary sessions, though smaller workshops depended on volunteers to take up this task. The role of translation in LLEGO's conference may just be the result of a U.S. Latino organization's oversight. After all, most of the organizational membership in LLEGO is English-speaking and it makes sense to take care first of the needs of that population. But at the same time, the question of language cannot be disengaged from other questions concerning representation. It is, on the one hand, a clear economic issue that concerns cost, but on the other it is also a political issue for an organization that is increasingly broadening its mandate to include Latino Americans south of Texas.

The problems in Puerto Rico went beyond issues of site (the conference hotel) and issues of language. The third problem was related to the concrete interventions that are possible in an internationalist setting. One of LLEGO's more conspicuous responses to national Puerto Rican affairs occurred the week the conference took place. A member of the Puerto Rican House of Representatives associated with the statehood political party introduced a congressional bill banning same-sex marriages. That this was sponsored by the statehood party is not without significance, for one of the party's aims is to reproduce the U.S. social fabric and discourse in the colony. This bill in particular mimicked others passed on the "mainland" as a result of the perceived threat of a possible Supreme Court decision authorizing the legality of same-sex unions. It was, of course, ironic that statehood proponents of the bill found themselves arguing for its passage by insisting on the *cultural* specificity of Puerto Ricans. The irony is that the party of assimilation wanted to pass a carbon copy of a U.S. law while at the same time arguing for the *exceptionality* of the Puerto Rican cultural construct. Gays and lesbians, as the bill stated, are "foreign influences" that seek to introduce "foreign" notions of minority acceptance within a culture perceived as "distinctly different."

Following a request by the Foundation for Human Rights, a Puerto Rican–based organization founded at the grassroots level to fight this legislation, LLEGO lent its support to a march in opposition to the bill, attended by about 250 from the estimated 800 participants in the conference—not a big turnout, in any case. Of course, as a political organization, LLEGO was obliged to take part in the march even though it ran the risk of paradoxically furthering those questionable statehood political agendas involved in the legislation, which saw gays and lesbians as "foreign" influences. In that case, the definition of "foreign" put forth by the statehood party was eminently facetious, considering the immense traffic back and forth between Puerto Ricans on the island and on the mainland—Puerto Ricans who claim allegiance to the island and to New York. But LLEGO's actions in terms of the national gay and lesbian press that covered this event once again show the disconnect between the base and the board. True to its mandate, LLEGO should have given Puerto Rican grassroots organizations primary billing in every possible venue. This LLEGO did not do, choosing to underscore its own participation in the march as a way of validating its mission. In fact, the article in the *Washington Blade* carried no opinions or quotes from any member of the Puerto Rican grassroots coalition that had formed to combat this bill.[32] Puerto Ricans, in the official article of the gay and lesbian paper of record, are referred to as "local" Puerto Ricans.[33]

Because of LLEGO's "internationalist" aspirations, it framed Puerto Rican culture as a minority discourse of the United States, a situation that is not the most productive one for gays and lesbians fighting very real social and political struggles in Puerto Rico. But this is, of course, the result of the ambiguities I mentioned earlier. The article in the *Washington Blade* was not addressed to the Puerto Rican population. Its readers were other board members of the Washington mainstream gay and lesbian organizations, and it served as a way to validate LLEGO as the only Latino organization around. It was evident that LLEGO attempted to work on two fronts, at the same time "local" and national. But LLEGO should have highlighted the grassroots component, while at the same time adding that the national organization facilitates what the vanguard requests.

The critique I level at this point is concerned solely with organizational structure. Debate within and outside an organization is important for preventing mistakes. In conversations regarding this conference and this choice of venue, I found that LLEGO did serve a positive function in the Puerto Rican arena. Participants in the march recall that the spectacle of hundreds of queers taking over the streets of San Juan was an immensely empowering event. The conference also served as a way of ventilating issues that do not appear as often as they should in the press or in other media on the island, and Puerto Rican organizations gained voice and respectability within Puerto Rican society. Last but not least, the conference also served as a clearinghouse for many Puerto Rican activists to engage in dialogue with their U.S. counterparts.

All of these are positive developments, particularly because or in spite of the fact that they take place in an organization that sees acculturation and assimilation as part of its political mandate. LLEGO's attempts at assimilating to other white gay and lesbian organizations led to its cosponsorship of the Human Rights Campaign's contentious millennium march in spite of the fact that this march was critiqued by many grassroots groups. LLEGO claims its own sense of difference from those organizations, but not to the extent that its notion of assimilating into U.S. politics is compromised.

In terms of political and ideological praxis LLEGO represents a very American mode of conducting politics. This form of politics will work in some instances, but in others it will not. A strict focus on identity, for example, will always produce marginal discourses within Latino communities. A lack of attention to issues of class and representation will also contribute to a disconnect between the organization and its base. And regardless of what positions LLEGO takes, it is clear that new and more progressive politics will always take place at the margins. Whether this happens *because* of LLEGO or *in spite of* its politics, or in some other way that entails a negotiation between these, is a point of debate.

Upstaging grassroots efforts, being insensitive to questions of language, choosing economy over ethics, and not consulting with local activists or consulting with them only in part—all these actions show the enormous disconnect between national representatives of the gay movement and those who fight "in the trenches." This is not to say that there are no activists in these organizations who understand the delicate positionalities involved in speaking from the position of economic and political power vis-à-vis non–U.S. groups. But frequently these activists' advice goes unheeded, or is lost in the organizations' general push for dollars and respect in the American context. In talking to Latino activists about their relationships with LLEGO, I found that critiques of the organization do not mean to deny that what happens within that space is important. In other words, conservative spaces produce a different type of discourse as a kind of remainder that spills over from its center. Many Latino activists, for example, level intense critiques of LLEGO as an organization, while at the same time they ascertain the fact that what happens outside it is more important than what happens within it. If LLEGO produces the show, the real action takes place elsewhere, and that would not be possible without the spectacle. Organizations like LLEGO, according to one point of view, should be sustained principally because of the spaces that they make possible. In other words, it is not important that the LLEGO conference produces stereotypes and false visions of the "national" (like the one quoted at the beginning of this section), for surely very important events took place in Tijuana outside the organizational structure in itself, and these are the events that will ultimately prove important in the long run.

I tend to agree with this position, though not without nuancing it a bit further. My own and very limited experience in Washington tells me that organizational models at this point are being functionally produced from top to bottom and not from the base up. This may be a result of the particular blinders involved in living in the seat of imperial power, but then again they may serve as cautionary remarks in terms of the ideologies produced in this space. The progressive sites where marginality is able to validate and recognize itself and at the same time engage in a discussion with the "mainstream" are reduced by this model of top-down organizing. This does not mean to foreclose the possibility for a creative reappropriation of those conservative discourses, but to critique the fact that imaginative politics is further and further consigned to even more marginal spaces, where it is localized and increasingly disregarded.

Crisis Politics

The relationship between mainstream organizations and marginal spaces has already been commented on in gay and lesbian studies in discussions on ethnic divisions created within "one" movement. Urvashi Vaid addresses the issue of ethnic divisiveness in *Virtual Equality*, and her critique of ethnic or racial identity-based organizations is generally quite trenchant: "Identity politics keeps the gay movement separated from straights, whites separated from blacks, lesbians separated from men, people of color separated from each other. We become a devolving series of specific identities instead of a broad community of people bonded by a shared egalitarian politics."[34] These separations are counterproductive: "In clinging to the idea of a fixed identity, we have gained and we have sacrificed. The question I pose is whether it has been effective for us to separate into singular racial, sexual, and gender categories. Who has benefited? And where does this identity-based organizing lead and leave our movement?"[35] In spite of the tenor of these words, she calls herself ambivalent in relation to organizing around issues of culture, ethnicity, or race. This may be a result of the fact that Vaid has mostly worked with the National Gay and Lesbian Task Force, and not with people of color communities. In other words, her experience is with national organizations rather than ethnic or racial ones. From the point of view of these organizations, and in spite of Vaid's objections, these separations are real, and not just simply produced by people of color. By organizing in terms of racial or ethnic identity, some groups are able to use difference as a catalyst for understanding; they can work together with mainstream (or white) organizations and still not be the same. Vaid herself admits that this organizing empowers communities of color and trains leaders who in turn speak for those communities—although in many of these organizations, she adds, there is certainly an "overrepresentation of well-educated, professional, middle-class people."[36] In spite of her desires to create a multiracial movement that will make those organizations effective, ultimately Vaid thinks that "race-based methods of organizing unacceptably maintain the status quo on racial prejudice."[37]

One problem with Vaid's discussion in *Virtual Equality* is that it presumes relatively stable ethnicities as well as sexualities. Here, the experiences of people of color community organizing show that the situation is quite different. Identities are not fixed entities—they are deployed, masked, or unmasked, and there is a degree to their masking and also a praxis to their deployment. The state, as well as other institutions that serve as its proxies—academia, social agencies, bureaucratic institutions—uses a fixed notion of identities in order to further politics that may not take into account subjects' sense of freedom. How does sexual "identity" collude or collide with other forms of identification? How does it relate to the subject's sense of belonging to a nation or engagement in gender politics? How does the particular oppression felt in terms of ethnicities, nationalities, or sexualities lead to, or produce, imperialist actions? How do minority voices in the United States export their ("our") notions of oppression and turn them into discourses of power in other contexts that may or may not be similar to our own?

All these questions are part of the histories of sexualities and imperialisms, and they are more clearly part of the histories of Latinos and modernity. The history of imperialism is sustained by oppressive discourses produced under the guise, or the illusion, of "liberating" populations from "oppressive" situations. What is different at this point is that since the 1980s, notions of modernity and progress have colluded in the United States with a debate in the areas of cultures, identities, and sexualities. These may be positive developments in the United States, though we should analyze in further detail their direct actions in other social contexts, attentive to the ways these organizations collude with a history of modernization that catalogues and defines. In the history of U.S. imperialism in Latino America, there is a very real fear that this discourse will replicate others that produce violent social change under various pretexts: hygiene and progress at the end of the nineteenth century, and identity at the end of the twentieth.

Globally, the "state of things" of which this essay speaks is one of extreme dissatisfaction even with dissatisfaction itself. There are successes within the movement—grassroots acts that speak of a nuanced sense of empowerment; intellectual thought within organizations that rivals and surpasses sophisticated analyses outside their purview, because they are combined with sheer brilliant political work. The people that produce these acts are not lonely voices, but they are also not representative of the majority that dominates the politics and the public voice of the movement. It may be good that they are not, but it is more important to ascertain that their marginality should not be sustained for long.

Like some of the writers profiled in the *Village Voice* issue on gay global networks, I engage in a productive ambivalence regarding an increasingly conservative gay politics and its grassroots base. I should also clarify that I am not trying to give the impression that any community is at a particular point of crisis, nor am I trying to explain how this crisis may or may not be symptomatic of a "healthy" skepticism. Walter Benjamin already warned of the rhetorical uses of the language of imminence: "The tradition of the oppressed teaches us that the 'state of emergency' in which we live is not the exception but the rule. We must attain to a conception of history that is in keeping with this insight."[38] Even if at the time of AIDS, crisis politics created wide coalitions that addressed the social, political, and emotional costs of the disease, it is also true that crisis politics generally produces desires to control and normatize, to fix and delimit. It also performs a sense of threat that invokes itself for the sake of a constant state of order. I am not interested in performing this sense of crisis nor in appealing to a sense of order.

For Latino lesbians and gays, there should be a way we can reintegrate ourselves into the communities from which we are forcibly exiled by the majoritarian gay movement. Sexual identities were reappropriated for the sake of a future utopian project based on access and representation, but instead of utopia we have the progressively more insidious alliances that elements of the Right have been manufacturing for the last fifteen years.[39] Faced with these alliances, we could invoke the multiple or even positional identifications and their histories in the United States. These are the basic tenets of projects like "U.S. Third World feminism," signaled by the publication in 1981 of Cherríe Moraga and Gloria Anzaldúa's *This Bridge Called My Back*. The book, as a project, argued for a specific coalition of social agents in order to negotiate gender, sexualities, and ethnicities. Moraga and Anzaldúa saw gender with inflections not registered within the context of white feminism, and they were also able to include the question of ethnicities and sexualities within a broad spectrum. They proposed modes of action that allowed women to communicate along different axes. In spite of any criticism that one may level at the project, it is clear that it saw the importance of claiming intersectionality as a key component of the question of identities. The model deserves to be invoked in a context in which desires for such intersectional dynamics have been taxonomized as not belonging to the mainstream and thus ignored.

The social and political future of the Latino gay, lesbian, bisexual, and transgender movement is not simply a question of adding more categories, like beads on a string, without listening to what those newly included have to say about themselves and about others. It entails asking what it means at this point to relate culture and sexuality, race and gender. In terms of the intersectional politics that they seek to pursue, Latino organizations should pay more attention to the ways Latin American social movements have been able to articulate their specific demands within broader contexts. At the same time, political work must take into account the specifically national traits of its areas of influence in order to develop progressive policies.

It is clear that social movements are always bound to change in terms of what is written from spaces that seem to fall outside majoritarian discourse. It is also clear that new spaces of contestation will open up while others that were previously marginalized will occupy the center. But this is a very detached way of looking at things and it belies a very national U.S.–based form of politics. As soon as it starts entering an international arena it is forced to contend with different forms of continuities that survive within other political and constitutional discontinuities.

What positions will these organizations take in the midst of constitutional crises that choose to validate only higher-class gay or lesbian communities and not lower-class ones? At what point will those organizations address the role that stigma and shame play in the realms of ethnicities and sexualities? Pride in terms of the choices we make is important, but it is also necessary to see how choices are significant political decisions in their own right. George Yúdice has explained that "to represent Latin America from a U.S. perspective, multicultural or not, is like jamming square pegs into round holes."[40] Those spaces that we have made possible by paying attention to issues of sexuality need to be validated and understood in their full complexity. This complexity will ultimately be useful and instructive for U.S. gay and lesbian organizations, not only by opening them up to different ways of conducting politics, but also by making them pay attention to the ways they unwittingly may find themselves in the wrong position—attempting to dictate policies in contexts that have nothing to do with their own.

Conclusion

Fires

Tropics of Desire offered bodies, archives, and masks. It aimed to seduce readers into exploring a space that promised some kind of denouement. The allure is always that there is some secret revealed in the act of masking. I explored the mask in its own circuit and I saw it as a positional tool, one that could be deployed in different settings and contexts, one that created broad coalitions in order to achieve visibility and civil rights. The mask was presented from the outset as a polemical intervention, but also as an effective one. It was effective insofar as it refused the certainties involved in a divided society, while also addressing the legacies of shame in Latin America so that shame was marked and reappropriated as such.

The book promised a conclusion that was then masked as an archive. The past in some way was allowed to clarify the present. There was a history to those activist forms of protest, as well as a context. The archive was deployed as a way of historicizing those gestures, but also as a way of encoding them within a tradition. This tradition may not see homosexuality within the same parameters for identity deployed at this point in the United States, but it has its own forms of social action, its own political and civil demands. In the first chapter of the book I saw the question of identity in a historical framework. The archive there was explored from its very surface: from the letters that members of different networks wrote to each other in order to foster a sense of contact predicated on notions of sexuality that were nowhere to be seen on paper. In this situation, the archive was engaged as a tool that spoke of the contradictory contacts made and the equally contradictory silences those contacts entailed in writing. At the same time, I argued the limits of seeing a notion of identity as providing a sense of solidarity to these writers. I thought it was more important to see the interaction of the identity with the law, with systems of control, including state systems of surveillance in the very form of the letters sent and the information contained in them.

I mentioned how this introduction to the archive was, somewhat paradoxically, "against the grain." I was interested in an ambivalent project in its own right: the construction and demolition of the archive itself, or rather, the freedom to construct the archive in whichever way we want—at a certain distance from notions of identity as these are understood in the United States, but also with the firm conviction that homosexuality is not merely an addendum to the tale, a festive afterthought. It could not be an afterthought in those letters precisely because it was *seldom* mentioned. This fact is what makes it all the more important. I then brought out other figures from the archive, once again with the intention of seeing what they had to say in terms of contemporary debates around homosexuality, but also in order to explore how these writers initially negotiated their positions within national discourses that were bound to marginalize them for their gender or their sexuality. In the case of Lydia Cabrera, I tried to decode a complex politics out of her anthropological work. This politics sends us back to a network of lesbian interventions that I thought were important to mark. In the case of Xavier Villaurrutia, I tried to understand his position in Mexican letters and the problems entailed in allowing our readings to be solely consumed with the issue of sexuality. Metaphysics and homosexuality can be part of the same interlocution, and the way these relate to each other gives a clearer account of Villaurrutia's positions on sex and sexuality than any other biographical gossip we may unearth. Finally, in the case of Virgilio Piñera, I explored issues that later reappeared in the chapter on *Strawberry and Chocolate*. In both essays, I was deeply suspicious of the act of outing a literary figure or even a composite social type within the context of state visibility. In the tragic case of Piñera, I argued, it collaborated against the very dramatic silence and ostracism that befell him in his later years.

How all this information is coded and uncoded allowed me to explore different forms of interaction with and within the Latino American milieu. Self-representation was the theme of the chapter on letters, just as sex and desire named the interventions seen in the case of Villaurrutia and Cabrera. The politics of silence cut a gash, which is also a running thread, in the work of Virgilio Piñera, and the relationship between revolution and sexuality is crucial for understanding the appearance of *Strawberry and Chocolate*.

The later chapters of the book move out of the archive and into a present signaled by the Cuban film. They keep the focus on different forms of artistic intervention but also spread that focus around in different directions. One could say that the book explodes after the figure of the homosexual is represented in the Cuban revolution. It goes on to examine the relationship between music and sexualities and gender, it speaks about the creation of a North American market built upon the fetishization of the Latino male, and it engages in a critique of the organizational politics of Latino gay and lesbian organizations based in the United States.

One of the questions I tried to answer in this book was about the relationship between the archive and the code, between the past and the present. Not that these are absolute terms: the code is part of the archive and vice versa. If the archive revealed a certain ambiguity as to the notion of sexual identities, what does that ambiguity mean in terms of the present, and what does it say about concrete issues facing us these days? The answer to this question migrates from chapter to chapter. Questions of identity do not immediately obtain in solving the situation of Latino gays and lesbians in the

United States or in Latin America. We must repeat and insist upon the difference of Latino American sociopolitical structures, and the examples given by the figures in the archive are also important to keep in mind. They negotiated their sexuality with a sense of fatality and damnation that they flung to their heirs, while also negotiating their own space within their societies and refusing acts of marginalization even as means to an end.

My qualified distance from the goals of identity politics manifested itself in the latter part of this book. One afternoon in class, a student asked what this book was all about. Without thinking about it (but also thinking about it at the same time), I showed him my copy of a Luis Miguel compact disc that I had been carrying around. The cover had the singer shadowed next to a microphone that looked like the shadow of a penis: "This is what it's all about." And I put the image squarely in front of him and we all laughed. And then I said, "I'm joking," but immediately I also said, "I am really not joking." And what he knew about the book is partly the snippets that I have let out here and there, like when I say the book is about Ricky Martin.

What I generally don't say when they ask about the book is that it is about gay and lesbian studies, or queer studies, or anything of the sort. This is not the result of my being in any way closeted but rather of the "celebrity" status that I sought for this book. Celebrities articulate a function at this time—they function more like the Morse code, the metonym, or the emblem for complex abstractions. The celebrity is not the symbol of anything but the emblem that compresses and expands temporality, that interpellates different audiences. That is why I always said the work was about Ricky Martin. But then, watching television late one night, Jay Leno remarked on *The Tonight Show* that *People* magazine had selected Ricky as this year's "Sexiest Man Alive." Immediately after the announcement, in the joke that followed, he adopted a fey prancing mode and tone of voice. The joke was unrelated to Ricky, but it referred to his presumed sexuality in an oblique manner. The joke that followed that one, significantly, was about Michael Jackson.

This book has a passport, but it is also clear that it is a hybrid book, over and beyond the systems of classification it may participate in. As a queer studies book, it also touches upon Latin American studies, and also "Latino studies." As a book on Latino American studies, it is about the queer inscriptions that we make. This sense of representation is out of the closet in this book from the first entry in the tourist brochure; it is important to mark the civil rights that secure freedom.

This book is marked by a form of desire that has not engaged in the same illusions of freedom that have been proclaimed by many in the gay and lesbian community. That desire at some times has assumed the form of resistance and at other times has been vocally in opposition to many of the received notions that inform narratives of sexuality in the United States. If at one point I wanted to claim cultural difference for the sake of explaining specificities involved in desire, at this point I am less interested in that notion of difference.

Tropics of Desire first aimed to explore the connection between genders, ethnicities, and sexualities by focusing on writers who placed themselves outside the normative definitions of nationality and sexuality given during their lifetimes. Xavier Villaurrutia, Lydia Cabrera, and Virgilio Piñera saw themselves in relation to national forms of identification, but also in terms of broader categories of meaning that linked them to others over and beyond their cultures of origin. Identifications in terms of sexuality created a "transnational" form of collaboration, while their work intervened in the national arenas where it originated. The way their various forms of identity discourse coalesced is not simple, and cannot simply be reduced to their interpellation as gay or lesbian subjectivity. The space of "high" culture, or even of a science such as anthropology, allowed for certain affective links to play themselves out, while at the same time it served to mask (or expose) their homosexuality. It is not that for these writers culture expressed a "gay" or "lesbian" identity, but rather that it accommodated a degree of complexity that allowed the subject to escape taxonomies based on simplified notions of object-choice or homosexual condemnation. It is clear that the works they produced were a form of escape and at the same time a form of coping with homophobia. But it is not clear to me that an assertion of homosexual identity would have in itself allowed for self-affirmation. I think, on the contrary, that an identity solely based on the reaffirmation of sexuality would have entailed an oppressive and oppressing mode of social articulation for these writers, and would have limited their sense of intervention in important ways.

I revisited these works as a way of trying to work out the impasse of a politics of identity in the United States. I see this identity politics as an oppressive and oppressing mode of social articulation. A simplified notion of gender, race, and class does not hold in a context where gender needs to be pluralized, and race need not fit the parameters of white and black, with class left aside. All these terms need to be mobilized, articulated, and rearticulated for the sake of a politics that goes beyond identity and its taxonomical imperative.

That these subjects played their work out in a "transnational" arena highlights the historical framework in which they lived, from the 1930s to the 1950s and beyond. It is clear that as gay and lesbian subjects, they allow us to grasp the profound transnational constellations of both North and South America, away from the imperial histories that always seek to create a center of discourse on identities and sexualities—Europe or the United States—and then peripheral societies that merely receive that discourse as part of a "modernizing" project. In fact, at various points in this book I see those peripheral societies articulating a more nuanced and progressive politics. Of course, we should not see the relationship between center and peripheries in a simplified way. But it is also clear that in a context in which the center aims to occupy the peripheries, there needs to be a way of opening up the center for the sake of an accommodation.

Tropics of Desire aims to be a kind of transdisciplinary object in itself: if the first part is more concerned with gay/lesbian relationships between the United States and Latin America, the second part focuses more on popular culture in the United States. The book works out of particular dissatisfactions with many discourses, objects of study, and even modes of articulation, particularly in the field of queer studies. There is a dissatisfaction with what is said about Latina/os and what we say about ourselves; dissatisfaction with identity politics; and dissatisfaction with recent political and cultural discourses in the United States in which gays and lesbians are classified under different taxonomical principles that are not allowed to communicate. What use is there for a queer studies that does not articulate a critique of class, or a women's studies that does not include race, or a postcolonial theory that does not take into account its own sense of privileged narrative?

Seven or eight years ago I was researching a project in Santiago de Chile when I decided to go to Valparaíso and Viña del Mar, on the coast, with a Chilean friend. We got to Viña late one night and then a cab took us to the adjoining city of Valparaíso, to a second-floor discotheque in what seemed to be a warehousing district. One entered by means of a metal or wooden staircase (I forget which) abutting the warehouse. Once inside we were at Discoteca Paraiso—or Disco Divine, I forget. I remarked to my friend that this was a much more interesting place than the upscale bar we went to back in Santiago. There were spandexed drag queens and drag queens with very cheap dresses. There were lesbians and men with beards, young and old, generally middle- or working-class, and then there were the two visitors from Santiago—one from abroad and the other one a fairly well known media figure. The show came and went and it was memorable precisely because of how unremarkable it was. It had its share of kinkiness and frisson, and an unbelievable plotline that concerned a visit to hell (a paper door on stage served as the prop), some devils carousing around, and references to Dante. It ended with a Beatrice who lip-synched the Spanish diva Rocio Durcal (not exactly young but still belting out a tune). I remember the evening as more than a happy occasion. I forget how many drinks I ordered and I have no idea if these made the show's plotline more incomprehensible to me. I did know the tunes, though, and I could even sing a number of them.

As I was finishing this book, I received a collection of essays published by Pedro Lemebel in Santiago. Lemebel is part of a duo called Las yeguas del Apocalipsis, which loosely translates as the Mares of the Apocalypse, and they sometimes dress in drag, or create performance shows, or work with installations. Lemebel also does literary chronicles and these, titled *La esquina es mi corazon* (The corner is my heart) were published by Editorial Cuarto Propio, which takes off from Woolf's idea of a room of one's own in order to create a publishing space that is open to progressive discourse of all kinds—particularly lesbian and gay. In one of these essays, Lemebel talks about how that disco burned down to the ground one night in Valparaíso, and how the authorities disregarded the event. It narrates, in an over-the-top and engaging prose that is ferocious in its sense of liberty, the night the queens died because of an arsonist. It evokes the raunchy smell of the wigs, the urinals that provided no escape, and all those rhinestones that are somehow still shining at night. It was Lemebel's protest and it was also his sadness. And nothing can take away that sense of rage at utter social disregard or collective condemnation. The fires can still be felt in the trace of those ashes, like the disco ball that Lemebel sees shining at night at the center of the dance floor.

Notes

All translations in the text and the notes are mine unless otherwise indicated.

Notes to the Introduction

1. Guy Hocquenghem, *Homosexual Desire*, trans. Daniella Dangoor (Durham: Duke University Press, 1993).

2. This has been noted by Donna Guy and Jorge Salessi. See Jorge Salessi, *Médicos maleantes y maricas: Higiene, criminología y homosexualidad en la construcción de la nación argentina (Buenos Aires, 1871–1914)* (Rosario: Beatriz Viterbo, 1995); and "The Argentine Dissemination of Homosexuality, 1890–1914," in *Entiendes? Queer Readings, Hispanic Writings*, ed. Emile Bergmann and Paul Julian Smith (Durham: Duke University Press, 1995), 49–91. Donna Guy, *Sex and Danger: Prostitution, Family and Nation in Argentina* (Lincoln: University of Nebraska Press, 1991). As Salessi has recalled, in Argentine texts at the end of the nineteenth century, the homosexual is a category, a "European" signifier that comes to disrupt the dream of the perfect binary and has already contaminated and "invaded" Europe and the United States (53). Since the homosexual is born into language, the naming of the homosexual follows a particular set of constraints. It is not my intention to dwell on the medico-legal discourse on homosexuality at the turn of the century. This has been the focus of, particularly, Salessi and Guy, among others. What I am more interested in for the sake of this project is the fact that the taxonomization, condemnation, and repression of homosexuality entailed the deployment of particular differential equations that have important consequences for the *present* study of homosexualities.

3. See Rob Buffington, "Los jotos: Contested Visions of Homosexuality in Modern Mexico," in *Sex and Sexuality in Latin America*, ed. Daniel Balderston and Donna J. Guy (New York: New York University Press, 1997), 118–32, 128.

4. In 1980, when the United States did not generally recognize homosexuality as legal grounds for immigration, some participants in the Mariel exodus from Cuba claimed their passive homosexual status as a way out of the island. For them, homosexuality was a valid reason for exile. Upon their arrival in the United States, this reason would be rewritten fundamentally in political terms.

5. Tomás Almaguer, "Chicano Men: A Cartography of Homosexual Identity and Behavior," in *The Lesbian and Gay Studies Reader*, ed. Henry Abelove, Michèle Aina Barale, and David M. Halperin (New York: Routledge, 1993), 255–73. Joseph Carrier, *De los otros: Intimacy and Homosexuality among Mexican Men* (New York: Columbia University Press, 1995); Octavio Paz, *The Labyrinth of Solitude and Other Writings*, trans. Lysander Kemp (New York: Grove Weidenfeld, 1985); Ian Lumsden, *Machos, Maricones and Gays: Cuba and Homosexuality* (Philadelphia: Temple University Press, 1996); Marvin Leiner, *Sexual Politics in Cuba: Machismo, Homosexuality and AIDS* (Boulder: Westview Press, 1994).

6. Roger N. Lancaster, *Life Is Hard: Machismo, Danger and the Intimacy of Power in Nicaragua* (Berkeley: University of California Press, 1992); see also his "Guto's Performance: Notes on the Transvestism of Everyday Life," in Balderston and Guy, *Sex and Sexuality in Latin America*, 9–32. Sylvia Molloy, "Disappearing Acts: Reading Lesbian in Teresa de la Parra," in Bergmann and Smith, *Entiendes?* 230–56. Licia Fiol Matta, "The Schoolteacher of America: Gender, Sexuality and Nation in Gabriela Mistral," in Bergmann and Smith, *Entiendes?* 201–29. Frances Negrón's *Brincando el charco* is discussed in chapter 8.

7. Yvonne Yarbro Bejarano, "Crossing the Border with Chabela Vargas: A Chicana Femme's Tribute," in Balderston and Guy, *Sex and Sexuality in Latin America*, 33–43.

8. "¿No será, acaso, peligrosa, si su existencia fuera comprobada? ¿Los homosexuales no estaremos cayendo en una trampa resaltando nuestra propia autoestima? ¿No le estaremos haciendo el juego a un poder que lo único que pretende es encasillar en compartimientos para alcanzar así ese 'divide y reinarás' maquiavélico?" Carlos Jáuregui, *La homosexualidad en Argentina* (Buenos Aires: Ediciones Tarso, 1987), 11–12.

9. "Es necesario que pensemos, a partir de esa realidad que es nuestra homosexualidad, cuáles son los tipos de relaciones que podemos establecer con el mundo, de qué forma podemos establecerlas y qué necesitamos inventar para hacerlo." Ibid., 12.

10. This is not to say that there are no polemics even within the issue of transnationality. For example, in 1993 the CHA objected to Jáuregui's use of the word "gay" in his organization Gays por los derechos civiles (Gays for Civil Rights) since the CHA thought that the use of the word "gay" leveled the cultural specificities of homosexuality as a condition and squarely made homosexuality part of a U.S.–centered mode of apolitical struggle, with the prospect of Argentinean homosexuals forgetting their political solidarity with the Left for the sake of the trappings of a U.S. "lifestyle" issue. Jáuregui's response to these polemics was situationist in the broader sense of the word. Since for most Argentineans the word "gay" had the positive connotations of modern, postindustrial societies, like those of Britain and the United States, Jáuregui opted to use the word as a way of allowing the connection to be there at the level of signifier, even if it was not at the level of the signified.

11. On the prudishness of history, see Daniel Balderston, *El deseo: Enorme cicatriz luminosa* (Caracas: Ediciones eXcultura, 1999), chap. 1, pp. 5–17.

12. Oscar Montero, "Modernismo and Homophobia: Darío and Rodó," in Balderston and Guy, *Sex and Sexuality in Latin America,* 101–17.

13. See John K. Walsh, "A Logic in Lorca's Ode to Walt Whitman," in Bergmann and Smith, *Entiendes?,* 257–78.

14. Ibid., 259.

15. Ibid., Walsh underscores the elitism of this publication: "It all came to a closed and private project, not to be released beyond the fringes: fifty carefully distributed copies from a poet whose *Romancero gitano* [Gypsy Ballads] was then being run off by the thousands and would become the most familiar cycle of poems of the century in any Western literature" (259).

16. See Neil Bartlett's stunning *Who Was That Man? A Present for Mr. Oscar Wilde* (London: Serpent's Tail, 1988). I am indebted to Daniel Balderston for leading me to this book.

17.

> *Federico y yo, solos, como dos amigos que no se han visto en muchos años, como dos personas que van a cotejar sus biografías, preparadas en distintos extremos de la tierra para gustar cada uno de cada otra. ¿En qué momento comenzamos a tutearnos? Yo llevaba fresco el recuerdo de su Oda a Walt Whitman, viril, valiente, preciosa, que en limitada edición acababan de imprimir en México los muchachos de Alcancía y que Federico no había visto. Pero no hablamos de literatura. Toda nuestra España fluía de sus labios en charla sin testigos, ávida de acercarse a nuestro México, que él miraba en el indiecito que descubría en mis ojos.*

Salvador Novo, "Buenos Aires," from *Continente vacío (Viaje a Sudamérica),* in *Toda la prosa* (México: Empresas Editoriales, 1964), 307.

18. Molloy, "Disappearing Acts," 230–56, 239.
19. Ibid., 241.
20. Ibid., 244.
21. It did assume center stage particularly after Lezama published *Paradiso*. Homosexuality also became an issue in postrevolutionary Cuban politics, as former members of *Orígenes* sought to explain to themselves the relationship of Lezama's acquiescence and inner exile to the closeted form in which he had always assumed his homosexuality. An interesting case concerns the Cuban poet and *Orígenes* fellow traveler Lorenzo García Vega in his *Los años de Orígenes* (Caracas: Monte Avila, 1978), who explicitly talks about Lezama's cultural project in its sublimated relationship to male homosexuality.
22. "Yo sé que no has hecho nada y que te dejas arrastrar por períodos insensatos y sensuales." José Lezama Lima to José Rodríguez Feo, in José Rodríguez Feo, *Mi correspondencia con Lezama Lima* (Havana: Ediciones Unión, 1989), 38.
23. "Despues de seis días en Firenze, estoy en esta playa deliciosa, dándome los baños de mar y contemplando estas bellezas italianas que surgen del mar como aquel Tadzio de Muerte en Venecia." José Rodríguez Feo to José Lezama Lima, in José Rodríguez Feo, *Mi correspondencia con Leazama Lima*, 137.

Notes to Chapter 1

1. Elizabeth Bishop, *One Art*, Letters, selected and edited by Robert Giroux (New York: Farrar, Straus, Giroux, 1994), 234–36. All page numbers in parentheses are from this edition.
2. At a later stage in the writing of this essay, I consulted Roxana Pagés-Rangel, *Del dominio público: Itinerarios de la carta privada* (Amsterdam: Rodopi, 1997). Pagés's brilliant book has many points of contact with this essay, and the act of finding and reading the book (actually, recalling at that particular time that another colleague had mentioned its existence) was important in reconfirming many of my ideas about correspondence—about its fragmentary existence, as well as about issues of the public or private nature of letters. My aim is different from that of Pagés, but it is important to point out its lucid intervention in this writing.
3. Pagés-Rangel mentions this as one of the most emblematic moments in the dis-

course of letters: the loss of one's own words to another. See *Del dominio público,* 13–14, 111.

4. Roland Barthes, *The Pleasure of the Text* (New York: Hill and Wang, 1975), 56. Representation can only be "embarrassed figuration" in Barthes's terms: "a space of alibis (reality, morality, likelihood, readability, truth, etc.)" (56).

5.

> *Los Angeles no tiene belleza sino en la noche irresistible. Los night clubs son preciosos y en ellos descanso, bebiendo cerveza antes de emprender una nueva ascensión al cielo de mi cuarto, en el noveno piso. Cuando crees que esa ascensión será la última de la noche, una tentación, una nueva oportunidad. No sé de qué color es el sueño de Los Angeles, sólo sé que estos son azules.*

Xavier Villaurrutia, *Cartas de Villaurrutia a Novo (1935–1936)* (Mexico: Instituto Nacional de Bellas Artes, 1966), 72.

6. Novo's memoirs have been published in Mexico as *La estatua de sal* (Mexico: Consejo Nacional para la Cultura y las Artes, 1998) with a brilliant introduction by Carlos Monsiváis. A part has appeared in English in *Now the Volcano,* ed. Winston Leyland (San Francisco: Gay Sunshine Press, 1979), 11–47. This is the first of two Gay Sunshine Anthologies of Latin American Gay Writers. The second volume, *My Deep Dark Pain Is Love,* was published in 1983.

7. Novo, "Memoir," in Leyland, *Now the Volcano,* 24–25.

8. *Nostalgia for Death: Poetry by Xavier Villarrutia,* trans. Eliot Weinberger, and *Hieroglyphs of Desire, by Octavio Paz,* trans. Esther Allen, ed. Eliot Weinberger (Port Townsend, WA: Copper Canyon Press, 1993). Cited as *Nostalgia for Death* from here on.

9. For a more complete recounting of homosexuality as a theme in Latin American writing, see Daniel Balderston, *El deseo: Enorme cicatriz luminosa* (Caracas: Ediciones eXcultura, 1999), particularly its first chapter.

10. A more thorough examination of all these codes can be found in Neil Bartlett's excellent *Who Was That Man? A Present for Mr. Oscar Wilde* (London: Serpent's Tail, 1988). The quote appears on pp. 140–41.

11. "Supongo que tus sentidos estarán más empavonados, con brillantina como si dijéramos, con el trato de todas esas firmas. ¿Qué tal parece un hombre disfrazado de firma? Muchos de esos respetables que tú enumeras, creía que nunca irían a la misma esquina con el farol que yo había escogido." José Lezama Lima to José

Rodríguez Feo, in José Rodríguez Feo, *Mi correspondencia con Lezama Lima* (Havana: Ediciones Unión, 1989), 94.

12. Severo Sarduy, *La simulación* (Caracas: Monte Avila, 1982).

13. "Atravesamos unos días egipcios, lo que está muerto se embalsama y los familiares siguen llevando comida y perfumes para seguir reyendo en una existencia petrificada." Lezama Lima to Rodríguez Feo in Rodríguez Feo, *Mi correspondencia con Lezama Lima*, 86.

14. On the relationship between absence and letter writing, see once again Pagés-Rangel, *Del dominio público*, 199. Letters, as Pagés-Rangel explains, are produced from the space of absence itself. Originating from absence, they then circulate in other contexts. This absence as foundational element in letters I see manifested in the question of homosexuality itself.

15. "Si la ciudad es fea de día, es maravillosa de noche. Ni en New York fluye, como aquí, el deseo y la satisfacción del deseo. El viernes y el sábado los pasé sin dormir casi." Villaurrutia, *Cartas de Villaurrutia a Novo*, 75.

16. "No estoy seguro de no extrañar, mañana, en México, lo que en un principio rechazaba aquí con toda la fuerza irracional de la nostalgia que sentía por mis costumbres allá." Ibid., 24–25.

17. "En Caracas no me atraen ni el deseo de gustar, los elogios me aburren mortalmente," Teresa de la Parra to Gonzalo Zaldumbide, April 14, 1928, in Teresa de la Parra, *Obra escogida*, vol. 2 (Caracas: Monte Avila Editores, 1992), 123.

18. "Yo también he sentido el charme de París en verano por los quais, pero yo estaba muy triste y muy sola, pensaba en mi muerte y la deseaba recordando las generaciones que habían caminado y sufrido de desencanto como yo por las mismas calles, frente al mismo Sena." Teresa de la Parra to Lydia Cabrera, August 1928, in Teresa de la Parra, *Obra escogida*, vol. 2, 128.

19. "Te veo siempre llegar hasta el borde y allí retroceder. Adelantas tus inquietas y minuciosas tropas hasta las puertas de Quebec, Terranova, Bunker Hill o New York, y aconsejado por tu inquieta pereza o por el grave destino, desistes y buscas otro centro de exploraciones geográficas," Lezama Lima to Rodríguez Feo, in Rodríguez Feo, *Mi correspondencia con Lezama Lima*, 57.

20. It is significant in this context that in the letter that precedes this one, from Rodríguez Feo to Lezama, the former talks about spending time with Paul Bowles in New York (see letter dated May 30, 1947, pp. 56–57). Bowles was, of course, the author of *The Sheltering Sky*, a novel that makes a clear distinction between travel and tourism.

21. Hart Crane to Waldo Frank, June 13, 1931, in *The Letters of Hart Crane, 1916–1932*, ed. Brom Weber (New York: Hermitage House, 1952), 372.

22. The comment is rescued by Octavio Paz in "Hieroglyphs of Desire: A Critical Study," in *Nostalgia for Death*. For an introduction to the "gay nonreading" of Whitman in Latin America, see Jorge Salessi and José Quiroga, "Errata sobre la erótica, or the Elision of Whitman's Body," in *Breaking Bounds: Whitman and American Cultural Studies*, ed. Betsy Erkkila and Jay Grossman (New York: Oxford University Press, 1996), 123–32. The two most recent and complete essays on Whitman in Latin America are Doris Sommer, "Supplying Demand: Walt Whitman as the Liberal Self," in *Reinventing the Americas: Comparative Studies of Literature of the United States and Spanish America*, ed. Bell Gale Chevigny and Gari Laguardia (Cambridge: Cambridge University Press, 1986), 68–91; and Enrico Mario Santí, "The Accidental Tourist: Walt Whitman in Latin America," in *Do the Americas Have a Common Literature?* ed. Gustavo Pérez-Firmat (Durham: Duke University Press, 1990), 156–76. Both of these works take as their polemical point of departure the now classic work by Fernando Alegría, *Walt Whitman en Hispanoamérica* (Mexico: Colección Studium, 1954).

23. "Y lo gracioso es que Mañach y Baralt y Sras. lo boycottearon. Yo tampoco fui. Por lo visto todos aquí se enteraron de qué clase de tipo es y su famosa seducción pasó de boca en boca empujada hábilmente por las lenguas chismosas de la Sra. de Mañach. Hasta Don Pedro Salinas oyó la historieta." Rodríguez Feo, *Mi correspondencia con Lezama Lima*, 67.

24. I have translated literally Rodríguez Feo's *pederastia* for its slanderous legalistic resonance. I have no information as to the details of the case and it most certainly involves ordinary sex acts.

Notes to Chapter 2

1. Robert McKee Irwin, "The Legend of Jorge Cuesta: The Perils of Alchemy and the Paranoia of Gender," in *Hispanisms and Homosexualities*, ed. Sylvia Molloy and Robert McKee Irwin (Durham: Duke University Press, 1998), 31.

2. *Nostalgia for Death*. The essay is a translation of Octavio Paz, *Xavier Villaurrutia en persona y obra* (Mexico: Fondo de Cultura Económica, 1978).

3. *Nostalgia for Death*, "Editor's Note," 1.

4. Ibid., 2.

5. Ibid., 1.

6. Guillermo Sheridan, *Los Contemporáneos ayer* (Mexico: Fondo de Cultura Económica, 1985), esp. 255–61.

7. Irwin, "The Legend of Jorge Cuesta," 32.

8. This was also the political tactic used by Virgilio Piñera in his essay "Ballagas en persona," where he chastised Cuban critics for not mentioning Ballagas's homosexuality. For more on Piñera and on this essay, see chapter 4.

9.

> *Even absent you're alive!*
> *I find you in the hollow*
> *of a form and the echo*
> *of some momentary sound;*
> *even my own saliva tastes of your shadowy taste,*
> *and in exchange for what's mine*
> *you've left me only the fear*
> *of finding even in taste*
> *the presence of this void.*

Nostalgia for Death, 88–89.

10. Paz, "Hieroglyphs of Desire," in *Nostalgia for Death*, 95.

11. Ibid., 96.

12. Ibid., 102.

13. Ibid., 109.

14. Leo Bersani, *Homos* (Cambridge: Harvard University Press, 1995). John Rechy, *The Sexual Outlaw: A Documentary: A Non-Fiction Account, with Commentaries, of Three Days and Nights in the Sexual Underground* (New York: Grove Press, 1977). Bersani does not mention Rechy in this book.

15. Some of that sex was recounted in Salvador Novo's racy memoirs, recently published in Mexico as *La estatua de sal* (Mexico: Consejo Nacional para la Cultura y las Artes, 1998), with an introduction by Carlos Monsiváis. A partial translation of this had already been published in English as "Memoir" in Winston Leyland, ed., *Now the Volcano* (San Francisco: Gay Sunshine Press, 1979), 11–47.

16. Paz speaks also of Villaurrutia in chapter 3 of *The Labyrinth of Solitude*, "The Day of the Dead," (New York: Grove Weidenfeld, 1985). For Paz, there is something essentially Mexican in Villaurrutia's notion of death as a return.

17. *Nostalgia for Death,* 79, 81.

> *O el miedo de llegar a ser uno mismo*
> *tan directa y profundamente*
> *que ni los años, ni la consunción ni la lepra,*
> *nada ni nadie*
> *nos distraiga un instante*
> *de nuestra perfecta atención a nosotros mismos,*
> *haciéndonos sentir nuestra creciente,*
> *irreversible parálisis.*

Villaurrutia, *Nostalgia de la muerte,* 78–80.

18. Villaurrutia, *Nostalgia de la muerte,* 12.

> *Find in the mirror the assassinated statue*
> *pull it out from the blood of its shadow,*
> *dress it in a flutter of eyes,*
> *caress it like a sister who suddenly appears,*
> *shuffle the chips of its fingers*
> *and repeat in its ear a hundred times a hundred*
> *hundred times*
> *until you hear it say: "I am dying of sleep."*

Nostalgia for Death, 13.

19. Villaurrutia uses the same metaphor of game pieces—*fichas*—as Foucault, when the latter remarks on SM as a chess game. Michel Foucault, *Foucault Live (Interviews, 1966–84),* trans. John Johnston, ed. Sylvère Lotringer (New York: Semiotext(e), 1989).

> *What interests the practitioners of S & M is that the relationship is at the same time regulated and open. It resembles a chess game in the sense that one can win and the other lose. . . . This mixture of rules and openness has the effect of intensifying sexual relations by introducing a perpetual novelty, a perpetual tension and a perpetual uncertainty which the simple consummation of the act lacks.*

226.

20. Villaurrutia, *Nostalgia de la muerte,* 4.

> *Everything the night sketches*

with its shadowy hand:
the pleasures it reveals,
the vices it undresses.

Nostalgia for Death, 5.

21. Villaurrutia, *Nostalgia de la muerte*, 6.

Everything
circulates through every branch
of the tree of my veins.
It caresses my thighs,
it pushes my head under,
it lives in my deadening eyes,
and dies on my hardening lips.

Nostalgia for Death, 7.

22. James Miller, "Dante on Fire Island: Reinventing Heaven in the AIDS Elegy," in *Writing AIDS: Gay Literature, Language and Analysis*, ed. Timothy F. Murphy and Suzanne Poirier (New York: Columbia University Press, 1993), 265–305, 266.

23. Ibid., 266–67.

24. Guy Hocquenghem, *Homosexual Desire*, trans. Daniella Dangoor (Durham: Duke University Press, 1993), 49–50.

25. *Nostalgia for Death*, 45.

Se diría que las calles fluyen dulcemente en la noche.
Las luces no son tan vivas que logren desvelar el secreto,
el secreto que los hombres que van y vienen conocen,
porque todos están en el secreto
y nada se ganaría con partirlo en mil pedazos
si, por el contrario,
es tan dulce guardarlo
y compartirlo sólo con la persona elegida.

Villaurrutia, *Nostalgia de la muerte*, 44.

26. Hocquenghem, *Homosexual Desire*, 131.

27. Mechanical scattering, as Hocquenghem says in relation to Thomas Mann's *Death in Venice*, is translated as "absence and substitution." Ibid., 131.

28. Villaurrutia, *Nostalgia del muerte*, 44–45.

29. Hocquenghem, *Homosexual Desire*, 131.

30. Ibid., 131–32.

31. *Nostalgia for Death,* 45.

Si cada uno dijera en un momento dado,
en solo una palabra, lo que piensa,
las cinco letras del DESEO formarían una enorme cicatriz luminosa,
una constelación más antigua, más viva aún que las otras.
Y esa constelación sería como un ardiente sexo
en el profundo cuerpo de la noche,
o, mejor, como los Gemelos que por vez primera en la vida
se miraran de frente, a los ojos, y se abrazaran ya para siempre.

Villaurrutia, *Nostalgia de la muerte,* 44.

32. Paul de Man, "Tropes (Rilke)," in *Allegories of Reading: Figural Language in Rousseau, Nietzsche, Rilke and Proust* (New Haven: Yale University Press, 1979), 20–56.

33. Ibid., 37.

34. I have used Jane Gallop's gloss on Lacan in *Reading Lacan* (Ithaca: Cornell University Press, 1985), esp. 74–92.

35. Dangerous Bedfellows, eds., *Policing Public Sex: Queer Politics and the Future of AIDS Activism* (Boston: South End Press, 1996). Odets argues for a differentiated approach to issues of prevention along the lines of HIV-negative and -positive men, allowing for the "relapses" from safer sex in these individuals; Thomas discusses how public sex has been unanimized for gay white men, and how the idea in itself works in communities of color; Allan Bérubé explains that the policing of sex will result in even more unsafe forms of sexual coupling.

36. For Rotello and Sullivan, gays (gay men in particular) should conform to "community standards" and should fight legally for issues such as the recognition of gay marriages, the full incorporation of gay men and lesbians into the armed forces, and a general lack of discrimination based on sexual orientation. For Sullivan, Rotello, and Bawer, the gay male community should attempt to "blend in" if it aims for a discourse of "inclusion" and legal rights under the law.

37. George Chauncey, *Gay New York: Gender, Urban Culture, and the Making of the Gay Male World, 1890–1940* (New York: Basic Books, 1994).

38. Gabriel Rotello, *Sexual Ecology: AIDS and the Destiny of Gay Men* (New York: Dutton, 1997), 41.

39. I focus on Rotello as one example of a generalized discourse that appears in certain segments of the gay community. Rotello, Sullivan, Bawer, and others have written books that, in the past two or three years, have proclaimed a new moment within the queer movement. The sense of distance that I have from this discourse is obvious, but I want to state that its implications go farther than just a mere reading of Rotello's book.

40. Villaurrutia, *Nostalgia de la muerte*, 14. I am departing from Weinberger's translation and offering my literal translation at this point:

And in the anguished game of one mirror in front of the other
my voice falls
And my voice that ripens
And my voice that burns
And my forest ripens
And my voice burns hard.

41. Weinberger could not exactly reproduce the same words; rather, he gives an idea of their effects in a brilliant solution:

In the miserable game of mirror to mirror
my voice is falling
and my voice incinerates
and my voice in sin narrates
and my voice in sin elates
and my poison scintillates.

Nostalgia for Death, 15.

Notes to Chapter 3

1. Other readers have remarked on the religious aspects of the book. For example, Eugenio Florit, in "Palabras sobre Lydia Cabrera y su obra," says that *El monte* is a "maravillosa colección de relatos y anécdotas en los que se reunen naturaleza, religión, fetichismo, plantas y animales, que los negros consideran como su biblia, así como hace siglos se formó el Popol-Vuh, la biblia del pueblo maya-quiché." In Reinaldo Sanchez et al., *Homenaje a Lydia Cabrera* (Miami: Ediciones Universal, 1978), 4.

2. There, the U.S. news media treated santería as a taxonomized "Cuban" religion, although its relationship with the Catholic hierarchy and with the governmental structures of power has always been tense, as I mention below.

3. I borrow the term from Kimberlé Crenshaw by way of José Esteban Muñoz, who defines intersectionality as a "critical hermeneutics that registers the copresence of sexuality, race, class, gender and other identity differentials as particular components that exist simultaneously with each other" (84). Intersectional strategy is one that does not pin down and is not bound by any particular code of identity or coherence, but rather seeks to turn incoherence or unintelligibility into its own kind of system. See José Esteban Muñoz, *Disidentifications: Queers of Color and the Performance of Politics* (Minneapolis: University of Minnesota Press, 1999).

4. Reinaldo Arenas, *Before Night Falls*, trans. Dolores M. Koch (New York: Viking Books, 1993), 290–91.

5. In the interviews I have read, Cabrera does not talk much about her mother. See Ana María Simo's introduction to *Lydia Cabrera: An Intimate Portrait* (New York: Intar Latin American Gallery, 1984) 6–7.

6. Ibid., 7–8.

7. Rosario Hiriart, *Más cerca de Teresa de la Parra (Diálogos con Lydia Cabrera)* (Caracas: Monte Avila, 1980), 51. In these transcripts of conversations between Hiriart and Cabrera, the latter claims that her dates are sometimes not to be trusted ("Mis fechas son siempre inseguras") (51).

8. "Una segunda madre y una amiga comprensiva y estimulante." Ibid., 56.

9. "Guardó por ella el luto riguroso que entonces se llevaba por una madre. En su mesa de noche estaba el retrato de Emilia que la acompañaba a todas partes." Ibid., 56.

10. Ibid., 117. Cabrera states that "Es curioso, pero cierto, que una puede querer a muertos que no ha conocido. Me hubiese agradado conservar copia de aquel retrato porque le tengo cariño a Emilia Barrios." Ibid., 57.

11. Ibid., 52.

12. Simo, *Lydia Cabrera*, 8.

13. Ibid., 60.

14. I am indebted to Sylvia Molloy's astounding "Disappearing Acts: Reading Lesbian in Teresa de la Parra," in *Entiendes? Queer Readings, Hispanic Writings*, ed. Emilie Bergmann and Paul Julian Smith (Durham: Duke University Press, 1995), 230–56.

Molloy reads carefully Parra and Cabrera's correspondence, noticing that the writing shows how "desire sees itself, the detours to which it resorts in order to name itself, the simulation it must engage in in order to 'pass,' the codes it uses in order to be recognized even as it masks itself, and even the repression it exerts against itself as it internalizes conventional prejudice" (241). Molloy's words have marked this essay from the outset.

15. This "random" or "improvisatory" writing tempts the reader to look for some kind of symbolic or even allegorical structure in them. I am less interested in whether allegory is or is not there; what I think is important is the *effect* the texts produce. Mariela Gutiérrez has published a morphological study that tries to understand the complexity of these tales by rendering them into particular schema. This complexity reveals how seductive Cabrera's work can be. See Mariela Gutiérrez. *Los cuentos negros de Lydia Cabrera* (un estudio morfológico) (Miami: Ediciones Universal, 1986).

16. I think it is important to clarify and underscore that the relationship of "art" to "life" is not as simple as it seems. For example, Cabrera's work—her stories, but also her work as an anthropologist—references a notion of destruction and construction that is not necessarily oppositional but dialectical. Cabrera understood anthropology, or ethnography, as a mode of preservation, but also as a form of engaging in the structural relationship between destruction and creation. A number of her *Cuentos negros* speak of a lack that is then supplemented, or an absence that needs to be repaired. An additional biographical detail that marks the element of destruction running through Cabrera's work is that before she met Parra, Cabrera wanted to become a painter, but in 1929 she burned all her paintings, and would not paint again for another forty years, after her exile in Miami. Simo, *Lydia Carbrera,* 8.

17. Parenthetically at least, it is important to recall the signs of the times: the Trocadero, the Dakar Djibouti expedition, Josephine Baker—marks of an exoticism that pretended to cure the wounds of the West. In terms that specifically relate to women, see Shari Benstock, *Women of the Left Bank: Paris, 1900–1940* (Austin: University of Texas Press, 1986).

18. Simo, *Lydia Cabrera,* 9.

19. Francis de Miomandre was also responsible for translating Miguel Angel Asturias's *Legendes de Guatemala*, also published in Paris. Asturias, who won the Nobel Prize for literature, was also another writer-ethnographer who collected his country's indigenous tales. Sara Soto, *Magia e historia en los "Cuentos negros," "Por que," y "Ayapá" de Lydia Cabrera* (Miami: Ediciones Universal, 1988). Miomandre was also, interestingly, the translator into French of Teresa de la Parra's *Ifigenia*. See Rosario Hiriart's prologue to a recent edition of Cabrera's *Cuentos negros de Cuba* (Barcelona: Icaria Editorial, Sociedad Estatal del V Centenario, 1989), 19.

20. Hiriart, *Más cerca de Teresa de la Parra*, 85.

21. According to Ana María Simo, "Had it not been for the double tragedy of Teresa's death and the war in Europe, Lydia might not have returned to Cuba, *El monte* would not have been written, and the voices of her centenarian Black informants would never have been known." Simo, *Lydia Cabrera*, 9.

22. Rosario Hiriart, *Lydia Cabrera: vida hecha arte* (New York: Eliseo Torres and Sons, 1978) 76.

23. The situation deserves to be explained in further detail, given the chained links in these lives. Cabrera meets Parra while she is in mourning for another woman, while later on María Teresa de Rojas meets Cabrera after Parra's death. They live together in the famous Quinta San José, which was owned by Rojas, a mansion located close to the Pogolotti neighborhood in Havana, where Cabrera found many of her native informants for *El monte*. María Teresa de Rojas would be Cabrera's lifelong companion, both in Cuba and in exile. Shortly after their departure from Cuba, the Quinta San José is destroyed, according to Simo, "by negligence, accident or arson: the circumstances are unclear, as is the fate of the priceless collection of antiques, books and research material inside the building." Simo, *Lydia Cabrera*, 11.

24. This does not reduce the book's publication—or its textual complexity—to a series of details in Cabrera's biography. But it does account for the tenor of the intervention, for the way women such as Parra or Cabrera stimulated each other to write within a patriarchal context that was generally uninterested in if not hostile to their writing. In her conversations with Hiriart, Cabrera underscores the fact that Emilia Barrios insisted that Teresa de la Parra write, and that Teresa then felt a responsibility to do the same for Cabrera, while much later on, the Chilean Nobel Prize–winning poet Gabriela Mistral also wanted Cabrera to publish her work, and advised her to bring out a Spanish edition of her *Contes nègres* in 1940. See the Hiriart interviews for these accounts. Mistral's role in the publication of Cabrera's *Cuentos negros* and her relationship to Cabrera are found on pp. 129–30.

25. Translating these fragments of *El monte* is a daunting task, but readers can here have an inkling of the particular way Cabrera writes, mixing African phrases throughout and at times twisting grammatical sense. The original reads,

> *Desde muy atrás se registra el pecado nefando como algo muy frecuente en la Regla lucumí. Sin embargo, muchos babalochas, omó-Changó, murieron castigados por un orisha tan varonil y mujeriego como Changó, que repudia este vicio. Actualmente, la proporción de pederastas en Ocha (no así en las sectas que se reclaman de congos, en las que se les desprecia profundamente y de las que se les expulsa) parece ser tan numerosa que es motivo continuo de indignación para los viejos santeros y devotos. ¡"A cada paso se tropieza uno un partido con un merengueteo"!*

Lydia Cabrera, *El monte* (Miami: Ediciones Universal, 1975), 56.

26. Ibid., 55.

27. "Este Papá Colás, que ha dejado tantos recuerdos entre los viejos, era famoso invertido y sorprendiendo la candidez de un cura, casó disfrazado de mujer, con otro invertido, motivando el escándalo que puede presumirse." Ibid., 56.

28. "Yewá, 'nuestra Señora de los Desamparados,' virgen, prohibe a sus hijas todo comercio sexual; de ahí que sus servidoras sean siempre viejas, vírgenes, o ya estériles, e Inlé, 'tan severo,' tan poderoso y delicado como Yewá, acaso exigía lo mismo de sus santeras, las cuales se abstenían de mantener relaciones sexuales con los hombres." Ibid., 59.

29. This is also Roger Lancaster's query during his time as an anthropologist in Nicaragua. See "Guto's Performance: Notes on the Transvestism of Everyday Life," *Sex and Sexuality in Latin America*, ed. Daniel Balderston and Donna J. Guy (New York: New York University Press, 1997), 9–32.

30. Cabrera, *El monte*, 65.

31. I refer to the reader as "he" in the translation to keep with Spanish conventioinal usage. "El lector, advertido de qué fuente procede el relato queda en libertad, como siempre, de creer lo que mejor le parezca. Por mi parte me inclino a aceptarlo como verídico, pues soy testigo de otros hechos que parecerán tanto más o igualmente inverosímiles." Ibid., 66.

32. "No se comprenderá a nuestro pueblo sin conocer al negro. . . . No nos adentraremos mucho en la vida cubana, sin dejar de encontrarnos con esta presencia africana *que no se manifiesta exclusivamente en la coloración de la piel.*" Ibid., 9 (my emphasis).

33. Ibid., 8.

34. Ibid.

35.

> *A la entrada del monte, donde idealmente hemos pagado nuestro tributo acompañándolo de unos granos de maíz y encendido una vela, o para ser más verídicos, ante el montón de tarjetas en que anoto las informaciones de los que saben propiciarse al dios Osaín y comprar efectivamente la voluntad inteligente de las plantas, me dice gravemente el nieto de un lucumí—"Cuando el padrino se da cuenta de que el ahijado llama a cada mata por su nombre conociendo lo que pueden, y sin confundirlas, ya lo manda a andar solo por el mundo."*

Ibid., 147.

36. Ibid., 8.

37. "The book is not the image of the world, despite the deeply rooted belief. It forms a rhizome with the world; there is an a-parallel evolution of the book and the world; the book insures the deterritorialization of the world, but the world effects a reterritorialization of the book, which is deterritorialized in its turn by being in the world (assuming the book is strong enough and capable of it)." Gilles Deleuze and Felix Guattari, *On the Line* (New York: Semiotext(e), 1983), 21–22.

38. Cabrera, *El monte*, 54.

39. Ibid., 186.

40. Morton Marks, "Exploring *El Monte*: Ethnobotany and the Afro-Cuban Science of the Concrete," in *En torno a Lydia Cabrera: Cincuentenario de los Cuentos Negros de Cuba, 1936–1986*, ed. Isabel Castellanos and Josefina Inclán (Miami: Ediciones Universal, 1987), 227–45.

> *While many readers approach El monte as essentially a literary work as ethnography, it may also be read as ethnobotany and even as ethnopharmacology. The book's second half contains a list of more than five hundred and fifty plants used magically and/or medicinally, and is one of the most complete sources of information on any New World botanical system. Its organization into an alphabetical order based on the entries' Spanish common names obscures a double system of classification, the first based on standard scientific binomials, the second on a folk taxonomy involving orisha ownership. A complete botanical entry in El monte thus consists of a Spanish common name, a scientific classification, the plant's Yoruba and Kongoo names, and an orisha "owner." (230)*

41. "¿Qué puedo decirte?, muchas cosas diferentes. . . . A las personas que hemos querido las sentimos presentes en algún objeto que haya estado en contacto con ellas." Hiriart, *Mas cerca de Teresa de la Parra*, 46–47.

42. Cabrera, *El monte*, 13.

43. Cabrera explains the ways one must enter "el monte":

> *Para entrar en el monte sombrero en mano o en el cementerio, donde en cada esquina se debe arrojar un grano de maíz y un centavo y "pagar antes de entrar," el palero o mayombero se identifica: "Ceiba es mi madre. Jagüey macho es mi padre. Camposanto es mi madrina." El Monte reconoce a un iniciado en sus misterios, "a un hijo," y le allana cualquier obstáculo.*

Ibid., 114.

44. "En La Habana, se considera 'un monte'—¡o sabana!—cualquier terreno baldío cubierto de matojos. . . . Al solar yermo de medidas más exiguas, la yerba silvestre que en él brota le da categoría de manigua, y sencillamente se le llamará 'un monte' o una 'manigua.'" ("In Havana one considers a 'monte'—or savannah!—any empty terrain full of weeds. . . . The empty plot of the smallest measures, the wild grass that you find in it is given the category of 'manigua' and will be simply called a 'monte' or a 'manigua.'") Ibid., 68.

45. Cabrera says that Teresa M. also has a lucumí name, Omí-Tomí, and Cabrera uses both names interchangeably.

46. 'Crecí en la sala como señorita blanca,' con todos los cuidados y la ternura excesiva que hubieran prodigado sus amas,—dos solteronas—a una hija. Y ambas llevaron su amor por la negrita,—negra como azabache, pero que vino a llenarles el vacío de la maternidad frustrada,—al extremo de nombrarla heredera universal de sus bienes." Cabrera, *El monte*, 26.

47. Cabrera insists that the practice is not totally based on race, but rather on culture. As a matter of fact, she insists that whites who adopt the santería pantheon are generally more hermetically secretive than blacks. "Y si el blanco estaba iniciado en la fe de su esclavo y se encomendaba en ocasiones a los dioses africanos, como ocurría tambien con harta frecuencia, era aún mucho más hermético que el negro." *El monte*, 42. This is in line with notes that Cabrera adds at other points in the text, as when she explains the relative ease with which people enter into possession: she talks about "gentes de color y . . . de los blancos de color" (30), thus attempting to mediate the opposition that would consign Afro-Cuban religion simply to a question of race.

48. "Contra toda calamidad el negro no duda en recurrir a la misma magia que puede provocarla, a las prácticas inmemoriales que el miedo y la credulidad mantienen tan vivas y firmes en nuestro pueblo, y sin duda en todos los pueblos del mundo." Ibid., 48.

49. Ortiz married Esther Cabrera, Lydia's older sister. See Simo, *Lydia Cabrera*, 13.

50.

> *No hay que olvidar que estos cuentos vienen a las prensas por una colaboración, la del folklore negro con su traductora blanca. Porque también el texto castellano es en realidad una traducción, y, en rigor sea dicho, una segunda traducción. Del lenguaje africano (yoruba, ewe o bantú) en que las fábulas se imaginaron, estas fueron vertidas en Cuba al idioma amestizado y dialectal de los negros criollos. Quizá la anciana morena que se las narró a Lydia ya las recibió de sus antepasados en lenguaje acriollado. Y de esta habla tuvo la coleccionista que pasarlas a una forma legible en castellano, tal como ahora se estamparán.*

Fernando Ortiz, "Prejuicio," in Lydia Cabrera, *Cuentos negros de Cuba* (1940) (Miami: Ediciones Universal, 1993), 8.

51. In his introduction to the English edition of *Cuban Counterpoint* (Durham: Duke University Press, 1995), Fernando Coronil explains the ways Ortiz has been marginalized and excluded from the canon of anthropology, in spite of how influential his notion of transculturation has been for anthropological studies. It is clear that Coronil intends to position Ortiz within this canon, and this is precisely what a presentation of Ortiz to the English-speaking public should do. In this way, Coronil argues that *Cuban Counterpoint* is "an invitation to question the conceits of modernity and postmodernity alike" (xiii) and it shows "that the constitution of the modern world has entailed the clash and disarticulation of peoples and civilizations together with the production of images of integrated cultures, bounded identities, and inexorable progress" (xiii). My aim in this essay has not been to inscribe Cabrera within the canon of anthropology, and not even within the canon of Cuban literature. I prefer to focus on Cabrera's queer space by also stopping short of claiming for her any significance for the field of gay and lesbian studies. That she has that significance for me is clear from the essay. But it is also clear that the discursive field of "gay and lesbian literature" is not one that I wish Cabrera to belong to. Despite Ortiz's very real contributions, which reposition the discourse of anthropology, the fact of marginality is no guarantee that patriarchal and power relations will not be reproduced vis-à-vis others who engage in work that is pursued by a double sense of marginality. I think there is no contradiction expressed in celebrating Ortiz's marginality while at the same time focusing on his rhetoric of power. It is interesting that Cabrera appears in Coronil's introduction only as a footnote that explains his choice of epigraph: "Un solo palo no hace monte" (One tree does not a forest make), and that he adds that Cabrera's *El monte* "is dedicated to Fernando Ortiz," xlviii.

52. Jacques Derrida, "Roundtable on Translation," in *The Ear of the Other: Autobiography, Transference, Translation*, ed. Christie McDonald, trans. Peggy Kamuf (Lincoln: University of Nebraska Press, 1988 [1985]), 152–53.

53. The question of transcription, or translation, is a particularly difficult one to pursue in Cabrera's work. It seems Cabrera insisted on calling her stories *transposiciones*, and that she assumed a particularly modest pose in terms of them. Cabrera, it seems, always limited her role to that of collector of tales, the mere receptor of the knowledge of others. This question is dealt with in Rosa Valdés Cruz, "Los cuentos de Lydia Cabrera: Transposiciones o creaciones?" in Sanchez et al., *Homenaje a Lydia Cabrera*, 93–99. For Valdés Cruz, Cabrera's method is to use folklore as a point of departure for a different purpose: "los motivos que Lydia Cabrera traslada del cuento folklórico sólo proveen el marco para que esta autora ejercita su fantasía y su talento artístico. Podemos asegurar que no es una colectora más de cuentos folklóricos" (99).

Notes to Chapter 4

1. Ewa Ziarek comments on *Trans-Atlantyk's* "jarring juxtaposition of modern experience of exile" and the "anachronism of its Baroque style." See "The Scar of the Foreigner and the Fold of the Baroque: National Affiliations and Homosexuality in Gombrowicz's *Trans-Atlantyk*," in *Gombrowicz's Grimaces: Modernism, Gender, Nationality*, ed. Ewa Plonowska Ziarek (Albany: State University of New York Press, 1998), 213–44, 216.

2. Witold Gombrowicz, *Trans-Atlantyk*, trans. Carolyn French and Nina Karsov (New Haven: Yale University Press, 1994), 57.

3. Marzena Grzegorczyk establishes Gombrowicz as a "border intellectual," one who does not leave "a clear corpus of academic and critical inquiry" and who used the kind of "linguistic transvestism" in *Trans-Atlantyk* as a disavowal of perfection. See

"Formed Lives, Formless Traditions: The Argentinean Legacy of Witold Gombrowicz," in Ziarek, *Gombrowicz's Grimaces: Modernism, Gender, Nationality*, 135–56.

4. Ziarek, "The Scar of the Foreigner," 229.

5. Rita Gombrowicz, *Gombrowicz en Argentine, 1939–1963* (Paris: Editions Denoël, 1984). On the Argentinean memory of Gombrowicz's influence, see Germán Leopoldo García, *Gombrowicz: El estilo y la heráldica* (Buenos Aires: Ediciones Atuel, 1992). An account of Piñera in Argentina can be found in Carlos Espinosa Domínguez, "El poder mágico de los bifes (La estancia argentina de Virgilio Piñera)," *Cuadernos hispanoamericanos* 471 (September 1989): 78–88. For a study of Gombrowicz and Piñera, see Daniel Balderston, "Estética de la deformación en Gombrowicz y Piñera," *Explicación de textos literarios* 19, no. 2 (1990–91): 1–7.

6. Ewa Ziarek mentions that "Alejandro Russovich suggests that the figure of Gonzalo could be influenced by . . . the friends of Virgilio Piñera, or by Piñera himself." She registers this but questions it, and prefers to see Gonzalo as "the distorted mirror image of Gombrowicz's own Argentinean homosexual experiences." Ziarek, "The Scar of the Foreigner," 242.

7. Virgilio Piñera, *Cold Tales*, trans. Mark Schafer, intro. Guillermo Cabrera Infante (Hygiene, CO: Eridanos Press, 1988), xi. Unless otherwise noted, all quotes in English are from this edition. Page numbers appear in parentheses in the text.

8. The account is found in Cabrera Infante's introduction to the volume cited above. *Teatro completo* was published by Ediciones R (1960).

9. For the best account of Piñera in Buenos Aires, see Espinosa Domínguez, "El poder mágico de los bifes." Recollections written by Piñera appear in Rita Gombrowicz's compilation of documents, *Gombrowicz en Argentine, 1939–1963,* esp. 69–88. The best essay on Piñera and Gombrowicz is Balderston, "Estética de la deformación en Gombrowicz y Piñera."

10. The obligatory essay on the relationship between Piñera and the revolution is still Reinaldo Arenas's verbal tour de force "La isla en peso con todas sus cucarachas," *Mariel* 21 (1983), reprinted in Reinaldo Arenas, *Necesidad de libertad. Mariel: Testimonios de un intellectual disidente* (Madrid: Kosmos, 1986). For a good account of the strained relationship between the revolution and gays, see Allen Young, *Gays under the Cuban Revolution* (San Francisco, Grey Fox Press, 1981). I will return to the question of homosexuality and revolution in the next chapter, in relation to *Strawberry and Chocolate*.

11. According to the *Diccionario de la literatura cubana* (Havana: Editorial Letras Cubanas, 1980), Piñera's last work was the volume of poems titled *La vida entera,* published in 1969.

12. Virgilio Piñera, *René's Flesh,* trans. Mark Schafer (New York: Marsilio, 1985), 104.

> *Igual que probamos una y otra vez el punto de la pluma y una vez cerciorados de su bondad lo hacemos correr a izquierda y derecha del papel, y a veces la mano se detiene porque el cerebro vacila entre un pensamiento u otro, así también Roger sacó su lengua y tomando un dedo del pie de René, la aplicó una y otra vez a fin de cerciorarse de la bondad de su punta. . . . Roger se asemejaba a esos calígrafos que pasan su pluma por los bordes del papel. Soltó el dedo y se trasladó a la cara. Pasó una mano por debajo de la cabeza de René y apoyó la otra en su pecho. Entonces, miró a Cochón.*
>
> *Este fue señalando las lenguas que debían secundar la de Roger. Una por cada parte del cuerpo: dos piernas, dos brazos. . . .*
>
> *—Roger, abra usted la sesión —dijo.*
>
> *Roger lamió profundamente la frente de René. Movió la cabeza con aire de duda. Pasó la lengua por los labios del rebelde. Volvió a mover la cabeza.*
>
> *—¿Qué pasa, Roger? —preguntó Cochón.*
>
> *—Pétrea —se limitó a decir Roger.*

Virgilio Piñera, *La carne de René* (Madrid: Alfaguara, 1985), 113.

13. Piñera, *René's Flesh,* trans. Schafer, 24. "Mira, tu cuerpo, el mío, el de tu madre, el de todo el mundo está hecho de carne. Esto es muy importante, y por olvidarlo con frecuencia, muchos caen víctima del cuchillo." Piñera, *La carne de René,* 14.

14. "Mi miedo es mi propio ser y ninguna revolución, ningún golpe de fortuna adversa podría derrocarle." Virgilio Piñera, "El enemigo," in *Cuentos frios* (Madrid: Alfoguara, 1983), 190.

15. "La tremenda perforación que él nos muestra es nada menos que la obra." Piñera, "El enemigo," 189.

16. "Como he sido iconoclasta / me niego a que me hagan estatua; / si en la vida he sido carne, / en la muerte no quiero ser mármol." Virgilio Piñera, *La vida entera* (Havana: UNEAC, 1969), 146.

17. "Como santa laica / con derecho a figurar en los altares del horror." Ibid., 129.

18. Piñera, *Cold Tales,* trans. Schafer, 267."El martes pasado, a las tres de la tarde, Damían me llamaba por teléfono." Piñera, *Cuentos frios,* 207.

19. Virgilio Piñera, "The Decoration," in *Cold Tales*, trans. Schafer, 127. "Cuando cumplí los quince años—momentos en que iba a desempeñar mi primer puesto como humilde empleado—mi padre me hizo un singular regalo." Piñera, *Cuentos fríos*, 97.

20. Virgilio Piñera, "Hot and Cold" in *Cold Tales*, trans. Schafer, 207. "Bueno, aquí me tienen. . . . Como no tengo quien me presente, lo haré yo mismo. Me llamo Rafael Sánchez Trevejo (Rafa para Rosita, mi mujer, la familia y los amigos)." Virgilio Piñera, "Frío en caliente," in *Cuentos frios*, 259.

21. For Fernando Valerio, this is part of the "coldness" of Piñera's cold tales. He relates it also to the fact that the text demands to be read, beckons a reading. See Fernando Valerio-Holguín, *Poética de la frialdad: La narrativa de Virgilio Piñera* (Lanham, MD: University Press of America, 1997), esp. 24–25.

22. Piñera, *Cold Tales*, trans. Schaefer, 183. "El libro se me cae de las manos, la música que escucho parece materia pegajosa y densa que obtura mis oídos; hablo con mi madre y siento que las palabras se me congelan en el borde de los labios; escribo una carta a M.—tengo mucho que contarle—pero a las dos líneas interrumpo la escritura." Piñera, *Cuentos fríos*, 217.

23. This definition and the one that follows are taken from Sigmund Freud, "Repression" (1915), *Standard Edition of Sigmund Freud*, trans. James Strachey, (London: Hogarth Press, 1957), 14:155, 157.

24. Piñera, *René's Flesh*, trans. Schafer, 74.

> *El dolor es nuestra estrella y nos guiará en este mar tempestuoso. Ustedes me dirán: ¿más por qué se nos pone mordazas si se debe dar rienda suelta al dolor? La ponemos porque nosotros estamos por el dolor contenido, concentrado y reconcentrado. La boca que se abre para gritar, desaloja automáticamente una preciosa cantidad de dolor. Si fuera a expresarme en términos de psicología le llamaría a eso una descarga. Y nosotros estamos, en todo y por todo, contra las descargas.*

Piñera, *La carne de René*, 84.

25. Piñera, *René's Flesh*, trans. Schafer, 75.

26. Ibid.

27. Ibid., 76.

28. Ibid.

29. Ibid., 77.

30. Ibid.

31. One interesting detail that I add here at the end of this section comes from Fernando Valerio, who speculates that René means "reborn" (renacido). See Valerio-Holguín, *Poética de la frialdad,* 49.

32.

> *Si los franceses escriben sobre Gide tomando como punto de partida el homosexualismo de este escritor; si los ingleses hacen lo mismo con Wilde, yo no veo por qué los cubanos no podamos hablar de Ballagas en tanto que homosexual. ¿Es que los franceses y los ingleses tienen la exclusiva de tal tema? No por cierto, no hay temas exclusivos ni ellos lo pretenderían, sino que franceses e ingleses nunca estarán dispuestos a hacer de sus escritores ese lechero de la Inmortalidad que tanto seduce a nuestros críticos.*

Virgilio Piñera, "Ballagas en persona," *Ciclón* 1, no. 5 (September 1955): 41–50, 42.

33. More of this may be found in Jonathan Dollimore, "Different Desires: Subjectivity and Transgression in Wilde and Gide," *Textual Practice* 1 (1987): 48–67. This is quoted by Paul Julian Smith in *The Body Hispanic: Gender and Sexuality in Spanish and Spanish American Literature* (Oxford: Clarendon Press, 1989), 136.

34. Daniel Balderston underscores the importance of this act of quoting while also stressing how partial it is: Piñera does not out himself, but an other. See *El deseo: Enorme cicatriz luminosa* (Caracas: Ediciones eXcultura, 1999), 10.

35. "Todos sus actos, comprendiendo en esos actos su obra entera, es el reflejo de esa lucha a brazo partido con el pecado. ¿Qué es esta obra, en definitiva, sino un largo y reiterado *De Profundis* del cual quizá Ballagas habría salido victorioso de no haber muerto tan joven?" Piñera, "Ballagas en persona," 42.

36. See Arrufat's perceptive rendering of Piñera's ideas concerning poets who focused on single themes (*poeta concentrado*) in *Virgilio Piñera: Entre él y yo* (Havana: Ediciones Unión, 1994). Arrufat is quoting one of Piñera's essays for *Lunes de Revolución,* titled "Poesía cubana del XIX": "En él se propone demostrar que los poetas cubanos importantes del siglo pasado padecían de un mal: la falta de concentración. Y esa carencia les vedó el acceso a la gran poesía" (27). Arrufat understands that Piñera is using a principle that has its origins in Baudelaire. For his reading of this aspect of Piñera's criticism as well as his critique, see pp. 26–29.

37. The Origenistas' critique on this generation can be seen in Cintio Vitier, *Lo cubano en la poesía* (Universidad Central de las Villas, Dept. de relaciones culturales, 1958).

38.

> *Hasta la muerte ejerció dos partes de su cuerpo. Una de ellas, el sexo, y la otra, la mente. Se acostaba dos o tres veces por semana, con uno de sus dos o tres "puntos fijos" cada vez, a los que pagaba menudas cantidades de dinero. A esto lo llamaba "sexuar." Pagar era otra manera de defender su libertad. En este caso la sentimental. Pagar a sus "puntos fijos" no lo comprometía ni ligaba sentimentalmente. Era pagar un servicio.*

Arrufat, *Virgilio Piñera*, 50.

39. "Claro que no podía saber a tan corta edad que el saldo arrojado por esas tres gorgonas: miseria, homosexualismo y arte, era la pavorosa nada." Some sections were published in *Lunes de Revolución* 100, no. 27 (March 1961); others in *Union: La Habana* 10 (1990). Finally some previously unpublished fragments appeared with an introduction by Daniel Samoilovich, in the Virgilio Piñera web page organized by Teresa Cristofani Barreto (http://www.fflcu.usp.br/sitesint/virgilio).

40.

> *En los años del setenta, calificados por Piñera de muerte civil, la burocracia de la década nos había configurado en esa "extraña latitud" del ser: la muerte en vida. . . . Nuestros libros dejaron de publicarse, los publicados fueron recogidos de las librerías y subrepticiamente retirados de los estantes de las bibliotecas públicas. Las piezas teatrales que habíamos escrito desaparecieron de los escenarios. Nuestros nombres dejaron de pronunciarse en conferencias y clases universitarias, se borraron de las antologías y de las historias de la literatura cubana compuestas en esa década funesta. No sólo estábamos muertos en vida: parecíamos no haber nacido ni escrito nunca. Las nuevas generaciones fueron educadas en el desprecio a cuando habíamos hecho o en su ignorancia. Fuimos sacados de nuestros empleos y enviados a trabajar donde nadie nos conociera, en bibliotecas alejadas de la ciudad, imprentas de textos escolares y fundiciones de acero.*

Arrufat, *Virgilio Piñera*, 42.

41. See Arenas, "La isla en peso con todas sus cucarachas." It is important to note that for many years Cubans closely identified with the revolutionary government refused to confirm that Piñera was indeed ostracized. Arenas was one of the first to insist on this repression. His account was followed, many years later, by Arrufat's.

42. See Lillian Manzor-Coats and Inés Martiatu Terry, "VI Festival Internacional de Teatro de La Habana: A Festival Against All Odds," *Drama Review* 39, no. 2 (summer

1995): 39–70, esp. 52–55 for a good account of Piñera's sardonic play *La niñita querida*, which had never been performed in Cuba before 1993.

43. The revaluation of the whole literary circle around *Ciclón* and *Lunes de Revolución* also involves, to an extent, the issue of sexuality and, more specifically, homosexuality, as can be seen in Roberto Pérez León, *Tiempo de Ciclón* (Havana: Ediciones Unión, 1995).

44. This line is best exemplified by Lourdes Argüelles and B. Ruby Rich, "Homosexuality, Homophobia, and Revolution: Notes toward an Understanding of the Cuban Lesbian and Gay Male Experience," parts 1 and 2, *Signs: Journal of Women in Culture and Society*, summer 1984, 683–99; autumn 1985, 120–36.

Notes to Chapter 5

1. See Van Gosse's illuminating *Where the Boys Are: Cuba, Cold War America and the Making of a New Left* (London: Verso, 1993).

2. See interviews with Carlos Delgado Linares collected in *El movimiento de la nueva trova cubana y la trova tradicional* (Caracas: Ediciones Namar, 1996). But the degree of governmental intervention in this movement can be seen in Martha Haya Jimenez, ed., *Movimiento de la nueva trova en su X aniversario* (Havana: Departamento de Información y Documentacion de la Cultura, 1982). This is a collection of documents, as well as an annotated bibliography. One of the documents goes so far as to prescribe the mode of presentation of the singers: "Erradicar de nuestras manifestaciones artísticas la ostentación, el despilfarro y la extravagancia en los vestuarios, teniendo en cuenta las reales condiciones de nuestro país. Ser capaces de actuar en todo momento con una conducta digna de un revolucionario, tanto en la escena como fuera de ella" (10). For a good novelistic account of the period, see Carlos Victoria, *La travesía secreta* (Miami: Ediciones Universal, 1994). Victoria talks about repression in terms of dress and behavior directed at young people during this time.

3. This point serves to explain the position of many dissident Cuban intellectuals associated with *Mariel* magazine in the 1980s, who exposed the New Left's solidarity with Cuba and with "liberation struggles" in general as primarily bourgeois affections whose outcome was to undermine, in Cuba, those same liberties that U.S. intellectuals apparently took for granted. In other words, for the *Mariel* writers the solidarity of the marginalized in the United States took the form of solidarity with the oppressors in the Third World states; the refusal to engage in that act of solidarity for exiles automatically seemed to guarantee them a place in the more reactionary discourse of the U.S. Right.

4. In a more recent version of this debate, there has been much discussion on the official government policy of sequestering HIV-positive individuals in treatment centers, once again for the sake of the common good of the society. An interesting account of the *sidatorios* appears in Jorge Cortiñas, "Laws That Say So: Dialogue with a Resident of Cuba's AIDS Sanatoriums," *Socialist Review* 23, no. 1 (1993).

5. This debate has always been at the core of the definition of homosexuality in the United States and elsewhere. Thus, in the formation of the first homophile movement in the United States during the 1950s, organizations such as the Mattachine Society and the Daughters of Bilitis tried to achieve a degree of tolerance so that homophiles or homosexuals could feel free from harassment or intimidation. In essence, this amounted to recognizing the fact that homosexuals were no different from the rest of society except in their choice of sexual partners. It was only by the influence of a New Left politics that a more identity-based notion of homosexuality came to assume center stage, by equating famously the personal with the political. See Martin Duberman, *Stonewall* (New York: Penguin, 1994), among others, for a good account of these debates.

6. An interesting example of this is given in Duberman, recounting the story of Jim Fouratt, a gay activist who helped form the first Venceremos brigade and who nevertheless was not allowed into Cuba in 1969 because "it was felt that his chief purpose in going to Cuba would be to organize gays and lesbians there, and that would not sit well with the revolutionary comrades." Duberman, *Stonewall*, 240.

7. See the discussion of Virgilio Piñera and his essay "Ballagas en persona" in chapter 4 of this book.

8. Andrew Parker, "Unthinking Sex: Marx, Engels and the Scene of Writing," in *Fear of a Queer Planet: Queer Politics and Social Theory*, ed. Michael Warner (Minneapolis: University of Minnesota Press, 1993), 19–41.

9. *Mariel* magazine was edited by Reinaldo Arenas, Reinaldo García Ramos, and Roberto Valero. It became the most important Cuban magazine outside Cuba, and produced important issues—in particular one dedicated to the topic of homosexuality in Cuba. Ana María Simo and Reinaldo García Ramos, "Hablemos claro," *Mariel: Revista de Literatura y Arte* 2, no. 5 (1984): 9–10.

10. This is also part of the strategy of a recent book published in Cuba by one of its best young poets, Victor Fowler, *La maldición: Una historia del placer como conquista* (Havana: Editorial Letras Cubanas, 1998). Fowler's book is a collection of essays on important male homosexual Cuban literary figures.
11. According to eyewitness accounts of audiences in Havana (more on this later), gay members of the audience identify with Diego to such an extent that they tend to annul him as an object of desire, choosing instead to drool over David and his other Communist Party friend, who are shown in a provocative scene in the shower.
12. "Desde la primera lectura se revelaba como una historia necesaria, como algo que seguramente todos queríamos escuchar." Quoted in Tomás Gutiérrez Alea, "De Fresa y chocolate," *Viridiana* (Madrid) 7 (1994): 119.
13. Paul Julian Smith, *Vision Machines: Cinema, Literature and Sexuality in Spain and Cuba, 1983–1993* (London: Verso, 1996).
14. Clarity and luminosity are underscored throughout Gutiérrez Alea's narration of the way the film was made. He praises Havana as a wonderful city even in the midst of its physical destruction—fragments of beauty almost at the point of disappearance. "En medio de su destrucción encontrábamos rincones de excepcional belleza a punto de desaparecer." Gutierrez Alea, "De Fresa y chocolate," 120.
15. The criteria of organicness entail the use of natural light as far as possible, and to include the spontaneous elements that arise from the mise-en-scène into the film itself:

> *Hemos tratado de reducir al mínimo la mediación de los recursos técnicos sin que esto afecte la calidad de la puesta en cámara. Al contrario, a menudo comprobamos, por ejemplo, que una utilización más racional de la luz natural nos permite no sólo trabajar con más soltura y con menos gasto, sino también alcanzar un resultado estéticamente más interesante. Lo mismo suele suceder cuando incorporamos a la escena los accidentes que van presentándose, los imprevistos, los obstáculos. . . . Es decir, tratamos de hacer una puesta en escena lo más orgánica posible. (We tried to keep to a minimum the mediation of technical recourses without affecting the qualitiy of the mise-en-scène. On the contrary, many times we realized, for example, that a more rational use of natural light allows us not only to work more smoothly and cheaply, but also to achieve a more interesting aesthetic result. The same thing generally happens when we incorporate onto the scene the accidents, the unforseen*

> *events, obstacles that appear here and there. . . . That is, we try to create a mise-en-scène that is as organic as possible.)*

Gutiérrez Alea, "De Fresa y chocolate," 122.

16. For a detailed assessment of the degree of technical proficiency this entailed, see Gutiérrez Alea's "De Fresa y chocolate" in *Viridiana*.

17. Gutiérrez Alea had imagined Diego as a much older man, closer to a forty-year-old. But he chose Perugorría since he was a "charismatic" actor who was "capable of awakening a great deal of affection, even from those who viscerally reject the slightest evidence of homosexuality" (un actor carismático, capaz de despertar una gran simpatía, aun en muchos que rechazan visceralmente la más leve manifestación de homosexualismo). Gutiérrez Alea, "De Fresa y chocolate," 121.

18.

> *En cuanto a su gestualidad, no estábamos muy seguros de qué nivel de afeminamiento debía manifestar el personaje. El cuento de Senel lo describía con modales marcadamente afeminados incluso, en ocasiones, agresivamente desenvuelto y provocador. Trabajamos con el actor para ver hasta qué punto era capaz de manifestarse en ese nivel sin que resultará chocante y, sobre todo, sin que se convirtiera en una caricatura. El actor llevó a cabo un trabajo delicado y riguroso hasta lograr que el aire afeminado brotara de una actitud interna más que de una gestualidad importada.*

Ibid.

19. Gilda Santana, "Fresa y chocolate: El largo camino de la literatura al cine," *Viridiana* 7 (1994): 131.

20. What is interesting is that in trying to give David the motivational urge to go to Diego's house, which seems to have been a particularly thorny problem for Paz and Santana ("éste [David] a pesar de sus principios y prejuicios termina por irse con aquél a su casa. ¿Cómo hacer que el espectador creyera en esta acción? ¿Cómo llevar a David a esa decisión? ¿Por qué David, que rechaza todo lo que representa Diego, se va con él?), the writers came upon the conceit of Diego's having photographs of David, so that, in a sense, David goes to Diego's house to rescue the aura of his own image. Ibid., 135.

21.

> *Pero es solamente en estos casos de escenas difíciles y con resoluciones trascendentales de los personajes donde se hace necesario examinar hasta la minuciosidad del*

> *modelo actancial cada microsecuencia. Este examen nos dirá, de la manera más exacta, por qué tal personaje actuó así, o en qué consiste ese aparente estancamiento de la acción. Estaremos entonces en poder de una visión del guión que va desde lo general (la historia que se nos cuenta) hasta sus más recónditas particularidades (el movimiento y el comportamiento interno de las acciones mediante las que se nos cuenta).*

Ibid., 136.

22. Senel Paz, "The Wolf, the Forest and the New Man," trans. Thomas Christensen, *Conjunctions*: 27, (1996): 62–87, 74–75, special issue on new Caribbean writing, ed. Robert Antoni and Bradford Morrow.

> *Los homosexuales caemos en otra clasificación aún más interesante que la que te explicaba el otro día. Esto es, los homosexuales propiamente dichos—se repite el término porque esta palabra conserva, aun en las peores circunstancias, cierto grado de recato—; los maricones—ay, también se repite—, y las locas, de las cuales la expresión más baja son las denominadas locas de carroza. Esta escala la determina la disposición del sujeto hacia el deber social o la mariconería. Cuando la balanza se inclina al deber social, estás en presencia de un homosexual. Somos aquellos—en esta categoría me incluyo—para quienes el sexo ocupa un lugar en la vida pero no el lugar de la vida. Como los héroes o los activistas políticos, anteponemos el Deber al Sexo. La causa a la que nos consagramos está antes que todo. En mi caso el sacerdocio es la Cultura nacional, a la que dedico lo mejor de mi intelecto y mi tiempo. . . . Los homosexuales de esta categoría no perdemos el tiempo a causa del sexo, no hay provocación capaz de desviarnos de nuestro trabajo. . . . Por nuestra inteligencia y el fruto de nuestro esfuerzo nos corresponde un espacio que siempre se nos niega. . . . Los maricones no merecen explicación aparte, como todo lo que queda a medio camino entre una y otra cosa: los comprenderás cuando te defina a las locas, que son muy fáciles de conceptualizar. Tienen todo el tiempo un falo incrustado en el cerebro y sólo actúan por y para él. La perdedera de tiempo es su característica fundamental. Si el tiempo que invierten en flirtear en parques y baños públicos lo dedicarán al trabajo socialmente útil, ya estaríamos llegando a eso que ustedes llaman comunismo y nosotros paraíso. Las más vagas de todas son las llamadas de carroza. A estas las odio por fatuas y vacías, y porque por su falta de discreción y tacto, han convertido en desafíos sociales actos tan simples y necesarios como pintarse las uñas de los pies. . . . Esta tipología es aplicable a los heterosexuales de uno y otro sexo. En el caso de*

> *los hombres, el eslabón más bajo, el que se corresponde con las locas de carroza y está signado por la perdedera de tiempo y el ansia de fornicación perpetua, lo ocupan los picha-dulce, quienes pueden ir a echar una carta al correo, pongamos por caso, y en el trayecto meterle mano hasta a una de nosotras, sin menoscabo de su virilidad, sólo porque no pueden contenerse.*

Senel Paz, "El bosque, el lobo y el hombre nuevo," (Mexico: Ediciones Era, 1991).

23. Compare, for example, Laura Gotkowitz and Richard Turits's 1984 account of an interview with Monika Krause, director of the National Working Group on Sex Education in Cuba. Their article in *Gay Community News* was in part a response to the fracas created around Néstor Almendros's *Improper Conduct* (8):

> *We asked Monika Krause why the books used for sex education were equivocal, and somewhat contradictory. She answered that the revolution has always been careful not to step far beyond the consciousness of the people or to alienate them. "We have to be patient, making steps forward little by little; in performing our sex education work, we have already very often broken the tolerance limits of our people."*

This jars, of course, with the more anthropologically "accurate" vision put out by Diego—a vision that is clearly meant to be more believable because it is validated by someone who is himself the victim of social repression. Laura Gotkowitz and Richard Turits, "Liberation Little by Little: Sex and Ideology in Cuba," *Gay Community News* 12, no. 11 (September 29, 1984): 8–10.

24. Before his untimely death, Gutiérrez Alea did his final film, *Guantanamera*, casting Perugorría again, but this time as a truck driver who is forced to participate in the travails involved in bringing a corpse from one end of the island to the other. *Guantanamera* received numerous accolades in Cuba and abroad, although in 1998 Fidel Castro gave an ominous speech condemning the demoralized portrayal of the revolution in literature and the arts, and singled out *Guantanamera* for criticism. This produced considerable scandal in Cuba, not only because Fidel spoke about a revered filmmaker after his death, but also because it presaged harder and more repressive times for all artists. Alfredo Guevara, the leading voice of the ICAIC (Instituto Cubano de Artes y Ciencias), openly threatened to resign in what was perceived as the first open sign of dissidence within the "historical" class of the revolutionary artistic "nomenclatura." The dispute apparently fizzled, though its ultimate conclusion at this point is unclear.

25. Michel Foucault, "Truth and Power," in *Power/Knowledge: Selected Interviews and*

Other Writings, 1972–1977, ed. Colin Gordon, trans. Colin Gordon, Leo Marshall, John Mepham, and Kate Soper (New York: Pantheon, 1980), 119.

Notes to Chapter 6

1. Rafael Castillo Zapata, *Fenomenología del bolero* (Caracas: Monte Avila, 1990), 16.
2. Ibid.
3.

> *Sin el contexto de lo que lo volvió necesario, Agustín Lara se va mostrando progresivamente anacrónico y patético. Su cursilería aislada es una catástrofe sólo recuperable a través de técnicas importadas como el camp. Pero estas técnicas o trucos de los sesentas más sepultan que redimen. . . . la indefensión literaria de las improvisaciones de Agustín Lara se esencializan si se les aplica la visión camp. [Lara no es] una opulencia de la forma a expensas de la ridiculez del contenido, sino la postrer defensa de un contenido primitivo que ve en lo exagerado su acceso a lo sublime. No es delirio de la forma, sino de las urgencias expresivas, del amor que se volverá "¡Cuna de plata de la mañana / que en la montaña se hace canción!"*

Carlos Monsiváis, *Amor Perdido* (Mexico: Ediciones Era, 1984), 86.
4. For a lucid account of boleros and modernity in Mexico City, see Juan Gelpí, "El bolero en Ciudad de México: Poesía popular urbana y procesos de modernización," *Cuadernos de literatura* 4, nos. 7–8 (January–December 1998): 197–212. Gelpí notes that there was a Decency League (Liga de la Decencia) formed by the bishop of Mexico that prohibited boleros from being performed on the radio because of their risqué sexual content.
5. Daniel Balderston, "Excluded Middle? Bisexuality in *Doña Herlinda y su hijo*," in *Sex and Sexuality in Latin America*, ed. Daniel Balderston and Donna J. Guy (New York: New York University Press, 1997), 190–99.

Notes to Chapter 7

1. Information about Billy, Carlos, and their parent company, Totem International, is all from Billyworld, his official Web site, at http://www.billyworld.com.
2. Eduardo Contreras, "Ricanlicious," *ñ*, issue 1 (spring–summer 1998): 14–15.
3. Totem has recently added a new "friend of Billy": Tyler, an African American re-

porter for a major TV network. One of the first wardrobe choices given to Tyler was "Army Tyler."

4. Walter Benjamin, "Toys and Play: Marginal Notes on a Monumental Work," in *Selected Writings*, vol. 2, *1927–1934*, trans. Rodney Livingstone et al., ed. Michael Jennings, Howard Eiland, and Gary Smith (Cambridge: Harvard University Press, 1999), 118–21, 118.

5. Walter Benjamin, "The Cultural History of Toys," in *Selected Writings*, 116.

6. Ibid.

7. This information is from "Shop Windows: Nigel Grimmer" at http://www.billyworld.com.

8. Maer Roshan, "Ricky Gets Real," *New York*, June 28–July 5, 1999, 43–45, 171.

Notes to Chapter 8

1. Richard Goldstein, "Gay Is Global," *Village Voice*, June 29, 1999, 50–52.

2. Martin Foreman, 'Yan Daudu' and Proud," *Village Voice*, June 29, 1999, 61, 67, 67.

3. Alisa Solomon, "We're Queer, We're Here," *Village Voice*, June 29, 1999, 78, 83.

4. Ibid., 83

5. Almodóvar is more interested in providing a vision of Madrid than he is in creating "gay" films. His homosexual plot narratives are incorporated within the city as a whole, and not merely within certain urban subcultures. For a good reading of Almodóvar in terms of postmodern narrative and cinema, see Alejandro Varderi, *Severo Sarduy y Pedro Almodóvar: Del barroco al kitsch en la narrativa y el cine postmodernos* (Madrid: Editorial Pliegos, 1996), 153–67.

6. Guy Hocquenghem, *Homosexual Desire*, trans. Daniella Dangoor (Durham: Duke University Press, 1993).

7. Cathy Cohen has expressed this in a very succinct manner:

> *in spite of the unequal power relationships located in marginal communities, I am still not interested in disassociating politically from these communities, for queerness, as it is currently constructed, offers no viable political alternative, since it invites us to put forth a political agenda that makes invisible the prominence of race, class, and to varying degrees gender in determining the life chances of those on both sides of the hetero/queer divide.*

Cathy J. Cohen, "Punks, Bulldaggers, and Welfare Queens: The Radical Potential of

Queer Politics?" *GLQ* 3 (1997): 437–65, 450. For an excellent account of the response of the African American community to AIDS, see her recent book *The Boundaries of Blackness: AIDS and the Breakdown of Black Politics* (Chicago: University of Chicago Press, 1999).

8. I hesitate to use terms like "a version of" because I do not want to validate origins and "translations." It is clear that in historical terms, the African American civil rights movements of the 1960s mobilized other minorities, and that the model for social change in the United States to this day follows its example. That each group had its own particular agenda, as well as social mode of action, is something that also needs to be underscored. For example, the Young Lords articulated themselves in terms of race but also in terms of ethnicity, since black, mulatto, and white Puerto Ricans in the United States were part of a unique American paradox—they were U.S. citizens yet, as migrants from the commonwealth of Puerto Rico, they formed a sort of permanent quasi-underclass. Mexican Americans or Chicanos also argued for civil rights, but also claimed not only an ethnic but also a historical sense of difference, since many Chicanos claimed allegiance to Aztlán—the Aztec term used to name what used to be Mexican territory until 1848. For a lucid account of these struggles, see Suzanne Oboler, *Ethnic Labels, Latino Lives: Identity and the Politics of Representation in the United States* (Minneapolis: University of Minnesota Press, 1995), esp. chap. 3, 'Establishing an Identity' in the Sixties: The Mexican-American/Chicano and Puerto Rican Movements," 44–79.

9. Ibid., 77.

10. "Since I'm talking about sexism, the second thing that made perhaps a greater impact on us was when we first heard about Gay Liberation. That's a whole other trip, because we found out it's a lot quicker for people to accept the fact that sisters should be in the front of the struggle, than saying we're gonna have gay people in the party." Pablo Guzmán, quoted in ibid., 55.

11. Lauren Berlant, *The Queen of America Goes to Washington City* (Durham: Duke University Press, 1997), 19.

12. Bernardo García, *The Development of a Latino Gay Identity* (New York: Garland, 1998), 35.

13. See Lisa Lowe, *Immigrant Acts* (Durham: Duke University Press, 1996), 9.

14. In this regard, the work of Chicana lesbians has been fundamental in exposing how nationalist myths are sexualized in an oppressive manner, particularly in the

Chicano movement. I am grateful to Emma Pérez's still unpublished essay "History's Imprints upon the Colonial Body: La Malinche as 'Phallic' Mother," delivered at the American Studies Association 1997 meeting, for these insights.

15. Chela Sandoval, "Cultural Studies and the Racialization of Theoretical Domains" (paper presented at the annual meeting of the American Studies Association, Washington, D.C., November 2, 1997).

16. Of particular importance are Tomás Almaguer, "Chicano Men: A Cartography of Homosexual Identity and Behavior," in *The Lesbian and Gay Studies Reader*, ed. Henry Abelove, Michèle Aina Barale, and David Halperin (New York: Routledge, 1993), 255–73; Gloria Anzaldúa, *Borderlands/La Frontera: The New Mestiza* (San Francisco: Spinsters/Aunt Lute, 1987); Cherríe Moraga and Gloria Anzaldúa, eds., *This Bridge Called My Back: Writings by Radical Women of Color* (New York: Kitchen Table Press, 1983).

17. One should take into account, of course, the present backlash against Latina feminists from the point of view of normative Chicano nationalist discourse. See, for example, Ignacio M. García, "Juncture in the Road: Chicano Studies since 'El plan de Santa Barbara,'" in *Chicanas/Chicanos at the Crossroads: Social, Economic and Political Change*, ed. David R. Mariel and Isidro D. Ortiz (Tucson: University of Arizona Press, 1996), 181–203. See, in particular, the following observations:

> *The lesbian Chicana scholars have even gone as far as promoting the idea that homosexuality is an integral part of Chicano culture. . . . It is even more likely that these scholars will further alienate themselves with their gender politics, which, unlike the politics of the Chicano Movement, are not based on what the predominantly working-class community thinks. The academy has become the only world for some of these scholars, because they have redefined the concept of community.*

190. I thank Javier Morillo for bringing this essay to my attention.

18. See "People Can Claim One or More Races on Federal Forms," *New York Times*, October 30, 1997, A1, A26. Thus, at present, racial and ethnic categories are being changed in federal forms for the first time since 1977, although the Clinton administration refused to recognize a "multiracial" classification that was pressured for by the Association of Multiethnic Americans. It is clear, however, that in categorizing in terms of race, the federal authorities are collapsing both race and ethnicity. Blacks, for example, will be termed "black or African-American," and the ethnic category of "Hispanic or Latino" will remain. Among other things, the discussion pits academics and demographers against civil rights groups, with the former arguing for more specific classifications, and civil rights groups for broader categories. It is presumed, then, that Latino civil rights groups are still immersed in pan-Latino definitions of identity, although I have found no independent confirmation of this.

19. It is clear that, as befits the economic nature of political representation and access in the United States, advertisers at times seem to be the most aware of the differing ethnic and national representations that divide and unite Latinos. By the same token, it at times seems as if consumer surveys are the ones that take into account the differing lines of gender, class, and racial avenues by means of which Latinos identify themselves—if only for the sake of participating much more directly in the construction of a pan-Latino consumer market.

20. Monique Wittig, "The Politics of the 'We,'" in *Eloquent Obsessions: Writing Cultural Criticism*, ed. Marianna Torgovnick (Durham: Duke University Press, 1994), 260–77.

21. See Coco Fusco, "Nationalism and Latinos, North and South: A Dialogue," in *English Is Broken Here: Notes on Cultural Fusion in the Americas* (New York: New Press, 1995), 159–68, 160.

22. The term "Latino" in itself is, to a certain extent, and particularly for recent middle- or upper-middle-class migrants, a marker of class.

23. I need to restate here that many middle- and upper-middle-class migrants from Latin America do not see themselves as "Latinos" but as Argentineans, Venezuelans, Colombians, and so on. Their children may not live within the same constructions of identity that we inhabit at present in the United States.

24. Robert Vázquez Pacheco, "At Night, All Cats Are Gray" (unpublished manuscript, 1994).

25. Michael Warner, *The Trouble with Normal: Sex, Politics and the Ethics of Queer Life* (New York: Simon and Schuster, 1999). "The politics of shame . . . includes vastly more than the overt and deliberate shaming produced by moralists. It also involves silent inequalities, unintended effects of isolation, and the lack of public access" (7).

26. "Identification is a process that keeps identity at a distance, that prevents identity from ever approximating the status of an ontological given, even as it makes possible the formation of an *illusion* of identity as immediate, secure, and totalizable." Diana Fuss, *Identification Papers* (New York: Routledge, 1995), 2. This is also important in terms of the "interior" sense of colonization that Fuss examines in relation to Frantz Fanon.

27. The participants in Bernardo García's study negotiate these two categories:

> *For all of the participants, both their Latino identity and their gay identity is important to them; however, for some, one identity and its maintenance is more important than the other. The majority of the men in this study reported participating more in the gay community than in their Latino communities. Some reported that they would not separate their Latino identities from their gay identity.*

For García, the integration of Latino and gay identities is "demonstrated through concentric circles." García, *Development of a Latino Gay Identity*, 109.

28. These identity markers may not have anything to do with the positionality entertained during sex, contra Tomás Almaguer's assertion of a fixed pattern along the active/passive axis that defines questions of identity along Latin American versus Anglo modes. See "Chicano Men: A Cartography of Homosexual Identity and Behavior."

29. Judith Butler, 447.

30. See once again Cohen, *The Boundaries of Blackness*:

> *Increasingly, in the third stage [of AIDS work in communities of color] professional social workers, policy wonks, and administrators have come to staff and head the few AIDS organizations centered in communities of color, especially those receiving significant amounts of state or federal funds. . . . these individuals have often come to their jobs devoid of any political focus except acquiring more funding for their agencies. Consequently, many organizations servicing people of color with AIDS pursue agendas structured around service provision and education, with little effort devoted to politics. (112)*

31. This is a position U.S. activists should also take in reference to the recent passage of the "mutual association pacts" (Pacte Civil de Solidarité) in France on October 13, 1999.

32. "Rhetoric of Hate: Anti-Gay Marriage Bill Hearings Coincide with LLEGO Gathering," *Washington Blade*, October 17, 1997, 1, 23.

33. Although it is clear that the LLEGO conference was successful in terms of gaining gay and lesbian visibility, it is not clear how and to what extent the movement is prepared to combat and effectively pursue the increasingly volatile issue of Latin American religious conservatives' alliance with the U.S. political Right, without understanding that in terms of these issues, the organization must take a back seat to local or national efforts, participating and collaborating with these, but making sure that those grassroots voices are heard in all their complexity. To do otherwise is a recipe for a disaster that will allow Latinos to be cast more and more as "foreigners" in a culture that is increasingly being reinvented by more conservative national voices in collusion with conservatives in the United States.

34. Urvashi Vaid, *Virtual Equality* (New York: Anchor Books, 1995), 294–95.

35. Ibid., 290.

36. Ibid., 269.

37. Ibid., 292. It is clear that Vaid stands on the side of those who are committed to broadening the gay and lesbian struggle as part of a broader movement of racial justice, one that builds out of coalition politics in order to pursue its goals. It is also clear that Vaid believes that "it will take nothing less than a new movement for us to move beyond identity and toward a shared progressive politics" (306). But it may be that the discussion itself, as Vaid defines it, does not allow for effective action.

38. Walter Benjamin, "Theses on the Philosophy of History," in *Illuminations*, ed. Hannah Arendt, trans. Harry Zohn (New York: Schocken Books, 1969), 257.

39. Of particular importance are the inroads that white fundamentalist denominations have achieved in the Latino community in order to isolate lesbian and gay Latinos. These denominations, such as the Assemblies of God, may mobilize their followers to vote for Proposition 187 (the bill that would prevent illegal immigrants from attending public school or gaining access to social services) while at the same time trying to create an alliance with Latino communities in order to condemn lesbians and gays. This volatile issue has finally prompted national organizations such as LLEGO to create links with Latino mainstream coalitions and organizations such as the National Hispanic Leadership Agenda and the National Council of La Raza. The results of LLEGO's balancing act are still to be seen, in particular given the fact that the organization has supported the controversial Human Rights Campaign in its efforts toward a millennium march in Washington, D.C., to the concern of many activists in the grassroots community who oppose the ideological premises of the march. LLEGO's attempt is to increasingly position itself within mainstream organizations—organized along an ethnic or sexual line. Whereas the issue of religion and its relationship to the LGBT Latino/a community is beyond the purview of this study, it does point to a growing divide between the national organizations and the community-based structures that may or may not support them. See Rhonda Smith, 'We Will Continue to Carry the Message': Strategies Put in Place to Counter Religious Right's Outreach to Latinos," *Washington Blade*, September 3, 1999, 5.

40. George Yúdice, "Transnational Cultural Brokering of Art," in *Beyond the Fantastic: Contemporary Art Criticism from Latin America*, ed. Gerardo Mosquera (Cambridge: MIT Press, 1996), 196–213, 212.

Index

ABOUT THE AUTHOR

José Quiroga is an associate professor of Spanish and Latin American studies at George Washington University. He has held visiting appointments at the University of California at Berkeley, Columbia University, and Emory University, among others. He has published articles and book reviews in the *San Juan Star* and the *Nation*, as well as in academic journals. He is also the author of *Understanding Octavio Paz*.